Fodor's
Norway

Reprinted from *Fodor's Scandinavia*

Fodor's Travel Publications, Inc.
New York • Toronto • London • Sydney • Auckland

Fodor's Norway

Editor: Nancy van Itallie
Contributors: David Brown, Andrew Collins, Melody Favish, Margaret Hunter, Hilary Jacobs, Caroline Liou, Mary King Nash, Karina Porcelli, Marcy Pritchard
Updater: Katrine Osa Aaby
Creative Director: Fabrizio La Rocca
Cartographer: David Lindroth
Illustrator: Karl Tanner
Cover Photograph: Hakan Ludwigsson

Design: Vignelli Associates

Special Sales

Fodor's Travel Publications are available at special discounts for bulk purchases for sales promotions or premiums. Special editions, including personalized covers, excerpts of existing guides, and corporate imprints, can be created in large quantities for special needs. For more information, contact your local bookseller or write to Special Markets, Fodor's Travel Publications, 201 East 50th Street, New York, NY 10022. Inquiries from Canada should be directed to your local Canadian bookseller or sent to Random House of Canada, Ltd., Marketing Department, 1265 Aerowood Drive, Mississauga, Ontario L4W 1B9. Inquiries from the United Kingdom should be sent to Fodor's Travel Publications, 20 Vauxhall Bridge Road, London, England SW1V 2SA.

Contents

Maps

Foreword

We would like to express our gratitude to Harald Hansen of the Norwegian Tourist Board in New York City for his valuable assistance during the preparation of this new edition of Fodor's *Norway*.

While every care has been taken to ensure the accuracy of the information in this guide, the passage of time will always bring change, and consequently the publisher cannot accept responsibility for errors that may occur.

All prices and opening times quoted here are based on information supplied to us at press time. Hours and admission fees may change, however, and the prudent traveler will avoid inconvenience by calling ahead.

Fodor's wants to hear about your travel experiences, both pleasant and unpleasant. When a hotel or restaurant fails to live up to its billing, let us know and we will investigate the complaint and revise our entries where the facts warrant it. Send your letters to the editors of Fodor's Travel Publications, 201 E. 50th Street, New York, NY 10022.

Highlights and Fodor's Choice

Highlights

Currently Norwegian voters remain undecided on whether to join the EC. The issue is creating divisions among the various elements of society, and the road to full membership seems remote for the moment, even though most Norwegians feel very much a part of western Europe. The pressures of the influx of eastern European and other refugees, however, may spur Norwegians to join other Europeans in coping with them.

The XVII Olympic Winter Games in Lillehammer, February 12–27 this year, have been planned with a view to the future. Great care was taken in the construction of the facilities to preserve the local ecology, and the installations are all intended for public use after the games are over.

Oslo will soon have a new airport, at Gardermoen, 40 kilometers (25 miles) outside the city. It is scheduled for completion by 1998 at a projected cost of NKr11.7 billion.

The XXVII Olympic Winter Games

Lillehammer draws crowds this year from February 12 to 27 for the 1994 Olympic Winter Games. Seven of the 12 Olympic winter sports, as well as opening and closing ceremonies, take place in **Olympiaparken** (the Olympic Park), near the center of town. In the heart of the Park is the newly built Lysgårdsbakkene Ski Jump Arena, with a total capacity of 50,000 spectators, and the Freestyle arena. The Birkebeineren Ski Stadium (on the eastern side of the Park) includes arenas for 18 cross-country skiing and biathlon events. The jewel of the Olympic Park is Håkon Hallen (the Håkon Hall), intended for ice-hockey contests, erected alongside the existing Kristin Hall, which will serve as a training center. The Olympic Village, built to accommodate 3,000 competitors and their managers, is in the northern end of the Park.

Parts of the ice-hockey competition are held south of Lillehammer in **Gjøvik**, in a massive cavern blasted out of rock. **Hamar**, also to the south, hosts the skating events in the unique Viking-ship hall, while Alpine disciplines are divided between the municipalities of **Øyer** and **Ringebu** to the north. The new Kvitfjell Alpine Center in Ringebu hosts women's and men's downhill and downhill combined. The upgraded Hafjell Alpine Center is the scene of the slalom competitions. The bobsleigh and luge tracks north of Lillehammer are built below ground level for environmental and safety reasons.

Fodor's Choice

No two people will agree on what makes a perfect vacation, but it can be fun and helpful to know what others think. We hope you'll have a chance to experience some of Fodor's Choices yourself while visiting Norway. For detailed information on individual entries, see the relevant sections of this guidebook.

Dining

Refnes Gods, Moss *(Expensive)*

Spisestuen (Alexandra Molde Hotel), Molde *(Expensive)*

Bryggestuen & Bryggeloftet, Bergen *(Moderate)*

Theatercafeen, Oslo *(Moderate)*

Lodging

Ambassadeur, Oslo *(Expensive)*

Alexandra, Loen *(Expensive)*

Kvikne's Hotel, Balestrand *(Moderate)*

Castles and Churches

Heddal Stave Church, Heddal

Akershus Slott, Oslo

Towns and Villages

Lyngør

Røros

Bryggen, Bergen

Parks and Gardens

Frogner Park, Oslo

Hardangervidda, Geilo

Jostedalsbreen (glacier), Loen

Briksdalsbreen, Olden

Museums

Norwegian Folk Museum, Bygdøy, Oslo

Vikingskiphuset, Bygdøy, Oslo

Sami Collections, Karasjok

Maihaugen, Lillehammer

Rock Carvings, Alta

Lakes, Fjords, and Islands

Lofoten Islands

Svalbard

Geirangerfjord

Nærøyfjord

Special Moments

Eating shrimp from the boats at the pier in Oslo and Bergen

Midsummer at the North Cape

Riding the train from Flåm to Myrdal

Driving the Atlantic Road from Molde to Kristiansund

A concert with the Oslo Philharmonic conducted by Mariss Janssons

Norway

World Time Zones

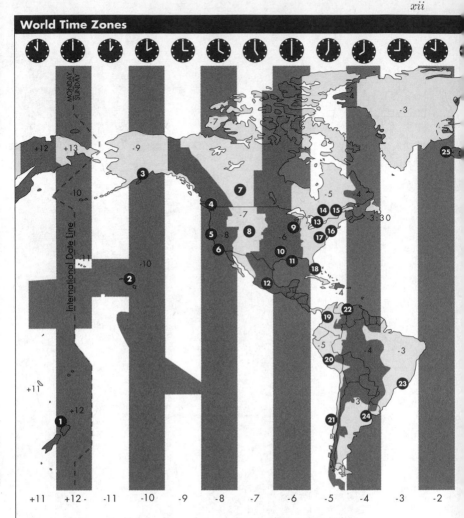

Numbers below vertical bands relate each zone to Greenwich Mean Time (0 hrs.).
Local times frequently differ from these general indications,
as indicated by light-face numbers on map.

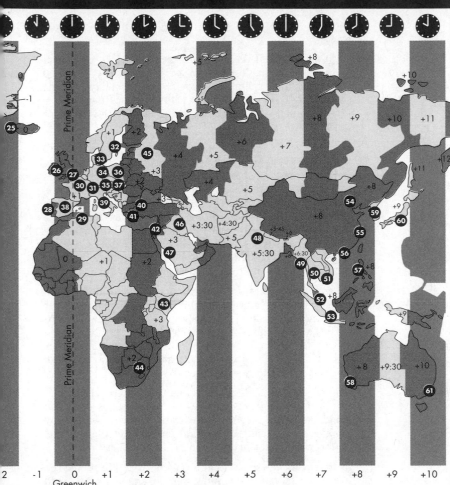

Introduction

By Melody Favish and Karina Porcelli

Just north of Lillehammer there lives a Norwegian family on the banks of the Mjøsa River. Every year they pack their bags and drive to their holiday retreat, where they bask in the warmth of the long, northern sun for four full weeks—then they pack up and drive the 100 yards back home again.

While most Norwegians vacation a bit farther from home, their sentiments—attachment to, pride in, and reverence for their great outdoors—remain the same as the feelings of those who journey across the street. Whether in the verdant dales of the interior, the brooding mountains of the north, or the carved fjords and archipelagoes of the coast, their ubiquitous *hytter*, or cottages, dot even the most violent landscapes. It's a question of perspective: To a Norwegian, it's not a matter of whether or not to enjoy the land, but how to enjoy it at this very moment.

In any kind of weather, blasting or balmy, inordinate numbers are out of doors, to fish, bike, ski, hike, and, whether they know it or not, strike the pose many foreigners regard as larger-than-life Norwegian: ruddy-faced, athletic, reindeer-sweatered. And all—cherubic children to decorous senior citizens—bundled up for just one more swoosh down the slopes, one more walk through the forest.

Although it's a modern, highly industrialized nation, vast areas of the country, up to 95%, remain forested or fallow; and Norwegians intend to keep them that way—in part by making it extremely difficult for foreigners, who may feel differently about the land, to purchase property.

Norwegians like to say that if Oslo remained fixed and the northern part of the country were swung south, it would reach all the way to Rome. Perched at the very top of the globe, this northern land is long and rangy, 2,750 kilometers (1,700 miles) in length, with only 4 million people scattered over it—making it the least densely populated land in Europe except for Iceland. Knuckled by snow-topped mountains, and serrated by Gulf-Stream–warmed fjords, this country has an abundance of magnificent views. No matter how or where your approach, if you fly above the clean ivory mountains of Tromsø in the winter, or tear by in a heart-stopping train north of Voss in the spring, getting there is often as eye-popping as arriving.

Thanks to the Gulf Stream, the coastal regions enjoy a moderate, temperate climate in winter, keeping the country green, while the interior has a more typical northern climate. Of course, throughout the land, winter temperatures can dip far below zero, but that doesn't thwart the activities of the Norwegians. As one North Caper put it, "We don't have good weather or bad weather, only a lot of weather."

Norwegians are justifiably proud of their native land, and of their ability to survive the elements and foreign invasions. The first people to appear on the land were reindeer-hunters and fisherfolk, who migrated north, following the path of the retreating ice. By the Bronze Age, settlements began to appear and, as rock carvings show (and modern school children are proud to announce), the first Norwegians began to ski—purely as a form a locomotion—some 4,000 years ago.

The Viking Age has perhaps left the most indelible mark on the country. The Vikings' travels and conquests took them to Iceland, England, Ireland (they founded Dublin in the 840s), and North America. Though they were famed as plunderers, their craftsmanship and fearlessness is revered by modern Norwegians, who place ancient Viking ships in museums, cast copies of thousand-year-old silver designs into jewelry, and adventure across the seas in sailboats to prove the abilities of their forefathers.

Harald I, better known as Harald the Fairhaired, swore he would not cut his hair until he united Norway, and in the 8th century he succeeded in doing both. But a millennium passed between that great era and Norwegian independence. Between the Middle Ages and 1905, Norway remained under the rule of either Denmark or Sweden, even after the constitution was written in 1814.

The 19th century saw the establishment of the Norwegian identity and a blossoming of culture. This romantic period produced some of the nation's most famous individuals, among them, composer Edvard Grieg, dramatist Henrik Ibsen, expressionist painter Edvard Munch, polar explorer Roald Amundsen, and explorer/humanitarian Fridtjof Nansen. Vestiges of national lyricism spangle the buildings of the era with Viking dragonheads and scrollwork, all of which symbolize the rebirth of the Viking spirit.

Faithful to their democratic nature, in 1905, when independence from Sweden became reality, Norwegians held a referendum to choose a king. Prince Carl of Denmark became King Haakon VII. His baby son Alexander's name was changed to Olav, and he, and later his son, presided over the kingdom for more than 85 years. When King Olav died in January 1991, the normally reserved Norwegians stood in line for hours to write in the condolence book at the Royal Palace. Rather than simply sign their names, they wrote personal letters of devotion to the man they called the "people's king." Thousands set candles in the snow outside the palace, transforming the winter darkness into a cathedral of ice and flame.

Harald V, Olav's son, is now king, with continuity assured by his own young-adult son, Crown Prince Haakon. Norwegians continue to salute the royal family with flag-waving and parades on May 17, Constitution Day, a spirited holiday of independence that transforms Oslo's main boulevard, Karl Johans gate, into a massive street party, when people of all ages, many in national costume, make a beeline to the Palace.

During both World Wars, Norway tried to maintain neutrality. World War I brought not only casualties and a considerable loss to the country's merchant fleet, but also financial gain through the repurchase of major companies, sovereignty over Svalbard (the islands near the North Pole), and the reaffirmation of Norway's prominence in international shipping. At the onset of World War II, Norway once again proclaimed neutrality and appeared more concerned with Allied mine-laying on the west coast than with national security. A country of mostly fisherfolk, lumber workers, and farmers, it was just beginning to realize its industrial potential when the Nazis invaded. Five years of German occupation and a burn-and-retreat strategy in the north finally left the nation ravaged. True to form, however, the people who had been evacuated returned to the embers of the north to rebuild their homes and villages.

In 1968, oil was discovered in the North Sea, and Norway was transformed from a fishing and shipping outpost to a highly developed industrial nation. Though still committed to a far-reaching social system, Norway developed in the next 20 years into a wealthy country, with one of the world's highest per capita standards of living and income, as well as long life expectancy.

Stand on a street corner with a map, and a curious Norwegian will show you the way. Visit a neighborhood, and within moments you'll be the talk of the town. As a native of Bergen quipped, "Next to skiing, gossip is a national sport." With one foot in modern, liberal Scandinavia and the other in the provincial and often self-righteous countryside, Norway, like her Nordic siblings, seems to be redefining her European identity. Famous for its social restrictiveness—smoking is frowned upon, liquor may not be served before 3 PM (and never on Sunday), and violence, even among cartoon characters, is closely monitored—Norway's government has applied to enter the European Community, thus paving the way for fewer limitations and more openmindedness. The next few years will define her course, as well as that of Scandinavia as a whole.

1 Essential Information

Before You Go

Government Tourist Offices

In the U.S. and Canada Scandinavian Tourist Board, 655 3rd Ave., New York, NY 10017, tel. 212/949–2333.

The U.S. Department of State's **Citizens Emergency Center** issues Consular Information Sheets, which cover crime, security, and health risks as well as embassy locations, entry requirements, currency regulations, and other routine matters. For the latest information, stop in at any passport office, consulate, or embassy; call the interactive hotline (tel. 202/647–5225); or, with your PC's modem, tap into the Bureau of Consular Affairs' computer bulletin board (tel. 202/647–9225).

In the U.K. Norwegian Tourist Board, 5 Lower Regent St., London SW1Y 4LX, tel. 071/839–6255, fax 071/839–4180.

Tours and Packages

Should you buy your travel arrangements to Norway packaged or do it yourself? There are advantages either way. Buying packaged arrangements saves you money, particularly if you can find a program that includes exactly the features you want. You also get a pretty good idea of what your trip will cost from the outset. Generally, you have two options: fully escorted tours and independent packages. Escorted tours are most often via motorcoach, with a tour director in charge. They're ideal if you don't mind having limited free time and traveling with strangers. Your baggage is handled, your time rigorously scheduled, and most meals planned. Escorted tours are therefore the most hassle-free way to see a destination, as well as generally the least expensive. Independent packages allow plenty of flexibility. They generally include airline travel and hotels, with certain options available, such as sightseeing, car rental, and excursions. Independent packages are usually more expensive than escorted tours, but your time is your own.

While you can book directly through tour operators, you will pay no more to go through a travel agent, who will be able to tell you about tours and packages from a number of operators. Whatever program you ultimately choose, be sure to find out exactly what is included: taxes, tips, transfers, meals, baggage handling, ground transportation, entertainment, excursions, sports, or recreation (and rental equipment if necessary). Ask about the level of hotel used, its location, the size of its rooms, the kind of beds, and its amenities, such as pool, room service, or programs for children, if they're important to you. Find out the operator's cancellation penalties. Nearly everyone charges them, and the only way to avoid them is to buy trip-cancellation insurance (*see* Trip Insurance, *below*). Also ask about the single supplement, a surcharge assessed to solo travelers. Some operators do not make you pay it if you agree to be matched up with a roommate of the same sex, even if one is not found by departure time. Remember that a program that has features you won't use, whether for rental sporting equipment or discounted museum admissions, may not be the most cost-wise choice for you.

Fully Escorted Tours Escorted tours are usually sold in three categories: deluxe, first-class, and tourist or budget class. The most important differences are the price, of course, and the level of accommodations. Some operators specialize in one category, while others offer a range.

Contact **Maupintour** (Box 807, Lawrence, KS 66044, tel. 800/255–4266 or 913/843–1211), **Tauck Tours** (11 Wilton Rd., Westport, CT 06881, tel. 800/468–2825 or 203/226–6911), and **Abercrombie & Kent** (1520 Kensington Rd., Oak Brook, IL 60521, tel. 800/325–7308 or 708/954–2944) in the deluxe category; **Bennett Tours** (270 Madison Ave., New York, NY 10016, tel. 800/221–2420 or 212/532–5060), **Caravan Tours** (401 N. Michigan Ave., Chicago, IL 60611, tel. 800/227–2826 or 312/321–9800), **Delta Dream Vacations** (tel. 800/872–7786), **Gadabout Tours** (700 E. Tahquitz Way, Palm Springs, CA 92262, tel. 800/952–5068 or 619/325–5556), **Globus-Gateway** (95–25 Queens Blvd., Rego Park, NY 11374, tel. 800/221–0090 or 718/268–7000), **SAS** (tel. 800/221–2350, press "3" for tour desk), and **Trafalgar Tours** (21 E. 26th St., New York, NY 10010, tel. 800/854–0103 or 212/689–8977) in the first-class category; and **Cosmos**, a sister company of Globus-Gateway (*see above*), in the budget category.

Most itineraries are jam-packed with sightseeing, so you see a lot in a short amount of time (usually one place per day). To judge just how fast-paced the tour is, review the itinerary carefully. If you are in a different hotel each night, you will be getting up early each day to head out, travel to your next destination, do some sightseeing, have dinner, and go to bed, then you'll start all over again. If you want some free time, make sure it's mentioned in the tour brochure; if you want to be escorted to every meal, confirm that any tour you consider does that. Also, when comparing programs, be sure to find out if the motorcoach is air-conditioned and has a restroom on board. Make your selection based on price and stops on the itinerary.

Independent Packages Independent packages, which travel agents call FITs (for foreign independent travel), are offered by airlines, tour operators who may also do escorted programs, and any number of other companies from large, established firms to small, new entrepreneurs.

Contact **Bennett Tours** (*see above*), **Delta Dream Vacations** (*see above*), **DER Tours** (11933 Wilshire Blvd., Los Angeles, CA 90025, tel. 800/937–1234 or 213/479–4140), **Gadabout Tours** (*see above*), **Jet Vacations** (1775 Broadway, New York, NY 10019, tel. 800/538–0999 or 212/247–0999), **SAS Tour Desk** (9 Polito Ave., Lyndhurst, NY 07071, tel. 800/221–2350), and **Travel Bound** (599 Broadway, Penthouse, New York, NY 10012, tel. 800/456–8656 or 212/334–1350).

Their programs come in a wide range of prices based on levels of luxury and options—in addition to hotel and airfare, sightseeing, car rental, transfers, admission to local attractions, and other extras. Note that when pricing different packages, it sometimes pays to purchase the same arrangements separately, as when a rock-bottom promotional airfare is being offered, for example. Again, base your choice on what's available at your budget for the destinations you want to visit.

Special-interest Travel Special-interest programs may be fully escorted or independent. Some require a certain amount of expertise, but most are for the average traveler with an interest and are usually hosted by experts in the subject matter. When the program is escorted, it enjoys the advantages and disadvantages of all escorted programs; because your fellow travelers are apt to be passionate or knowledgeable about the subject, they can prove as enjoyable a part of your travel experience as the destination itself. The price range is wide, but the cost is usually higher—sometimes a lot higher—than for ordinary escorted tours and packages, because of the expert guiding and special activities.

Biking **Backroads** (1516 5th St., Suite Q333, Berkeley, CA 94710, tel. 800/245–3874 or 510/527–1555) offers a seven-day inn trip through Norway, in July and August.

Educational **Arrangements Abroad** (50 Broadway, New York, NY 10004, tel. 212/514–8921) specializes in educational programs for alumni groups and museum members.

When to Go

Every season has its charm and its enthusiasts. Winter means skiing at resorts in the country's midsection, where snow is abundant and facilities are first-rate. Winter in Oslo means evenings at the theater or at the concert house. Skiing on the lit trails surrounding Oslo is almost as good as that farther afield. On the down side, winter means little daylight, few organized tours, restricted opening hours at museums, and higher hotel rates except on weekends. Avoid Easter, the traditional "last ski trip of the year" for many Norwegians. Christmas is similar, with families retreating to the privacy of their own homes for much of the holiday, which begins on December 24, and, for many, does not end until January 2 or 3. May is one of the best times to visit Norway, for the days are long and sunny, the cultural life in the city is still going strong, tourists are few, and *Syttende mai* (Constitution Day, May 17), with all the festivities, is worth a trip for its own sake. For enjoying the outdoors, September is a delightful time to hike in the hills. Most people come to Norway in the summer, and the months of July and August offer the most travel bargains. Hotels everywhere have special rates, and transportation packages of all kinds are available. In the far north, summer's main attraction is the midnight sun, visible at the North Cape from May 13 through July 29. In winter, the northern lights illuminate the sky.

Climate Coastal Norway enjoys mild winters, with more rain than snow in the southern areas. The temperature in Oslo seldom drops below 20°F, thanks to the Gulf Stream. It is dark, though, and if there's no snow, Oslo can look bleak. Summers in Norway are equally mild; days are relatively warm, but nights can be chilly. Inland and up north, winters are very long, cold, snowy, and dark, while summers are short, warm, intense, and endowed with an indescribably clear light.

What follows are average daily maximum and minimum temperatures for Oslo.

Oslo	**Jan.**	28F	– 2C	**May**	61F	16C	**Sept.**	60F	16C
		19	– 7		43	6		46	8
	Feb.	30F	– 1C	**June**	68F	20C	**Oct.**	48F	9C
		19	– 7		50	10		38	3
	Mar.	39F	4C	**July**	72F	22C	**Nov.**	38F	3C
		25	– 4		55	13		31	– 1
	Apr.	50F	10C	**Aug.**	70F	21C	**Dec.**	32F	0C
		34	1		54	12		25	– 4

Information Sources For current weather conditions for cities in the United States and abroad, plus the local time and helpful travel tips, call the **Weather Channel Connection** (tel. 900/932–8437; 95¢ per minute) from a touch-tone phone.

National Holidays

The following are national holidays in 1994: January 1, Easter (April 1–4), Labor Day (May 1), Constitution Day (May 17), Ascension (May 12), Whitmonday (May 23), December 25–26.

Festivals and Seasonal Events 1994

1994: 200th anniversary of the city of Tromsø.
January: Northern Light Festival, Tromsø, features classical, contemporary, and chamber music.
February 12–27: Winter Olympics at Lillehammer.
March: The **Holmenkollen Ski Festival** in Oslo features international Nordic events, including ski jumping. The **Birkebeiner Race** commemorates a centuries-old cross-country ski race from Lillehammer to Rena.
April: The **Karasjok Easter Festival** features traditional Sami entertainment and folklore and reindeer racing.
May 17: Constitution Day brings out every flag in the country and crowds of marchers for the parade in Oslo.
May: The **Grete Waitz Race,** a 5-kilometer street marathon in Oslo challenges women only.
June 23: Midsummer Eve, called "Sankt Hans," is celebrated nationwide with bonfires, fireworks, and outdoor dancing.
June: The annual **Bergen Music Festival** is customarily opened by the king. The **Emigration Festival.** Exhibitions and concerts in Stavanger commemorate the emigration to the United States. The **North Norwegian Cultural Festival** at Harstad includes plays, concerts, ballet, and art exhibitions. The **North Cape March** brings hikers from around the world to walk the 70 kilometers from Honningsvåg to the North Cape and back. The **Great Endurance Test** is a bicycle race (560 km) from Trondheim to Oslo.
July: The **Bislett Games** attract the best international track and field stars to Bislett Stadium. The **Molde International Jazz Festival** is Norway's best-known jazz festival. The **Stiklestad Festivals** honor Olav the Holy (Haraldsson) with outdoor theater performances.
Mid-August: The **European Sea Fishing Championships** are held at Tananger, outside Stavanger.
August: Oslo Chamber Music Festival draws participants from around the world.
September: Oslo Marathon, 42 kilometers through the streets of Oslo, draws men and women.
December 1: The Christmas tree at University Square in Oslo is lit.

December 10: The **Nobel Peace Prize** is awarded in Oslo.
December: Christmas concerts, fairs, and crafts workshops are
held at museums and churches throughout the country.

What to Pack

Clothing   Casual clothing is the rule in Norway, although it is a good idea
for men to pack a sport jacket for cool evenings. Women might
want to bring a dress or suit, preferably with a jacket, for evenings. A jacket or neat casual dress might be required when going out at night. A windbreaker, good walking shoes, and
sunglasses are a must. Summer in Norway can be both chilly
and rainy, so bring a raincoat (with lining for the fringe seasons) and an umbrella. Winter weather demands heavy outer-
wear but normal indoor clothing, as Norwegian buildings are
well heated. If you are traveling north in winter, bring heavy,
impermeable boots and some kind of snow suit. However, if
you're going on an organized outing (particularly dog- or rein-
deer-sledding), most outfitters provide both.

Miscellaneous   Most hotels do not provide washcloths, so if you prefer them,
bring your own. Many hotel bathrooms are equipped with
converter outlets for shavers only, so if you bring a hair dryer,
make sure that it is convertible. If you prefer decaffeinated coffee, bring some individual envelopes as many restaurants do
not serve it. If you can't sleep when it is light and you are traveling during summer, bring a comfortable eye-mask, so you won't
wake up automatically at the 4 AM sunrise. If you are going north
in summer, bring along the best mosquito repellent you can find.

Because of the far northern latitude, the sun slants at angles un-
seen elsewhere on the globe, and a pair of dark sunglasses can
prevent eyestrain. Bring an extra pair of eyeglasses or contact
lenses. If you have a health problem that may require you to purchase a prescription drug, pack enough to last the duration of the
trip, or have your doctor write a prescription using the drug's ge-
neric name, since brand names vary from country to country.
And don't forget to pack a list of the addresses of offices that supply refunds for lost or stolen traveler's checks.

Electricity   The electrical current in Norway is 220 volts, 50 cycles alternating current (AC); the United States runs on 110-volt, 60-cy-
cle AC current. Unlike wall outlets in the United States, which
accept plugs with two flat prongs, outlets in Norway take plugs
with two round prongs.

Adapters,   To plug in U.S.-made appliances abroad, you'll need an adapter
Converters,   plug. To reduce the voltage entering the appliance from 220 to
Transformers   110 volts, you'll also need a converter, unless it is a dual-voltage
appliance, made for travel. There are converters for high-watt-
age appliances (such as hair dryers), low-wattage items (such
as electric toothbrushes and razors), and combination models.
Hotels sometimes have outlets marked "For Shavers Only"
near the sink; these are 110-volt outlets for low-wattage appliances; don't use them for a high-wattage appliance. If you're
traveling with a laptop computer, especially an older one, you
may need a transformer—a type of converter used with elec-
tronic-circuitry products. Newer laptop computers are auto-
sensing, operating equally well on 110 and 220 volts (so you
need only the appropriate adapter plug). When in doubt, consult your appliance's owner's manual or the manufacturer. Or
get a copy of the free brochure "Foreign Electricity is No Deep

Dark Secret," published by adapter-converter manufacturer Franzus (Murtha Industrial Park, Box 142, Beacon Falls, CT 06403, tel. 203/723–6664; send a stamped, self-addressed envelope when ordering).

Luggage Regulations Free baggage allowances on an airline depend on the airline, the route, and the class of your ticket. In general, on domestic flights and on international flights between the United States and foreign destinations, you are entitled to check two bags—neither exceeding 62 inches, or 158 centimeters (length + width + height), or weighing more than 70 pounds (32 kilograms). A third piece may be brought aboard as a carryon; its total dimensions are generally limited to less than 45 inches (114 centimeters), so it will fit easily under the seat in front of you or in the overhead compartment. There are variations, so ask in advance. The single rule, a Federal Aviation Administration safety regulation that pertains to carry-on baggage on U.S. airlines, requires only that carryons be properly stowed and allows the airline to limit allowances and tailor them to different aircraft and operational conditions. Charges for excess, oversize, or overweight pieces vary, so inquire before you pack.

If you are flying between two foreign destinations, note that baggage allowances may be determined not by the piece method but by the weight method, which generally allows 88 pounds (40 kilograms) of luggage in first class, 66 pounds (30 kilograms) in business class, and 44 pounds (20 kilograms) in economy. If your flight between two cities abroad *connects* with your transatlantic or transpacific flight, the piece method still applies.

Safeguarding Your Luggage Before leaving home, itemize your bags' contents and their worth; this list will help you estimate the extent of your loss if your bags go astray. To minimize that risk, tag them inside and out with your name, address, and phone number. (If you use your home address, cover it so that potential thieves can't see it.) At check-in, make sure that the tag attached by baggage handlers bears the correct three-letter code for your destination. If your bags do not arrive with you, or if you detect damage, do not leave the airport until you've filed a written report with the airline.

Taking Money Abroad

Traveler's Checks Although you will want plenty of cash when visiting small cities or rural areas, traveler's checks are usually preferable. The most widely recognized are **American Express, Citicorp, Thomas Cook,** and **Visa,** which are sold by major commercial banks. American Express also issues *Traveler's Cheques for Two*, which can be counter-signed and used by you or your traveling companion. Some checks are free; usually the issuing company or the bank at which you make your purchase charges 1%–2% of the checks' face value as a fee. Be sure to buy a few checks in small denominations to cash toward the end of your trip, when you don't want to be left with more foreign currency than you can spend. Always record the numbers of checks as you spend them, and keep this list separate from the checks.

Currency Exchange Banks and bank-operated exchange booths at airports and railroad stations are usually the best places to change money. Hotels, stores, and privately run exchange firms typically offer less favorable rates.

Before your trip, pay attention to how the dollar is doing vis-à-vis Norway's currency. If the dollar is losing strength, try to pay as many travel bills as possible in advance, especially the big ones. If it is getting stronger, pay for costly items overseas, and use your credit card whenever possible—you'll come out ahead, whether the exchange rate at which your purchase is calculated is the one in effect the day the vendor's bank abroad processes the charge, or the one prevailing on the day the charge company's service center processes it at home.

To avoid lines at airport currency-exchange booths, arrive in a foreign country with a small amount of the local currency already in your pocket—a so-called tip pack. **Thomas Cook Currency Services** (630 5th Ave., New York, NY 10111, tel. 212/757–6915) supplies foreign currency by mail.

Getting Money from Home

Cash Machines Automated-teller machines (ATMs) are proliferating; many are tied to international networks such as **Cirrus** and **Plus.** You can use your bank card at ATMs away from home to withdraw money from an account and get cash advances on a credit-card account (providing your card has been programmed with a personal identification number, or PIN). Check in advance on limits on withdrawals and cash advances within specified periods. Ask whether your bank-card or credit-card PIN number will need to be reprogrammed for use in the area you'll be visiting—a possibility if the number has more than four digits. Remember that on cash advances you are charged interest from the day you get the money from ATMs as well as from tellers. And note that, although transaction fees for ATM withdrawals abroad will probably be higher than fees for withdrawals at home, Cirrus and Plus exchange rates tend to be good.

Be sure to plan ahead: Obtain ATM locations and the names of affiliated cash-machine networks before departure. For specific foreign Cirrus locations, call 800/424–7787; for foreign Plus locations, consult the Plus directory at your local bank.

American Express Cardholder Services The company's **Express Cash** system lets you withdraw cash and/or traveler's checks from a worldwide network of 57,000 American Express dispensers and participating bank ATMs. You must *enroll first* (call 800/227–4669 for a form and allow two weeks for processing). Withdrawals are charged not to your card but to a designated bank account. You can withdraw up to $1,000 per seven-day period on the basic card, more if your card is gold or platinum. There is a 2% fee (minimum $2.50, maximum $10) for each cash transaction, and a 1% fee for traveler's checks (except for the platinum card), which are available only from American Express dispensers.

At AmEx offices, cardholders can also cash personal checks for up to $1,000 in any seven-day period (21 days abroad); of this $200 can be in cash, more if available, with the balance paid in traveler's checks, for which all but platinum cardholders pay a 1% fee. Higher limits apply to the gold and platinum cards.

Wiring Money You don't have to be a cardholder to send or receive an **American Express MoneyGram** for up to $10,000. To send one, go to an American Express MoneyGram agent, pay up to $1,000 with a credit card and anything over that in cash, and phone a transaction reference number to your intended recipient, who needs only present identification and the reference number to the nearest MoneyGram agent to pick up the cash. There are MoneyGram agents in more than 60 countries (call 800/543–4080 for locations). Fees range from 5% to 10%, depending on the amount and how you pay. You can't use American Express, which is really a convenience card—only Discover, Master-Card, and Visa credit cards.

You can also use **Western Union.** To wire money, take either cash or a check to the nearest office. (Or you can call and use a credit card.) Fees are roughly 5%–10%. Money sent from the United States or Canada will be available for pick up at agent locations in Norway within minutes. (Note that once the money is in the system it can be picked up at *any* location. You don't have to miss your train waiting for it to arrive in City A, because if there's an agent in City B, where you're headed, you can pick it up there, too.) There are approximately 20,000 agents worldwide (call 800/325–6000 for locations).

Norwegian Currency

The unit of currency in Norway is the *krone* (plural: *kroner*), which translates as "crown," written officially as NOK. Price tags are seldom marked this way, but rather read "Kr." and then the amount, such as Kr10. (In this book, the Norwegian krone is abbreviated NKr.) One krone is divided into 100 *øre*, and coins of 10 and 50 øre, 1, 5, and 10 kroner are in circulation. Bills are issued in denominations of 50, 100, 500, and 1,000 kroner. In summer 1993, the exchange rate was NKr6.91 to U.S.$1, NKr10.70 to £1, and NKr5.45 to C$1. These rates fluctuate, so be sure to check them when planning a trip.

What It Will Cost

Sample Prices Cup of coffee, from $2 in a cafeteria to $3.50 or more in a restaurant; a 20-pack of cigarettes, $5.90; a half-liter of beer, $4.50–$6.50; the smallest hot dog (with bun plus *lompe*—a Norwegian tortilla—mustard, ketchup, and fried onions) at a convenience store, $2.10; cheapest bottle of wine from a government store, $8; the same bottle at a restaurant, $15–$25; urban transit fare in Oslo, $2.10; soft drink, from $2.75 in a cafeteria to $4 in a better restaurant; one adult movie ticket, $6; shrimp or roast beef sandwich at a cafeteria, $6; one-mile taxi ride, $6–$7 depending upon time of day.

Passports and Visas

If your passport is lost or stolen abroad, report it immediately to the nearest embassy or consulate and to the local police. If you can provide the consular officer with the information contained in the passport, they will usually be able to issue you a new passport. For this reason, it is a good idea to keep a copy of the data page of your passport in a separate place, or to leave the passport number, date, and place of issuance with a relative or friend at home.

U.S. Citizens All U.S. citizens, even infants, need a valid passport to enter Norway for stays of up to three months. Note that this three-month period is calculated from the time you enter any Scandinavian country. You can pick up new and renewal application forms at any of the 13 U.S. Passport Agency offices and at some post offices and courthouses. Although passports are usually mailed within two weeks of your application's receipt, it's best to allow three weeks for delivery in low season, five weeks or more from April through summer. Call the Department of State Office of Passport Services' information line (1425 K St. NW, Washington, DC 20522, tel. 202/647–0518) for fees, documentation requirements, and other details.

Canadian Citizens Canadian citizens need a valid passport to enter Norway for stays of up to three months. Note that this three-month period is calculated from the time you enter any Scandinavian country. Application forms are available at 23 regional passport offices as well as post offices and travel agencies. Whether applying for a first or subsequent passport, you must apply in person. Children under 16 may be included on a parent's passport but must have their own passport to travel alone. Passports are valid for five years and are usually mailed within two weeks of an application's receipt. For fees, documentation requirements, and other information in English or French, call the passport office (tel. 514/283–2152).

U.K. Citizens Citizens of the United Kingdom need a valid passport to enter Norway for stays of up to three months. Applications for new and renewal passports are available from main post offices as well as at the six passport offices, located in Belfast, Glasgow, Liverpool, London, Newport, and Peterborough. You may apply in person at all passport offices, or by mail to all except the London office. Children under 16 may travel on a parent's passport when accompanying them. All passports are valid for 10 years. Allow a month for processing.

A British Visitor's Passport is valid for holidays and some business trips of up to three months to Norway. It can include both partners of a married couple. Valid for one year, it will be issued on the same day that you apply. You must apply in person at a main post office.

Customs and Duties

On Arrival Any adult can bring in duty-free ¾ liter of alcohol (not exceeding 60% alcohol by volume) and one liter of wine (not exceeding 21% alcohol by volume). As most liquor is sold in 1-liter bottles, the allowance is flexible on that point. Two liters of beer also can be imported duty-free. Anyone over 16 years old can import 200 cigarettes or 250 grams of other tobacco products duty-free. Importing alcohol over the above limit is not recommended.

Returning Home Provided you've been out of the country for at least 48 hours *U.S. Customs* and haven't already used the exemption, or any part of it, in the past 30 days, you may bring home $400 worth of foreign goods duty-free. So can each member of your family, regardless of age; and your exemptions may be pooled, so one of you can bring in more if another brings in less. A flat 10% duty applies to the next $1,000 of goods; above $1,400, the rate varies with the merchandise. (If the 48-hour or 30-day limits apply, your duty-free allowance drops to $25, which may not be pooled.)

Travelers 21 or older may bring back 1 liter of alcohol duty-free, provided the beverage laws of the state through which they reenter the United States allow it. In addition, 100 non-Cuban cigars and 200 cigarettes are allowed, regardless of your age. Antiques and works of art more than 100 years old are duty-free.

Gifts valued at less than $50 may be mailed duty-free to stateside friends and relatives, with a limit of one package per day per addressee (do not send alcohol or tobacco products, nor perfume valued at more than $5). These gifts do not count as part of your exemption, unless you bring them home with you. Mark the package "Unsolicited Gift" and include the nature of the gift and its retail value.

For a copy of "Know Before You Go," a free brochure detailing what you may and may not bring back to the United States, rates of duty, and other pointers, contact the **U.S. Customs Service** (Box 7407, Washington, DC 20044, tel. 202/927–6724).

Canadian Customs Once per calendar year, when you've been out of Canada for at least seven days, you may bring in $300 worth of goods dutyfree. If you've been away less than seven days but more than 48 hours, the duty-free exemption drops to $100 but can be claimed any number of times (as can a $20 duty-free exemption for absences of 24 hours or more). You cannot combine the yearly and 48-hour exemptions, use the $300 exemption only partially (to save the balance for a later trip), or pool exemptions with family members. Goods claimed under the $300 exemption may follow you by mail; those claimed under the lesser exemptions must accompany you on your return.

Alcohol and tobacco products may be included in the yearly and 48-hour exemptions but not in the 24-hour exemption. If you meet the age requirements of the province through which you reenter Canada, you may bring in, duty-free, 1.14 liters (40 imperial ounces) of wine or liquor *or* two dozen 12-ounce cans or bottles of beer or ale. If you are 16 or older, you may bring in, duty-free, 200 cigarettes, 50 cigars or cigarillos, and 400 tobacco sticks or 400 grams of manufactured tobacco. Alcohol and tobacco must accompany you on your return.

Gifts may be mailed to friends in Canada duty-free. These do not count as part of your exemption. Each gift may be worth up to $60—label the package "Unsolicited Gift—Value under $60." There are no limits on the number of gifts that may be sent per day or per addressee, but you can't mail alcohol or tobacco.

For more information, including details of duties on items that exceed your duty-free limit, ask the Revenue Canada Customs and Excise Department (Connaught Bldg., MacKenzie Ave., Ottawa, Ont., K1A OL5, tel. 613/957–0275) for a copy of the free brochure "I Declare/Je Déclare."

U.K. Customs If your journey was wholly within EC countries, you no longer need to pass through customs when you return to the United Kingdom. According to EC guidelines, you may bring in 800 cigarettes, 400 cigarillos, 200 cigars, and 1 kilogram of smoking tobacco, plus 10 liters of spirits, 20 liters of fortified wine, 90 liters of wine, and 110 liters of beer. If you exceed these limits, you may be required to prove that the goods are for your personal use or are gifts.

From countries outside the EC, you may import duty-free 200 cigarettes, 100 cigarillos, 50 cigars, or 250 grams of tobacco; 1 liter of spirits or 2 liters of fortified or sparkling wine; 2 liters of still table wine; 60 milliliters of perfume; 250 milliliters of toilet water; plus £36 worth of other goods, including gifts and souvenirs.

For further information or a copy of "A Guide for Travellers," which details standard customs procedures as well as what you may bring into the United Kingdom from abroad, contact HM Customs and Excise (New King's Beam House, 22 Upper Ground, London SE1 9PJ, tel. 071/620–1313).

Traveling with Cameras, Camcorders, and Laptops

About Film and Cameras If your camera is new or if you haven't used it for a while, shoot and develop a few rolls of film before leaving home. Pack some lens tissue and an extra battery for your built-in light meter, and invest in an inexpensive skylight filter, to both protect your lens and provide some definition in hazy shots. Store film in a cool, dry place—never in the car's glove compartment or on the shelf under the rear window.

Films above ISO 400 are more sensitive to damage from airport security X-rays than others; very high speed films, ISO 1,000 and above, are exceedingly vulnerable. To protect your film, don't put it in checked luggage; carry it with you in a plastic bag and ask for a hand inspection. Such requests are honored at American airports, but are up to the inspector abroad. Don't depend on a lead-lined bag to protect film in checked luggage—the airline may very well turn up the dosage of radiation to see what you've got in there. Airport metal detectors do not harm film, although you'll set off the alarm if you walk through one with a roll in your pocket. Call the Kodak Information Center (tel. 800/242–2424) for details.

About Camcorders Before your trip, put new or long-unused camcorders through their paces, and practice panning and zooming. Invest in a skylight filter to protect the lens, and check the lithium battery that lights up the LCD (liquid crystal display) modes. As for the rechargeable nickel-cadmium batteries that are the camera's power source, take along an extra pair, so while you're using your camcorder you'll have one battery ready and another recharging. Most newer camcorders are equipped with the battery (which generally slides or clicks onto the camera body) and, to recharge it, with what's known as a universal or worldwide AC adapter charger (or multivoltage converter) that can be used whether the voltage is 110 or 220. All that's needed is the appropriate plug.

About Videotape Unlike still-camera film, videotape is not damaged by X-rays. However, it may well be harmed by the magnetic field of a walk-through metal detector. Airport security personnel may want you to turn the camcorder on to prove that that's what it is, so make sure the battery is charged when you get to the airport. Note that although the United States, Canada, Japan, Korea, Taiwan, and other countries operate on the National Television System Committee video standard (NTSC), Norway uses PAL/SECAM technology. So you will not be able to view your tapes through the local TV set or view movies bought there in your home VCR. Blank tapes bought in Norway can be used for NTSC camcorder taping, however—although you'll probably find they cost more abroad and wish you'd brought an adequate supply along.

About Laptops Security X-rays do not harm hard-disk or floppy-disk storage. Most airlines allow you to use your laptop aloft but request that you turn it off during takeoff and landing so as not to interfere with navigation equipment. Make sure the battery is charged when you arrive at the airport, because you may be asked to turn on the computer at security checkpoints to prove that it is what it appears to be. If you're a heavy computer user, consider traveling with a backup battery. For international travel, register your laptop with U.S. Customs as you leave the country, providing it's manufactured abroad (U.S.-origin items cannot be registered at U.S. Customs); when you do so, you'll get a certificate, good for as long as you own the item, containing your name and address, a description of the laptop, and its serial number, that will quash any questions that may arise on your return. If your laptop is U.S.-made, call the consulate of the country you'll be visiting to find out whether it should be registered with customs in that country upon arrival. Some travelers do this as a matter of course and ask customs officers to sign a document that specifies the total configuration of the system, computer and peripherals, and its value. In addition, before leaving home, find out about repair facilities at your destination, and don't forget any transformer or adapter plug you may need (*see* Electricity, *above*).

Language

Every Norwegian receives at least seven years of English instruction, starting in the second grade. Norwegian has three additional vowels, æ, ø, and å. Æ is pronounced as a short "a." The ø, sometimes printed as *oe*, is the same as ö in German and Swedish, pronounced very much like a short "u." The å is a contraction of the archaic aa and sounds like long "o." These three letters appear at the end of alphabetical listings.

There are two officially sanctioned languages, Bokmål and Nynorsk. Bokmål is used by 84% of the population and is the main written form of Norwegian, the language of books, as the first half of its name indicates. Nynorsk, which translates as "new Norwegian," is actually a compilation of older dialect forms from rural Norway, which evolved during the national romantic period around the turn of this century. All Norwegians have to study both languages.

The Sami (incorrectly called Lapp) people have their own language, which is more akin to Finnish than to Norwegian.

Staying Healthy

Finding a Doctor The **International Association for Medical Assistance to Travellers** (IAMAT, 417 Center St., Lewiston, NY 14092, tel. 716/754–4883; 40 Regal Rd., Guelph, Ontario N1K 1B5; 57 Voirets, 1212 Grand-Lancy, Geneva, Switzerland) publishes a worldwide directory of English-speaking physicians whose qualifications meet IAMAT standards and who have agreed to treat members for a set fee. Membership is free.

Assistance Companies Pretrip medical referrals, emergency evacuation or repatriation, 24-hour telephone hot lines for medical consultation, dispatch of medical personnel, relay of medical records, up-front cash for emergencies, and other personal and legal assistance are among the services provided by several membership organizations specializing in medical assistance to travelers. Among them are **International SOS Assistance** (Box 11568, Philadelphia, PA 19116, tel. 215/244–1500 or 800/523–8930; Box 466, Pl. Bonaventure, Montréal, Qué. H5A 1C1, tel. 514/874–7674 or 800/363–0263), **Near Services** (450 Prairie Ave., Suite 101, Calumet City, IL 60409, tel. 708/868–6700 or 800/654–6700), and **Travel Assistance International** (1133 15th St. NW, Suite 400, Washington, DC 20005, tel. 202/331–1609 or 800/821–2828), part of Europ Assistance Worldwide Services, Inc. Because these companies will also sell you death-and-dismemberment, trip-cancellation, and other insurance coverage, there is some overlap with the travel-insurance policies discussed below, which may include the services of an assistance company among the insurance options or reimburse travelers for such services without providing them.

Insurance

For U.S. Residents Most tour operators, travel agents, and insurance agents sell specialized health-and-accident, flight, trip-cancellation, and luggage insurance as well as comprehensive policies with some or all of these features. But before you make any purchase, review your existing health and homeowner policies to find out whether they cover expenses incurred while traveling.

Health-and-Accident Insurance Supplemental health-and-accident insurance for travelers is usually a part of comprehensive policies. Specific policy provisions vary, but they tend to address three general areas, beginning with reimbursement for medical expenses caused by illness or an accident during a trip. Such policies may reimburse anywhere from $1,000 to $150,000 worth of medical expenses; dental benefits may also be included. A second common feature is the personal-accident, or death-and-dismemberment, provision, which pays a lump sum to your beneficiaries if you die or to you if you lose one or both limbs or your eyesight. This is similar to the flight insurance described below, although it is not necessarily limited to accidents involving airplanes or even other "common carriers" (buses, trains, and ships) and can be in effect 24 hours a day. The lump sum awarded can range from $15,000 to $500,000. A third area generally addressed by these policies is medical assistance (referrals, evacuation, or repatriation and other services). Some policies reimburse travelers for the cost of such services; others may automatically enroll you as a member of a particular medical-assistance company.

Flight Insurance This insurance, often bought as a last-minute impulse at the airport, pays a lump sum to a beneficiary when a plane crashes and the insured dies (and sometimes to a surviving passenger who loses eyesight or a limb); thus it supplements the airlines' own coverage as described in the limits-of-liability paragraphs on your ticket (up to $75,000 on international flights, $20,000 on domestic ones—and that is generally subject to litigation). Charging an airline ticket to a major credit card often automatically signs you up for flight insurance; in this case, the coverage may also embrace travel by bus, train, and ship.

Baggage Insurance In the event of loss, damage, or theft on international flights, airlines limit their liability to $20 per kilogram for checked baggage (roughly about $640 per 70-pound bag) and $400 per passenger for unchecked baggage. On domestic flights, the ceiling is $1,250 per passenger. Excess-valuation insurance can be bought directly from the airline at check-in but leaves your bags vulnerable on the ground.

Trip Insurance   There are two sides to this coin. **Trip-cancellation-and-interruption insurance** protects you in the event you are unable to undertake or finish your trip. **Default** or **bankruptcy insurance** protects you against a supplier's failure to deliver. Consider the former if your airline ticket, cruise, or package tour does not allow changes or cancellations. The amount of coverage to buy should equal the cost of your trip should you, a traveling companion, or a family member get sick, forcing you to stay home, plus the nondiscounted one-way airline ticket you would need to buy if you had to return home early. Read the fine print carefully; pay attention to sections defining "family member" and "preexisting medical conditions." A characteristic quirk of default policies is that they often do not cover default by travel agencies or default by a tour operator, airline, or cruise line if you bought your tour and the coverage directly from the firm in question. To reduce your need for default insurance, give preference to tours packaged by members of the United States Tour Operators Association (USTOA), which maintains a fund to reimburse clients in the event of member defaults. Even better, pay for travel arrangements with a major credit card, so that you can refuse to pay the bill if services have not been rendered—and let the card company fight your battles.

Comprehensive Policies   Companies supplying comprehensive policies with some or all of the above features include **Access America, Inc.,** underwritten by BCS Insurance Company (Box 11188, Richmond, VA 23230, tel. 800/284–8300); **Carefree Travel Insurance,** underwritten by The Hartford (Box 310, 120 Mineola Blvd., Mineola, NY 11501, tel. 516/294–0220 or 800/323–3149); **Tele-Trip** (Mutual of Omaha Plaza, Box 31762, Omaha, NE 68131, tel. 800/228–9792), a subsidiary of Mutual of Omaha; **The Travelers Companies** (1 Tower Sq., Hartford, CT 06183, tel. 203/277–0111 or 800/243–3174); **Travel Guard International,** underwritten by Transamerica Occidental Life Companies (1145 Clark St., Stevens Point, WI 54481, tel. 715/345–0505 or 800/782–5151); and **Wallach and Company, Inc.** (107 W. Federal St., Box 480, Middleburg, VA 22117, tel. 703/687–3166 or 800/237–6615), underwritten by Lloyds, London. These companies may also offer the above types of insurance separately.

U.K. Residents   Most tour operators, travel agents, and insurance agents sell specialized policies covering accident, medical expenses, personal liability, trip cancellation, and loss or theft of personal property. Some policies include coverage for delayed departure and legal expenses, winter-sports, accidents, or motoring abroad. You can also purchase an annual travel-insurance policy valid for every trip you make during the year in which it's purchased (usually only trips of less than 90 days). Before you leave, make sure you will be covered if you have a preexisting medical condition or are pregnant; your insurers may not pay for routine or continuing treatment, or may require a note from your doctor certifying your fitness to travel.

For advice by phone or a free booklet, "Holiday Insurance," that sets out what to expect from a holiday-insurance policy and gives price guidelines, contact the **Association of British Insurers** (51 Gresham St., London EC2V 7HQ, tel. 071/600–3333; 30 Gordon St., Glasgow G1 3PU, tel. 041/226–3905; Scottish Provincial Bldg., Donegall Sq. W, Belfast BT1 6JE, tel. 0232/249176; call for other locations).

Car Rentals

Driving through Norway is delightful; you'll notice that drivers keep their headlights on even during the day—it is required by law. Take a good pair of sunglasses—the slanting sunlight creates a lot of glare.

Most major car-rental companies are represented in Norway, including **Avis** (tel. 800/331–1084, 800/879–2847 in Canada); **Budget** (tel. 800/527–0700); **Dollar** (tel. 800/800–6000); **Hertz** (tel. 800/654–3001, 800/263-0600 in Canada); **National** (tel. 800/227–3876), known internationally as InterRent and Europcar. In cities, unlimited-mileage rates range from $118 per day for an economy car to $206 for a large car; weekly unlimited-mileage rates range from $300 to $408. This does not include VAT, which in Norway is 22% on car rentals.

Requirements Your own U.S., Canadian, or U.K. driver's license is acceptable. An International Driver's Permit, available from the American or Canadian Automobile Association, is a good idea.

Extra Charges Picking up the car in one city or country and leaving it in another may entail drop-off charges or one-way service fees, which can be substantial. The cost of a collision or loss-damage waiver (*see below*) can be high, also. Automatic transmissions and air-conditioning are not universally available abroad; ask for them when you book if you want them, and check the cost before you commit yourself to the rental.

Cutting Costs If you know you will want a car for more than a day or two, you can save by planning ahead. Major international companies have programs that discount their standard rates by 15%–30% if you make the reservation before departure (anywhere from two to 14 days), rent for a minimum number of days (typically three or four), and prepay the rental. Ask about these advance-purchase schemes when you call for information. More economical rentals are those that come as part of fly/drive or other packages, even those as bare-bones as the rental plus an airline ticket (*see* Tours and Packages, *above*).

Other sources of savings are the several companies that operate as wholesalers—companies that do not own their own fleets but rent in bulk from those that do and offer advantageous rates to their customers. Rentals through such companies must be arranged and paid for before you leave the United States. Among them are **Auto Europe** (Box 1097, Camden, ME 04843, tel. 207/236–8235 or 800/223–5555, 800/458–9503 in Canada) and **Kemwel** (106 Calvert St., Harrison, NY 10528, tel. 914/835–5555 or 800/678–0678). You won't see these wholesalers' deals advertised; they're even better in summer, when business travel is down. Always ask whether the prices are guaranteed in U.S. dollars or foreign currency and if unlimited mileage is available. Find out about any required deposits, cancellation penalties, and drop-off charges, and confirm the cost of the CDW.

One last tip: Remember to fill the tank when you turn in the vehicle, to avoid being charged for refueling at what you'll swear is the most expensive pump in town.

Insurance and Collision Damage Waiver The standard rental contract includes liability coverage (for damage to public property, injury to pedestrians, etc.) and coverage for the car against fire, theft (not included in certain countries), and collision damage with a deductible—most commonly $2,000–$3,000, occasionally more. In the case of an accident, you are responsible for the deductible amount unless you've purchased the collision damage waiver (CDW), which costs an average of $12 a day, although this varies depending on what you've rented, where, and from whom.

Because this adds up quickly, you may be inclined to say "no thanks"—and that's certainly your option, although the rental agent may not tell you so. Planning ahead will help you make the right decision. By all means, find out if your own insurance covers damage to a rental car while traveling (not simply a car to drive when yours is in for repairs). And check whether charging car rentals to any of your credit cards will get you a CDW at no charge. Note before you decline that deductibles are occasionally high enough that totaling a car would make you responsible for its full value.

Rail Passes

The **EurailPass,** valid for unlimited first-class train travel through 17 countries, including Norway, is an excellent value if you plan to travel around the Continent. The ticket is available for periods of 15 days ($460), 21 days ($598), one month ($728), two months ($998), and three months ($1,260). For two or more people traveling together, a 15-day rail pass costs $390 each. Between April 1 and September 30, you need a minimum of three in your group to get this discount. For those younger than 26, there is the **Eurail Youthpass,** for one or two months of unlimited second-class train travel at $508 and $698. If you like to spread out your train journey, you can use the **Eurail Flexipass.** With a Flexipass you can choose between 5, 10, or 15 days unlimited first-class train travel within a period of two months. You pay $298, $496, and $676 for the **Eurail Flexipass,** sold for first-class travel; and $220, $348, $474 for the **Eurail Youth Flexipass,** available to those under 26 on their first travel day, sold for second-class travel. Ask also about the **EurailDrive** Pass, which lets you combine four days of train travel with three days of car rental (through Hertz or Avis) at any time within a two-month period. Charges vary according to size of car, but two people traveling together can get the basic package for $289 per person. The **EurailPass** is available only if you live outside Europe and North Africa. You can apply through an authorized travel agent or through **Rail Europe** (226–230 Westchester Ave., White Plains, NY 10604, tel. 914/682–5172 or 800/848–7245 from the East and 800/438–7245 from the West).

The **Scanrail Pass** is valid for unlimited rail travel in Scandinavia, and offers free and discounted crossings on several ferry lines. A second-class pass costs $155 for 4 travel days within a period of 15 days, $265 for 9 days travel within 21 days, and $369 for 14 travel days within one month. The first-class rates are $189, $325, and $475, respectively. If you want the flexibility of a car combined with the speed and comfort of the train, try **Scanrail 'n Drive** (from $289 per person, based on two adults sharing an economy car). This pass gives you a four- or nine-day Scanrail pass, plus three days of car rental to use within a 14- or

21-day period. Both of these passes can be purchased from Rail Europe (*see above*) or from NBS Travel Agency in London.

Don't make the mistake of assuming that your rail pass guarantees you seats on the trains you want to ride. Seat reservations are required on some trains, particularly high-speed trains, and are a good idea on trains that may be crowded. You will also need reservations for overnight sleeping accommodations. Rail Europe can help you determine if you need reservations and can make them for you (about $10 each, less if you purchase them in Europe at the time of travel). (*See also* Staying in Norway: Getting Around by Train, *below*).

Student and Youth Travel

Oslo offers a special **City Card,** which entitles the holder to unlimited, reduced-rate travel on public transportation as well as free or discounted admission to museums, theaters, and other attractions. The cards can be purchased at tourist offices and major rail stations.

Travel Agencies The foremost U.S. student travel agency is **Council Travel,** a subsidiary of the nonprofit Council on International Educational Exchange. It specializes in low-cost travel arrangements, is the exclusive U.S. agent for several discount cards, and, with its sister CIEE subsidiary, **Council Charter,** is a source of airfare bargains. The Council Charter brochure and CIEE's twice-yearly *Student Travels* magazine, which details its programs, are available at the Council Travel office at CIEE headquarters (205 E. 42nd Street, New York, NY 10017, tel. 212/661–1450) and at 37 branches in college towns nationwide (free in person, $1 by mail). The **Educational Travel Center** (ETC, 438 N. Francis St., Madison, WI 53703, tel. 608/256–5551) also offers low-cost rail passes, domestic and international airline tickets (mostly for flights departing from Chicago), and other budgetwise travel arrangements. Other travel agencies catering to students include **Travel Management International** (TMI, 18 Prescott St., Suite 4, Cambridge, MA 02138, tel. 617/661–8187) and **Travel Cuts** (187 College St., Toronto, Ont. M5T 1P7, tel. 416/979–2406).

Discount Cards For discounts on transportation and on museum and attractions admissions, buy the **International Student Identity Card** (ISIC) if you're a bona fide student, or the **International Youth Card** (IYC) if you're under 26. In the United States the ISIC and IYC cards cost $15 each and include basic travel accident and sickness coverage. Apply to **CIEE** (*see* address *above*, tel. 212/661–1414; the application is in *Student Travels*). In Canada the cards are available for $15 each from **Travel Cuts** (*see above*). In the United Kingdom they cost £5 and £4, respectively, at student unions and student travel companies, including Council Travel's London office (28A Poland St., London W1V 3DB, tel. 071/437–7767).

Hosteling An **International Youth Hostel Federation** (IYHF) membership card is the key to more than 5,300 hostel locations in 59 countries; the sex-segregated, dormitory-style sleeping quarters, including some for families, go for $7–$20 a night per person. Membership is available in the United States through **American Youth Hostels** (AYH, 733 15th St. NW, Washington, DC 20005, tel. 202/783–6161), the American link in the worldwide chain, and costs $25 for adults 18–54, $10 for those under 18,

$15 for those 55 and over, and $35 for families. Volume 1 of the two-volume *Guide to Budget Accommodation* lists hostels in Europe and the Mediterranean ($13.95, including postage). IYHF membership is available in Canada through the **Canadian Hostelling Association** (CHA, 1600 James Naismith Dr., Suite 608, Gloucester, Ont. K1B 5N4, tel. 613/748–5638) for $26.75, and in the United Kingdom through the **Youth Hostel Association of England and Wales** (8 St. Stephen's Hill, St. Albans, Herts. AL1 2DY, tel. 0727/55215) for £9.

Traveling with Children

Families visiting Norway in summer may enjoy renting an authentic *rorbu* (fisherman's shanty) at the seaside. Accommodations are simple yet adequate, and rowboats usually are available for rent. For more information contact **Borton Overseas** (5516 Lyndale Ave. S, Minneapolis, MN 55419, tel. 800/843–0602). Information on farming holidays in Norway is available from **Nortra** (Nortravel Marketing; Box 499, Sentrum, N-0105 Oslo, tel. 22/42–70–44).

Publications *Family Travel Times,* published 10 times a year by **Travel With**
Newsletter **Your Children** (TWYCH, 45 W. 18th St., 7th Floor Tower, New York, NY 10011, tel. 212/206–0688; annual subscription $55), covers destinations, types of vacations, and modes of travel.

Books *Traveling with Children—And Enjoying It,* by Arlene K. Butler ($11.95 plus $3 shipping per book; Globe Pequot Press, Box 833, Old Saybrook, CT 06475, tel. 800/243–0495, or 800/962–0973 in CT) helps plan your trip with children, from toddlers to teens. *Innocents Abroad: Traveling with Kids in Europe,* by Valerie Wolf Deutsch and Laura Sutherland ($15.95 or $4.95 paperback, Penguin USA, *see above*), covers child- and teen-friendly activities, food, and transportation.

Tour Operators **GrandTravel** (6900 Wisconsin Ave., Suite 706, Chevy Chase, MD 20815, tel. 301/986–0790 or 800/247–7651) offers international and domestic tours for grandparents traveling with their grandchildren. The catalogue, as charmingly written and illustrated as a children's book, positively invites armchair traveling with lap-sitters aboard. **Families Welcome!** (21 W. Colony Pl., Suite 140, Durham, NC 27705, tel. 919/489–2555 or 800/326–0724) packages and sells family tours to Europe. **Rascals in Paradise** (650 5th St., Suite 505, San Francisco, CA 94107, tel. 415/978–9800 or 800/872–7225) specializes in programs for families.

Getting There On international flights, the fare for infants under 2 not occupy-
Airfares ing a seat is generally 10% of the accompanying adult's fare; children ages 2–11 usually pay half to two-thirds of the adult fare. On domestic flights, children under 2 not occupying a seat travel free, and older children currently travel on the "lowest applicable" adult fare.

Baggage In general, infants paying 10% of the adult fare are allowed one carry-on bag, not to exceed 70 pounds or 45 inches (length + width + height). The adult baggage allowance applies for children paying half or more of the adult fare. Check with the airline for particulars, especially regarding flights between two foreign destinations, where allowances for infants may be less generous than those above.

Safety Seats The FAA recommends the use of safety seats aloft and details approved models in the free leaflet **"Child/Infant Safety Seats Recommended for Use in Aircraft"** (available from the Federal Aviation Administration, APA–200, 800 Independence Ave. SW, Washington, DC 20591, tel. 202/267–3479). Airline policy varies. U.S. carriers must allow FAA-approved models, but because these seats are strapped into a regular passenger seat, they may require that parents buy a ticket even for an infant under 2 who would otherwise ride free. Foreign carriers may not allow infant seats, may charge the child's rather than the infant's fare for their use, or may require you to hold your baby during takeoff and landing, thus defeating the seat's purpose.

Facilities Aloft Airlines do provide other facilities and services for children, such as children's meals and freestanding bassinets (to those sitting in seats on the bulkhead, where there's enough legroom to accommodate them). Make your request when reserving. The annual February/March issue of **Family Travel Times** gives details of the children's services of dozens of airlines ($10; *see above*). "Kids and Teens in Flight" (free from the U.S. Department of Transportation, tel. 202/366–2220) offers tips for children flying alone.

Getting Around Children are entitled to discount tickets (often as much as 50% off) on buses, trains, and ferries throughout Norway, as well as reductions on special City Cards. During summer months children under 12 are entitled to special discounts on airfare.

Lodging In most Norwegian hotels children stay free or at reduced rates when sharing their parents' rooms; there is a nominal charge for an extra bed.

Baby-sitting Services For information on local baby-sitting agencies, contact the tourist office in the city or region you are visiting.

Hints for Travelers with Disabilities

The Norwegian Association of the Disabled offers a leaflet detailing hotels with facilities for disabled visitors. (Norges Handikapforbund, Box 9217 Grønland N-0134, Oslo, tel. 22/17–02–55).

Organizations Several organizations provide travel information for people with disabilities, usually for a membership fee, and some publish newsletters and bulletins. Among them are the **Information Center for Individuals with Disabilities** (Fort Point Pl., 27–43 Wormwood St., Boston, MA 02210, tel. 617/727–5540 or 800/462–5015 in MA between 11 and 4, or leave message; TDD/TTY tel. 617/345–9743); **Mobility International USA** (Box 3551, Eugene, OR 97403, voice and TDD tel. 503/343–1284), the U.S. branch of an international organization based in Britain (*see below*) and present in 30 countries; **MossRehab Hospital Travel Information Service** (1200 W. Tabor Rd., Philadelphia, PA 19141, tel. 215/456–9603, TDD tel. 215/456–9602); the **Society for the Advancement of Travel for the Handicapped** (SATH, 347 5th Ave., Suite 610, New York, NY 10016, tel. 212/447–7284, fax 212/725–8253); the **Travel Industry and Disabled Exchange** (TIDE, 5435 Donna Ave., Tarzana, CA 91356, tel. 818/368–5648); and **Travelin' Talk** (Box 3534, Clarksville, TN 37043, tel. 615/552–6670).

In the United Kingdom Main information sources include the **Royal Association for Disability and Rehabilitation** (RADAR, 25 Mortimer St., London

W1N 8AB, tel. 071/637–5400), which publishes travel information for the disabled in Britain, and **Mobility International** (228 Borough High St., London SE1 1JX, tel. 071/403–5688), the headquarters of an international membership organization that serves as a clearinghouse of travel information for people with disabilities.

Travel Agencies and Tour Operators **Directions Unlimited** (720 N. Bedford Rd., Bedford Hills, NY 10507, tel. 914/241–1700), a travel agency, has expertise in tours and cruises for the disabled. **Evergreen Travel Service** (4114 198th St. SW, Suite 13, Lynnwood, WA 98036, tel. 206/776–1184 or 800/435–2288) operates Wings on Wheels Tours for those in wheelchairs, White Cane Tours for the blind, and tours for the deaf and makes group and independent arrangements for travelers with any disability. **Flying Wheels Travel** (143 W. Bridge St., Box 382, Owatonna, MN 55060, tel. 800/535–6790 or 800/722–9351 in MN), a tour operator and travel agency, arranges international tours, cruises, and independent travel itineraries for people with mobility disabilities. **Nautilus,** at the same address as TIDE (*see above*), packages tours for the disabled internationally.

Publications In addition to the fact sheets, newsletters, and books mentioned above are several free publications available from the Consumer Information Center (Pueblo, CO 81009): "New Horizons for the Air Traveler with a Disability," a U.S. Department of Transportation booklet describing changes resulting from the 1986 Air Carrier Access Act and those still to come from the 1990 Americans with Disabilities Act (include Department 608Y in the address), and the Airport Operators Council's *Access Travel: Airports* (Dept. 5804), which describes facilities and services for the disabled at more than 500 airports worldwide.

Twin Peaks Press (Box 129, Vancouver, WA 98666, tel. 206/694–2462 or 800/637–2256) publishes the *Directory of Travel Agencies for the Disabled* ($19.95), listing more than 370 agencies worldwide; *Travel for the Disabled* ($19.95), listing some 500 access guides and accessible places worldwide; the *Directory of Accessible Van Rentals* ($9.95) for campers and RV travelers worldwide; and *Wheelchair Vagabond* ($14.95), a collection of personal travel tips. Add $2 per book for shipping.

Lodging Some hotels are suitable for unaccompanied travelers, but, in many others, individuals will require the assistance of an able-bodied companion. Contact the organizations listed above for further information.

The **Best Western** chain (tel. 800/528–1234) has a hotel with wheelchair-accessible rooms in Oslo. If wheelchair rooms are not available, ground-floor rooms are provided.

Hints for Older Travelers

Visitors over 67 are automatically entitled to a 50% reduction on all first- and second-class train tickets. Senior-citizen tickets can be purchased at all rail stations. For additional information on senior discounts and seasonal savings plans, contact the Scandinavian Tourist Board (*see* Government Tourist Offices, *above*), and HT Reiser with Pensjonistenes Reisesenter (Travel Center for the Retired; tel. 22/36–20–40 in Oslo).

Organizations The **American Association of Retired Persons** (AARP, 601 E St. NW, Washington, DC 20049, tel. 202/434–2277) provides independent travelers the Purchase Privilege Program, which offers discounts on hotels, car rentals, and sightseeing, and arranges group tours, cruises, and apartment living through AARP Travel Experience from American Express (400 Pinnacle Way, Suite 450, Norcross, GA 30071, tel. 800/927–0111); these can be booked through travel agents, except for the cruises, which must be booked directly (tel. 800/745–4567). AARP membership is open to those 50 and over; annual dues are $8 per person or couple.

Two other membership organizations offer discounts on lodgings, car rentals, and other travel products, along with such nontravel perks as magazines and newsletters. The **National Council of Senior Citizens** (1331 F St. NW, Washington, DC 20004, tel. 202/347–8800) is a nonprofit advocacy group with some 5,000 local clubs across the United States; membership costs $12 per person or couple annually. **Mature Outlook** (6001 N. Clark St., Chicago, IL 60660, tel. 800/336–6330), a Sears Roebuck & Co. subsidiary with 800,000 members, charges $9.95 for an annual membership.

Note: When using any senior-citizen identification card for reduced hotel rates, mention it when booking, not when checking out. At restaurants, show your card before you're seated; discounts may be limited to certain menus, days, or hours. If you are renting a car, ask about promotional rates that might improve on your senior-citizen discount.

Educational Travel **Elderhostel** (75 Federal St., 3rd floor, Boston, MA 02110, tel. 617/426–7788) is a nonprofit organization that has offered inexpensive study programs for people 60 and older since 1975. Programs take place at more than 1,800 educational institutions in the United States, Canada, and 45 other countries; courses cover everything from marine science to Greek myths and cowboy poetry. Participants generally attend lectures in the morning and spend the afternoon sightseeing or on field trips; they live in dorms on the host campuses. Fees for two- to three-week international trips—including room, board, and transportation from the United States—range from $1,800 to $4,500.

Interhostel (University of New Hampshire, 6 Garrison Ave., Durham, NH 03824, tel. 800/733–9753), a slightly younger enterprise than Elderhostel, caters to a slightly younger clientele—that is, 50 and over—and runs programs overseas in some 25 countries. But the idea is similar: Lectures and field trips mix with sightseeing, and participants stay in dormitories at cooperating educational institutions or in modest hotels. Programs are usually two weeks in length and cost $1,500–$2,100, not including airfare from the United States.

Tour Operators **Saga International Holidays** (222 Berkeley St., Boston, MA 02116, tel. 800/343–0273), which specializes in group travel for people over 60, offers a selection of variously priced tours and cruises covering five continents. If you want to take your grandchildren, look into **GrandTravel** (*see* Traveling with Children, *above*).

Further Reading

A *History of the Vikings* (Oxford University Press, 1984) re-counts the story of the aggressive warriors and explorers who, by the time of their defeat at Hastings in 1066, had influenced a large portion of the world, from Constantinople to America. Gwyn Jones's lively account makes learning the history enjoyable.

Norway's major writers offer intense and moving experiences of the Norwegian sensibility. The plays of Henrik Ibsen (1828–1906), such as *The Doll's House, Ghosts, Hedda Gabler,* and *The Master Builder,* are gems of psychological insight, symbol-ism, and social criticism. Among Norway's three literary No-bel prizewinners of the early 20th century, the dramatist, novelist, and critic Bjørnstjerne Bjørnson linked Norwegian history and legends with modern ideals; and the novelists Knut Hamsun (*Hunger*) and Sigrid Undset (*Kristin Lavransdatter*) explored the tension between society and the individual, and the plight of women, respectively. More recently, Tarjei Vesaas (1897–1970) captured the spare Norwegian taste for al-legory and symbolism in the novels *The Ice Palace* and *Birds* and in his *Selected Poems.*

Arriving and Departing

From North America by Plane

Flights are either nonstop, direct, or connecting. A **nonstop** flight requires no change of plane and makes no stops. A **direct** flight stops at least once and can involve a change of plane, al-though the flight number remains the same; if the first leg is late, the second waits. This is not the case with a **connecting** flight, which involves a different plane and a different flight number.

Airports and Airlines **Oslo Fornebu Airport** is the gateway to Norway for most vis-itors. Once called a "cafeteria with a landing strip," it is currently being transformed into a modern airport worthy of a capital city. Other international airports include **Bergen, Kristiansand S., Sandefjord, Stavanger,** and **Trondheim.**

Scandinavian Airlines (SAS) (tel. 800/221–2350) has daily non-stop flights to Oslo from New York, daily connections to Oslo via Copenhagen from Chicago, Los Angeles, and Seattle, and twice-weekly connections (also via Copenhagen) from Toronto and Anchorage. During the summer months, **Delta Airlines** (tel. 800/221–1212) has daily nonstop flights from New York to Oslo. **Icelandair** (tel. 800/223–5500) flies from New York to Oslo via Reykjavik.

Flying Time A nonstop flight from New York to Oslo takes about 8½ hours.

Cutting Flight Costs The Sunday travel section of most newspapers is a good source of deals. When booking, particularly through an unfamiliar company, call the Better Business Bureau to find out whether any complaints have been registered against the company, pay with a credit card if you can, and consider trip-cancellation and default insurance (*see* Insurance, *above*).

Promotional Airfares All the less expensive fares, called promotional or discount fares, are round-trip and involve restrictions. The exact nature of the restrictions depends on the airline, the route, and the season and on whether travel is domestic or international, but you must usually buy the ticket—commonly called an APEX (advance purchase excursion) when it's for international travel—in advance (seven, 14, or 21 days are usual). You must also respect certain minimum- and maximum-stay requirements (for instance, over a Saturday night or at least seven and no more than 30, 45, or 90 days), and you must be willing to pay penalties for changes. Airlines generally allow some changes for a fee. But the cheaper the fare, the more likely the ticket is nonrefundable; it would take a death in the family for the airline to give you any of your money back if you had to cancel. The cheapest fares are also subject to availability; because only a certain percentage of the plane's total seats will be sold at that price, they may go quickly.

Consolidators Consolidators or bulk-fare operators—also known as bucket shops—buy blocks of seats on scheduled flights that airlines anticipate they won't be able to sell. They pay wholesale prices, add a markup, and resell the seats to travel agents or directly to the public at prices that still undercut the airline's promotional or discount fares. You pay more than on a charter but ordinarily less than for an APEX ticket, and, even when there is not much of a price difference, the ticket usually comes without the advance-purchase restriction. Moreover, although tickets are marked nonrefundable so you can't turn them in to the airline for a full-fare refund, some consolidators sometimes give you your money back. Carefully read the fine print detailing penalties for changes and cancellations. If you doubt the reliability of a company, call the airline once you've made your booking and confirm that you do, indeed, have a reservation on the flight.

The biggest U.S. consolidator, C.L. Thomson Express, sells only to travel agents. Well-established consolidators selling to the public include **UniTravel** (Box 12485, St. Louis, MO 63132, tel. 314/569–0900 or 800/325–2222); **Council Charter** (205 E. 42nd St., New York, NY 10017, tel. 212/661–0311 or 800/800–8222), a division of the Council on International Educational Exchange and a longtime charter operator now functioning more as a consolidator; and **Travac** (989 6th Ave., New York, NY 10018, tel. 212/563–3303 or 800/872–8800), also a former charterer.

Charter Flights Charters usually have the lowest fares and the most restrictions. Departures are limited and seldom on time, and you can lose all or most of your money if you cancel. (Generally, the closer to departure you cancel, the more you lose, although sometimes you will be charged only a small fee if you supply a substitute passenger.) The charterer, on the other hand, may legally cancel the flight for any reason up to 10 days before departure; within 10 days of departure, the flight may be canceled only if it becomes physically impossible to operate it. The charterer may also revise the itinerary or increase the price after you have bought the ticket, but if the new arrangement constitutes a "major change," you have the right to a refund. Before buying a charter ticket, read the fine print for the company's refund policy and details on major changes. Money for charter flights is usually paid into a bank escrow account, the name of which should be on the contract. If you don't pay by credit card, make your check payable to the escrow account (unless you're dealing with a travel agent, in which case, his or her check should be payable to the escrow account). The Department of Transportation's Consumer Affairs Office (I–25, Washington, DC 20590, tel. 202/366–2220) can answer questions on charters and send you its "Plane Talk: Public Charter Flights" information sheet.

Discount Travel Clubs
Travel clubs offer their members unsold space on airplanes, cruise ships, and package tours at nearly the last minute and at well below the original cost. Suppliers thus receive some revenue for their "leftovers," and members get a bargain. Membership generally includes a regular bulletin or access to a toll-free telephone hot line giving details of available trips departing anywhere from three or four days to several months in the future. Packages tend to be more common than flights alone, so if airfares are your only interest, read the literature before joining. Reductions on hotels are also available. Clubs include **Discount Travel International** (114 Forrest Ave., Suite 203, Narberth, PA 19072, tel. 215/668–7184; $45 annually, single or family), **Moment's Notice** (425 Madison Ave., New York, NY 10017, tel. 212/486–0503; $45 annually, single or family), **Travelers Advantage** (CUC Travel Service, 49 Music Sq. W, Nashville, TN 37203, tel. 800/548–1116; $49 annually, single or family), and **Worldwide Discount Travel Club** (1674 Meridian Ave., Miami Beach, FL 33139, tel. 305/534–2082; $50 annually for family, $40 single).

Enjoying the Flight
All flights to Norway are night flights, unless you prefer to take a morning flight to London and stay overnight before continuing on. Because the air aloft is dry, drink plenty of beverages while on board; remember that drinking alcohol contributes to jet lag, as do heavy meals. Sleepers usually prefer window seats to curl up against; restless passengers ask to be on the aisle. Bulkhead seats, in the front row of each cabin, have more legroom, but since there's no seat ahead, trays attach awkwardly to the arms of your seat, and you must stow all possessions overhead. Bulkhead seats are usually reserved for the disabled, the elderly, and people traveling with babies.

Smoking
Since February 1990, smoking has been banned on all domestic flights of less than six hours duration; the ban also applies to domestic segments of international flights aboard U.S. and foreign carriers. On U.S. carriers flying to Norway and other destinations abroad, a seat in a no-smoking section must be provided for every passenger who requests one, and the section must be enlarged to accommodate such passengers if necessary as long as they have complied with the airline's deadline for check-in and seat assignment. If smoking bothers you, request a seat far from the smoking section.

Foreign airlines are exempt from these rules but do provide no-smoking sections, and some nations, including Canada as of July 1, 1993, have gone as far as to ban smoking on all domestic flights; other countries may ban smoking on flights of less than a specified duration. The International Civil Aviation Organization has set July 1, 1996, as the date to ban smoking aboard airlines worldwide, but the body has no power to enforce its decisions.

From the United Kingdom by Plane

SAS (tel. 071/734–6777, fax 071/465–0125) flies from Heathrow to Oslo and Stavanger, and from Aberdeen to Stavanger. **Braathens SAFE** operates flights from Newcastle to Stavanger and Oslo, and from London Gatwick to Oslo. **AirUK** has several flights weekly from Aberdeen to Stavanger and Bergen. Flying time from London to Oslo is about 1¾ hours and about 1½ hours to Stavanger.

British Airways (tel. 081/897–4000) offers nonstop flights from Heathrow to Bergen, Oslo, and Stavanger. **Aer Lingus** (tel. 0345/01–01–01; in Ireland, 0001/377–777), **Cimber Air** (tel. 0652/688491), **Business Air** (tel. 0382/66345), **Midtfly** (tel. 0224/723357), and **Icelandair** (tel. 071/388–5599; or 081/745–7051 at Heathrow Airport) all have flights between Great Britain or Ireland and major Scandinavian cities. The flying time from London to Oslo is about 1¾ hours.

From the United Kingdom by Train and Boat

By Train Traveling from Britain to Norway by train is not difficult. The best connection leaves London's Victoria Station at noon and connects at Dover with a boat to Oostende, Belgium. From Oostende there is a sleeping-car-only connection to Copenhagen that arrives the next morning at 8:25. The train to Oslo leaves at 9:45 AM and arrives at 7:42 PM. A number of special discounted trips are available, including the **InterRail Pass,** which is now available for European residents of all ages.

By Boat Only one ferry line serves Norway from the United Kingdom, **Color Line** (Tyne Commission Quay, North Shields [near Newcastle] LEN29 6EA, tel. 091/296–1313, or Skoltegrunnskaien, 5000 Bergen, tel. 55/32–27–80), which has three departures a week between Bergen, Stavanger, and Newcastle during the summer season (May 22–Sept. 10), two during the rest of the year. Crossings take about 20 hours. Monday sailings stop first in Stavanger and arrive in Bergen six hours later, while the other trips stop first in Bergen. **Scandinavian Seaways** has a crossing between Harwich and Göteborg, Sweden, a 4½-hour drive from Oslo.

Staying in Norway

Getting Around

The southern part of Norway can be considered fairly compact—all major cities are about a day's drive from one another (although Trondheim–Stavanger is pushing it). The distances make themselves felt on the way north, where Norway becomes narrower as it inches up to and beyond the Arctic Circle and hooks over Sweden and Finland to touch the Soviet Union. Because distances are so great, it is virtually impossible to visit the entire country from one base.

By Plane SAS (EuroClass, tel. 22/17–00–10; Tourist, tel. 22/17–00–20) serves most major cities, including Svalbard. **Braathens SAFE** (SAFE stands for the "South Asian and Far Eastern" routes of the parent shipping company; tel. 22/83–44–70) is the major domestic airline, serving cities throughout the country and along the coast as far north as Tromsø and Svalbard. It also has international routes from Oslo to Billund (Denmark), Malmö (Sweden), and Newcastle (England). **Widerøe** (tel. 22/73–65–00) serves smaller airports (with smaller planes), mostly along the coast, and in northern Norway. **Norsk Air** (tel. 33/46–90–00), a subsidiary of Widerøe, provides similar services in the southern part of the country. **Coast Air** (tel. 52/83–41–10) and **Norlink** (tel. 77/67–57–80), an SAS subsidiary, are commuter systems linking smaller and larger airports.

A number of special fares are available within Norway year-round, including air passes, family tickets, weekend excursions, youth (up to the age of 26), and senior (over 67). Youth fares are cheapest when purchased from the automatic ticket machines at the airport on the day of departure. All Norwegian routes have reduced rates from July through the middle of August, and tickets can be purchased on the spot. Outside of these times, a minifare during low traffic hours is probably the cheapest way to fly.

All flights within Scandinavia are nonsmoking, as are all airports in Norway, except in designated areas.

By Train **NSB,** the Norwegian State Railway System, has five main lines originating from the **Oslo S Station.** The longest runs north to Trondheim, then extends onward as far as Fauske and Bodø. The southern line hugs the coast to Stavanger, while the western line crosses some famous scenic territory on the way to Bergen. An eastern line through Kongsvinger links Norway with Sweden to Stockholm, while another southern line through Gothenburg is the main connection with Continental Europe. Narvik, north of Bodø, is the last stop on Sweden's Ofot line, which runs from Stockholm via Kiruna, the world's northernmost rail system. It is possible to take a five-hour bus trip between Bodø and Narvik to connect with the other train.

Discounted fares include family, senior citizen (including not-yet-senior spouses), and off-peak fares, which must be purchased a day in advance. NSB gives student discounts only to foreigners studying at Norwegian institutions.

NSB trains are clean, comfortable, and punctual. Most have special compartments for the disabled and for families with children under two years old. Both first- and second-class tickets are available. Both seat and sleeper reservations are required on long journeys. Prices vary according to one-, two-, or three-bunk cabins.

Most trains have food service, ranging from simple sandwiches and beverages to a buffet car selling hot dogs, pizza, and perhaps an entrée. Only the Oslo-Bergen route has a full-service dining car, where reservations are essential.

Train tickets can be purchased in railway stations or from travel agencies. NSB has its own travel agency in Oslo (Stortingsgt. 28, tel. 22/83–88–50).

NSB offers many kinds of passes, including the **Nordturist Card,** good for unlimited rail travel in Denmark, Sweden, Norway, and Finland and is valid on many ferries. The 21-day card costs about $380 (first class) or $285 (second class). Tickets can be bought at any train station in the four countries. Young people ages 12 to 25 pay about three-fourths, and children 4 to 11, half price. Rebates of up to 50% are granted on some other ferries and coaches and by some hotels. The Nordturist Card can also be purchased from NSB Travel Agency in London.

By Bus Every end station of the railroad is supported by a number of bus routes, some of which are operated by NSB, others by local companies.

Long-distance buses usually take longer than the railroad and fares are only slightly lower. Virtually every settlement on the mainland is served by bus, and for anyone with a desire to get off the beaten track, a pay-as-you-go open-ended bus trip is the best way to see Norway. **Nor-Way Bussekspress** (Bussterminalen, Galleri Olso, tel. 22/17–52–90, fax 22/17–59–22) has more than 40 different bus services, covering 10,000 kilometers (6,200 miles) and 500 destinations in its organization and can arrange any journey. One of its participating services, **Feriebussen** (Østerdal Billag A/S, 2560 Alvdal, tel. 62/48–74–00) offers five package tours with English guides.

Discounted tickets are available for children, people over 60, families, students, and military personnel.

By Boat Ferries and passenger ships remain important means of transportation. Along west-coast fjords, car ferries are a way of life. Once you know your route, buy tickets for those ferries that allow advance purchase—this lets you drive to the front of the line.

More specialized boat service includes hydrofoil/catamaran trips between Stavanger, Haugesund, and Bergen. There are also fjord cruises out of these cities and others in the north. **Color Line** (Box 1422 Vika 0115, Oslo, tel. 22/94–44–00, fax 22/83–07–76) is a major carrier in Norwegian waters.

Norway's most renowned boat trip is **Hurtigruten,** or the Coastal Express, which departs from Bergen and stops at 36 ports in six days, ending with Kirkenes, near the Russian border, before turning back. Tickets can be purchased for the whole journey or for individual legs. Shore excursions are arranged at all ports. Tickets are available through travel agents or directly from the companies that run the service: FFR (9600 Hammerfest, tel. 78/41–10–00), OVDS (8501 Narvik, tel. 76/92–37–00), Nordenfjeldske Dampskibsselskab A/S (Kjøpmannsgt. 52, 7011 Trondheim, tel. 73/51–51–20, fax 73/51–51–46), and TFDS (9000 Tromsø, tel. 77/68–60–88).

By Car All vehicles registered abroad are required to carry international liability insurance and an international accident report form, which can be obtained from automobile clubs. Collision insurance is recommended. One important rule when driving in Norway: Yield to the vehicle approaching from the right.

Dimmed headlights are mandatory at all times, as is the use of seatbelts and children's seats (when appropriate) in both front and rear seats. All cars must carry red reflecting warning triangles to be placed a safe distance from a disabled vehicle.

Four-lane highways are the exception and are found only around major cities. Outside of main coastal routes, roads tend to be narrow and sharply twisting, with only token guardrails and during the summer, roads are always crowded. Along the west coast, waits for ferries can be significant.

Driving is on the right. Norwegian roads are well marked with directional, distance, and informational signs. Some roads, particularly those over mountains, can close for all or part of the winter.

The maximum speed limit is 90 kilometers per hour (55 miles per hour) on major motorways. On other highways, the limit is 80 kph (50 mph). The speed limit in cities and towns is 50 kph (30 mph), and 30 kph (18 mph) in residential areas.

Gas stations are plentiful, and unleaded gasoline and diesel fuel are sold virtually everywhere from self-service gas pumps. Those marked *kort* are 24-hour pumps, which take oil company credit cards or bank cards, either of which is inserted directly into the pump.

Norway has strict drinking and driving laws, and routine road-side checks, especially on Friday and Saturday nights, are common. The legal limit is a blood alcohol percentage of 0.05%, which corresponds to a glass of wine or a bottle of low-alcohol beer. If you are stopped for a routine check, you may be re-quired to take a breath test. If that result is positive, you must submit to a blood test. No exceptions are made for foreigners, who can lose their licenses on the spot.

Speeding is also punished severely. Most roads are monitored by gray metal boxes equipped with radar and cameras. Signs warning of *Automatisk Trafikkontroll* (Automatic Traffic Monitoring) are posted periodically along appropriate roads. Norway has recently been in the process of changing the numbers of some of its routes and highways, especially those beginning with "E." Make sure you double check all directions and have an up-to-date maps before you venture out.

By Taxi Even the smallest villages have some form of taxi service. Towns on the railroad normally have taxi ranks just outside the station. Look in the telephone book under "Taxi" or "Drosje." All city taxis are connected with a central dispatching office, so there is only one main telephone number, the taxi central.

Telephones

The telephone system is modern and efficient, and international direct service is available throughout the country. Phone numbers are six digits in the cities, eight digits throughout the country.

Public telephones are of two types. Push-button phones, which accept NKr1, 5, and 10 coins, are easy to use: Lift the receiver, listen for the dial tone, insert the coins, dial the number, and wait for a connection. The digital screen at the top of the box indicates the amount of money in your "account."

Older rotary telephones sometimes have a grooved slope at the top for NKr1 coins, allowing them to drop into the phone as needed. Place several in the slope, lift off the receiver, listen for the dial tone, dial the number, and wait for a connection. When the call is connected, the telephone will emit a series of beeps, allowing coins to drop into the telephone.

Both types of telephones have warning signals (short pips) indicating that the purchased time is almost over.

Local Calls Local calls cost NKr2 (about 30 cents) from a pay phone and about NKr3 from hotel phones.

Long-distance Calls All eight digits are required when dialing in Norway, both for local and long-distance calls. Rates vary according to distance and time of day.

International Calls Dial the international access code, 095, then the country code, and number. (Beginning in 1995, the new international access code will be 00.) All telephone books list country code numbers, including the United States and Canada (1), Great Britain (44), and Australia (61). Norway's code is 47. For operator-assisted calls, dial 117 for national calls and 115 for international calls. All international operators speak English.

Information Dial 180 for information for Norway and the other Scandinavian countries, 181 for international telephone numbers.

Mail

The letter rate for Norway is Nkr3.50, Nkr4 for the other Nordic countries, NKr4.40 for Europe, and NKr5.50 for outside Europe for a letter weighing up to 20g (¾ ounce).

Tipping

Tipping is kept to a minimum in Norway because service charges are added to most bills. It is, however, handy to have a supply of NKr5 or 10 coins for less formal service. Tip only in local currency.

Airport and railroad porters (if you can find them) have fixed rates per bag, so they will tell you how much they should be paid. Tips to doormen vary according to the type of bag and the distance carried—NKr5–10 each, with similar tips for porters carrying bags to the room. Room service usually has a service charge included already, so tipping is discretionary.

Round off a taxi fare to the next round digit, or anywhere from NKr5 to NKr10, a little more if the driver has been helpful with luggage.

All restaurants include a service charge ranging from 12% to 15% in the bill. It is customary to add an additional 5% for exceptional service, but it is not obligatory. Maitre d's are not tipped, and coat checks have flat rates, ranging from NKr5 to NKr10 per person.

Opening and Closing Times

Banks are open weekdays 8 to 3:30, Thursday until 6. Most shops are open 9 or 10 to 5 weekdays, Thursday until 7, Saturday 9 to 2, closed Sunday. Some large shopping centers are open until 8 weekdays. Supermarkets are open until 8 or 10 weekdays and until 6 on Saturdays. During the summer, most shops close weekdays at 4 and at 1 on Saturday, while banks open at 8:15 and close at 3, with a Thursday closing at 5. Most post offices are open weekdays 8 to 5:30, Saturday 8 to 1.

Shopping

Good buys include handicrafts, handknitted sweaters, yarn, embroidery kits, textiles, pewter, rustic ironwork, silverware, wooden bowls and spoons, hand-dipped candles, and Christmas ornaments made from natural materials. *Husfliden* (homecraft) outlets are located in almost every city. The **classic knitting designs**, with snowflakes and reindeer, have been bestsellers for years and can be bought at most Husfliden and specialty stores, while more modern sweaters, made of combinations of brightly colored yarns, can be purchased from yarn shops. *Juleduk* (Christmas tablecloths) with typical Norwegian themes, are for sale year-round at embroidery shops. **High-fashion textiles** include coats and jackets in wool blanket material with nature motifs. Other handmade items include **candlesticks** of both pewter and wrought iron, **handblown glass,** and handturned **wood bowls** and **platters** made of birch roots. All Husfliden stores and many gift shops sell **Christmas ornaments** handmade from straw and wood shavings. Other, more off-beat, items include **cheese planes** (*osteøvel* in Norwegian) and graduated forms for making almond ring cakes (*kransekakeformer*). Hobby gardeners will appreciate the *krafse,* a practical tool somewhere between a spade and a hoe, while the outdoor person will like the *supertrøye,* a gossamer thin, insulated undershirt. Because Norwegian children spend so much time out of doors, practical clothing is a must, and good buys include **Helly-Hansen rain gear** and **insulated boots.**

Norwegian silver companies produce a wide range of patterns. At 830 parts to 1,000, compared with 925 parts in sterling, Norwegian silver is stronger than English or American, and the price is very competitive.

Norwegian rustic antiques may not be exported. Even the simplest corner shelf or dish rack valued at $50 is considered a national treasure if it is known to be over 100 years old.

Value-added Tax Refunds   Value-added tax, MVA for short, but called *moms* all over Scandinavia, is a hefty 22% on all services and purchases except books; it is normally included in the prices of goods. All purchases of consumer goods totaling over NKr300 ($45) for export by nonresidents are eligible for value-added tax refunds.

Shops subscribing to "Norway Tax-Free Shopping" provide customers with vouchers, which they must present, together with their purchases, upon departure in order to receive an on-the-spot refund of 16.25% of the tax.

Shops that do not subscribe to this program have slightly more detailed forms, which must be presented to the Norwegian Customs Office along with the goods to obtain a refund by mail. This refund is closer to the actual amount of the tax.

It's essential to have both the forms and the goods available for inspection upon departure. Make sure that the appropriate stamps are on the voucher or other forms before leaving the country.

Sports and Outdoor Activities

Norway is a sports lover's paradise. Outdoor sports have always been popular, while indoor facilities have been built nationwide. Close to 100 recreational and competitive sports are recognized in Norway, each with its own national association, 57 of which are affiliated with the **Norges Idrettsforbund** (Norwegian Confederation of Sports, Hauger Skolevei 1, 1351 Rud, tel. 67/15–46–00). The tourist board's Norway brochure, which lists sporting- and active-holiday resources and contacts, is a more helpful starting point for visitors.

Bicycling   Most cities have marked bike routes and paths. Bicycling on country roads away from traffic is a favorite national pastime, but as most routes are hilly, this demands good physical condition. All cyclists are required to wear protective helmets and use lights at night.

The **Norwegian Mountain Touring Association** (PB 1963 Vika N–0125 Oslo 1, tel. 22/83–25–50, fax 22/83–24–78) provides inexpensive lodging for cyclists planning overnight trips. You can also contact the helpful **Syklistens Landsforening** (Maridalsun. 60, N–0458 Oslo 4, tel. 22/71–92–93) for general information and maps, as well as the latest weather conditions.

Bird-watching   Northern Norway contains some of northern Europe's largest bird sanctuaries and teems with fantastic numbers of seabirds, including cormorants, razorbills, auks, guillemots, eider ducks, puffins, and even eagles. For organized tours, contact **Borton Overseas** (tel. 800/843–0602), **California Nature Tours** (tel. 619/241–2322), or, in Canada, **Quest Nature Tours** (tel. 800/387–1484).

Camping   Norway offers more than 900 inspected and classified campsites, many with showers, bathrooms, and hookups for electricity. Most also have cabins or chalets to rent by the night or longer. For more information contact local tourist offices or the **Norwegian Automobile Federation** (Storgt. 2, N–0155, Oslo 1, tel. 22/34–14–00), the **National Camping Site Organization** (FOS, Pilestredet 27, N–0164 Oslo 1, tel. 22/11–53–50), or, for a list of sites, the Norwegian Tourist Board.

Canoeing   There are plenty of lakes and streams for canoeing in Norway, as well as rental facilities. Contact **Norges Kajakkforbund** (Hauger Skolevej 1, N–1351 Olso, tel. 67/13–77–00) for a list of rental companies and regional canoeing centers.

Fishing   Whether it is fly-fishing for salmon or trout in western rivers or deep-sea fishing off the northern coast, Norway has all kinds of angling possibilities. Fishermen are required to buy an annual fishing tax card at the post office and a local license from the sporting goods store nearest the fishing site. Live bait is prohibited, and imported tackle must be disinfected before use.

Golf   Golf came to Norway only recently, but the country has gone golf-crazy—there is even a course on arctic Spitsbergen! For information about guest privileges and greens fees, contact **Oslo Golfklubb** (Bogstad, 0740 Oslo 7, tel. 22/50–44–02); **Bergen Golfklubb** (Boks 470, 5001 Bergen, tel. 55/18–20–77); **Stavanger Golfklubb** (Longebakken 45, 4042 Hafrsfjord, tel. 51/55–54–31); or **Trondheim Golfklubb** (Boks 169, 7001 Trondheim, tel. 73–53–18–85).

Hiking   Every city has surrounding trails and many have cabins where guests can rest, eat, and even spend the night. **Den Norske Turistforening** (DNT, Boks 1963 Vika, 0125 Oslo 1, tel. 22/83–25–50) and affiliated organizations administer cabins and tourist facilities in the central and northern mountainous areas of the country and will arrange group hikes. They have English brochures that can be ordered by mail.

Horseback Riding   Most cities and resort areas have stables, which rent chunky Norwegian fjord ponies and horses. **Steinseth Ridesenter** (Sollivn. 74, 1370 Asker, tel. 66/78–75–46), is a 30-minute drive from Oslo. Many resorts specialize in mountain pack trips; riding camps are in operation every summer.

Mountaineering The mountains of the Lofoten Islands and the Lyngen area of Troms County offer Alpine-class mountaineering. The **DNT** (*see* Hiking, *above*) has information. Oslo rock climbers practice on the Kolsås cliffs, a 20-minute drive west of the city, while the pros go to the Trolltindene peaks in Romsdal, near Åndalsnes.

Orienteering Norway's top mass-participation sport is based on running or hiking over territory with a map and compass to find control points marked on a map. Special cards can be purchased at sports shops to be punched at control points found during a season. It's an enjoyable, inexpensive family sport, and gear can be purchased at any sports shop.

Rafting Rafting excursions are offered throughout Norway. For more information, contact: **Flåteopplevelser** (pb 227, 2051 Jessheim, tel. 63/97–29–04); **Norwegian Wildlife and Rafting** (2254 Lundersæter, tel. 62/82–97–24); **Dagali-Voss Rafting** (Dagali, 3580 Geilo, tel. 22/23–75–09 or 32/08–78–20); or **Schulstad Adventure** (Stabbursdal, 9710 Indre Billegjord, tel. 78/46–47–66).

Running Grete Waitz and Ingrid Kristiansen have put Norway on the marathon runners' map in recent years. The first national marathon championships were held in Norway in 1897 and the Oslo Marathon always attracts a large following. For the recreational runner, **Norges Friidretts Forbund** (Karl Johans Gate 2, 0104 Oslo, tel. 22/42–03–03) has information about local clubs and competitions.

Sailing Both the late King Olav V and the present King Harald V won Olympic gold medals in sailing. Sailing in Oslo fjord and among the islands of the southern coast is a favorite summer pastime. Contact **Norges Seilforbund** (Hauger Skolevei 1, 1351 Rud, tel. 67/15–46–00) about facilities around the country; for the Oslo region, contact **KNS** (The Royal Norwegian Sailing Association; Huk Aveny 1, 0287 Oslo 2, tel. 22/43–74–10).

Skating Norway had one of the first indoor rinks in the world in the early 20th century. Some rinks have a few hours of public figure skating on weekends and just about every school in the country floods its playground in winter.

Skiing The ski is Norway's contribution to the world of sports. Norway's skiing season lasts from November to Easter. In February the 1994 Winter Olympics will be held in Lillehammer, which, along with other Norwegian resorts, regularly hosts World Cup competitions. Cross-country skiing needs only basic equipment and rentals are readily available; every city has lit trails for evening skiing. In addition to downhill and cross-country, the 100-year-old **Telemark Style** is enjoying a revival across the country. It involves a characteristic deep knee bend in the turns and traditional garb, including heavy boots attached to the skis only at the toe. **Skiforeningen** (Kongevn. 5, 0390 Oslo 3, tel. 22/92–32–00) provides national snow condition reports. Ski centers in operation over the summer include: **Finse Skisenter** (3590 Finse, tel. 55/52–67–144); **Galdhøpiggen Sommerskisenter** (2687 Bøverdalen, tel. 61/01–21–42); and **Stryn Sommerskisenter** (6880 Stryn, tel. 57/87–19–95).

Swimming Most towns have indoor swimming pools, while larger cities have heated outdoor pools. Many resorts also have swimming pools.

Tennis   Municipal courts are usually booked in advance for a season at a time, while private tennis clubs have covered courts that are in use year-round. Many resorts have tennis courts.

Windsurfing   The best windsurfing (a new sport here) is in western Norway. Centers include: **BT Brettseilerskole** (Nygårdsgt. 5/11, 5015 Bergen, tel. 55/21–45–00); **Selje Sjøsportsenter** (6740 Selje, tel. 57/85–66–06); and **Stavanger Surfsenter** (Paradisvn. 33, 4012 Stavanger, tel. 51/52–31–08).

Sports for the Disabled   Norway encouraged active participation in sports for the disabled long before it became popular elsewhere and has many Special Olympics medal winners. **Beitostølen Helsesportsenter** (2953 Beitostølen, tel. 61/34–12–00) has sports facilities for the blind and other physically challenged people as well as training programs for instructors. Sports offered include skiing, hiking, running, and horseback riding.

Beaches

Many Norwegians enjoy bathing in the summer, but low water temperatures, from 14°C to 18°C (57°F to 65°F), are enough to deter all but the most hardy. The beaches around **Mandal** in the south and **Sola** near Stavanger are the country's finest, with fine white sand, but all along the Oslo fjord there are many fine beaches. Be aware that some might have sharp pebbles and broken mussel shells, making rubber bathing shoes a necessity. The western fjords are warmer and calmer than the open beaches of the south, and inland freshwater lakes are chillier still than Gulf Stream-warmed fjords.

Dining

For centuries, Norwegians regarded food as fuel, and their dining habits still bear traces of this.

Breakfast is a fairly big meal, usually with a selection of crusty bread, herring, cold meat, and cheese. *Geitost* (a sweet, caramel-flavored whey cheese made wholly or in part from goats' milk) is on virtually every table. It is eaten in thin slices, cut with a cheese plane or slicer, a Norwegian invention, on buttered brown bread.

Lunch is simple, usually open-faced sandwiches. Most businesses have only a 30-minute lunch break, so unless there's a company cafeteria, most people eat home-packed sandwiches. Big lunchtime buffet tables, *koldtbord*, where one can sample most of Norway's special dishes all at once, are primarily for special occasions and visitors.

Dinner, the only hot meal of the day, is early, from 1–4 in the country, 1–5 in the city, and many cafeterias serving home-style food close by six or seven in the evening.

Traditional, home-style Norwegian food is stick-to-the-ribs fare, served in generous portions and blanketed with gravy. The most popular meal is *kjøttkaker* (meat cakes), which resemble salisbury steaks, served with boiled potatoes and brown gravy. Almost as popular are *medisterkaker* (mild pork sausage patties), served with brown gravy and caraway-seasoned sauerkraut, and *reinsdyrkaker* (reindeer meatballs), served with cream sauce and lingonberry jam. Other typical meat dishes include *får i kål*, a great-tasting lamb and cabbage stew, and *stek* (roast meat), always served well-done. Fish dishes include poached *torsk* (cod) or *laks* (salmon), served with a creamy sauce called Sandefjord butter, *seibiff* (fried pollack and onions), and *fiskegrateng*, something between a fish souffle and a casserole, usually served with carrot slaw.

Norway is known for several eccentric, often pungent fish dishes, but these are not representative—both *rakfisk* (fermented trout) and *lutefisk* (dried cod soaked in lye and then boiled) are acquired tastes, even for natives.

Traditional desserts include the ubiquitous *karamellpudding* (creme caramel), and *rømmegrøt* (sour cream porridge served with cinnamon-sugar and a glass of raspberry juice). The latter, a typical farm dish, tastes rather like warm cheesecake batter—delicious. Christmas time brings with it a delectable array of light, sweet, and buttery pastries.

Norwegian restaurant food has undergone major changes in the last few years. Until recently, fine restaurants were invariably French, and fine food usually meant meat. Today, seafood and game have replaced beef and veal. Fish, from common cod and skate to the noble salmon, have a prominent place in the new Norwegian kitchen, and local cappelin roe, golden caviar, is served instead of the imported variety. Norwegian lamb, full of flavor, is now in the spotlight, and game, from birds to moose, is prepared with sauces made from the wild berries that are part of their diet. These dishes are often accompanied by native root vegetables.

Desserts, too, often feature fruit and berries. Norwegian strawberries and raspberries ripen in the long early summer days and are sweeter and more intense than those grown farther south. Red and black currants are also used. Two berries native to Norway are *tyttebær* (lingonberries), which taste similar to cranberries but are much smaller, and *multer* (cloudberries), which look like orange raspberries, but which have an indescribable taste. These wild berries grow above the tree line and are a real delicacy.

Category	Cost
Very Expensive	over NKr450
Expensive	NKr300–NKr450
Moderate	NKr125–NKr300
Inexpensive	under NKr125

Prices are for a three-course meal, including tax and 12½% service charge.

Lodging

Norway is a land of hard beds and hearty breakfasts. Hotel standards are high, and even the simplest youth hostels provide good mattresses with fluffy down comforters and clean showers or baths. Breakfast, usually served buffet-style, is almost always included in the room price at hotels, while hostels often charge extra for the morning meal.

Norway has several hotel chains. **SAS**, which is a division of the airline, has a number of luxury hotels aimed at the business traveler. Many are above the Arctic Circle and are the "only game in town." **Rica** hotels, also a luxury chain, has expanded extensively in the last few years. The most interesting and individual hotel chain is **Home** hotels (Swedish-owned), which has successfully converted existing historic buildings into modern functional establishments in the middle price range. All Home hotels provide an evening meal, jogging suits, free beer, and other amenities designed to appeal to the single, usually business, traveler. As far as value for money is concerned, they are Norway's best buy. The **Farmer's Association** operates simple hotels in most towns and cities. These reasonably priced accommodations usually have **-heimen** as part of the name, such as Bondeheimen in Oslo. The same organization also operates cafeterias serving traditional Norwegian food, usually called **Kaffistova**. All these hotels and restaurants are alcohol-free.

Many hotels offer summer rates, although some require advance booking or hotel passes that also must be purchased in advance. **Inter Nor Hotels** (Dronningen Gate 40, 0154 Oslo, tel. 22/33–42–00, fax 22/33–69–06), a group of independently run hotels, offers a summer pass worth up to 50% off regular rates. It costs about $23 for two adults and two children and is valid at 250 hotels in Norway, 130 in the Nordic countries. **Fjord Pass** (Fjord Tours A/S PB 1752, 5024 Bergen, tel. 55/32–65–50, fax 55/31–86–56), which costs NKr50 (about $8) is valid at 298 establishments, from fancy hotels to simple mountain cabins.

Hostels Norway has 87 youth hostels, but in an effort to appeal to vacationers of all ages, the name has been changed to **vandrerhjem** (travelers' homes). Norwegian hostels are among the best in the world, squeaky clean and with excellent facilities—rooms sleep from two to six, and many have private showers. Membership can be arranged at any vandrerhjem, or you can buy a coupon book good for seven nights, which includes the membership fee. Linens are usually rented per night, so it's a good idea to bring your own—if you haven't, you can buy a *lakenpose* (sheet sleeping bag) at specialty stores. For more information and a list of vandrerhjem in Norway, contact **Norske Vandrerhjem** (Dronningensgt. 26, 0154 Oslo 1, tel. 22/42–14–10, fax 22/42–44–76).

Home Exchange This is an inexpensive solution to the lodging problem, because house-swapping means living rent-free. You find a house, apartment, or other vacation property to exchange for your own by becoming a member of a home-exchange organization, which then sends you its annual directories listing available exchanges and includes your own listing in at least one of them. Arrangements for the actual exchange are made by the two parties to it, not by the organization. Principal clearinghouses include **Intervac U.S./International Home Exchange** (Box 590504, San Francisco, CA 94159, tel. 415/435–3497), the oldest, with thousands of foreign and domestic homes for exchange in its three annual directories; membership is $62, or $72 if you want to receive the directories but remain unlisted. The **Vacation Exchange Club** (Box 650, Key West, FL 33041, tel. 800/638–3841), also with thousands of foreign and domestic listings, publishes four annual directories plus updates; the $50 membership includes your listing in one book. **Loan-a-Home** (2 Park La., Apt. 6E, Mount Vernon, NY 10552, tel. 914/664–7640) specializes in long-term exchanges; there is no charge to list your home, but the directories cost $35 or $45 depending on the number you receive.

Ratings

Category	Cost
Very Expensive	over NKr1,300
Expensive	NKr1,000–NKr1,300
Moderate	NKr800–NKr1,000
Inexpensive	under NKr800

All prices are for a standard double room, including service and 22% V.A.T.

Credit Cards

The following credit card abbreviations have been used: AE, American Express; D, Discover; DC, Diners Club; MC, Mastercard; V, Visa. It's always a good idea to call ahead and confirm an establishment's credit card policy.

2 Portraits of Norway

Norway at a Glance: A Chronology

c 1200 BC The earliest human settlers reach Norway.

2,000 BC Tribes from Southern Europe migrate toward Denmark. The majority of early settlers in Scandinavia were of Germanic origin.

c AD 770 The Viking Age begins. For the next 250 years, Scandinavians set sail on frequent expeditions stretching from the Baltic to the Irish seas and even to the Mediterranean as far as Sicily, employing superior ships and weapons and efficient military organization.

c 870 The first permanent settlers arrive in Iceland from western Norway.

c 900 Norwegians unite under Harald I Haarfager.

995 King Olaf I Tryggvasson introduces Christianity into Norway.

1000 Leif Eriksson visits America. Olaf I sends a mission to Christianize Iceland.

1016–1028 King Olaf II Haraldsson (St. Olaf) tries to complete conversion of Norway to Christianity. Killed at Stiklestad in battle with Danish king, he becomes patron saint of Norway.

1028–1035 Canute (Knud) the Great is king of England, Denmark (1018), and Norway (1028).

1045–1066 King Harald III (Hardraade) fights long war with Danes, then participates in and is killed during Norman invasion of England.

1217 Haakon IV becomes king of Norway, beginning its "Golden Age." His many reforms modernize the Norwegian administration; under him, the Norwegian empire reaches its greatest extent when Greenland and Iceland form unions with Norway in 1261. The Sagas are written during this time.

1319 Sweden and Norway form a union that lasts until 1335.

1349 The Black Death strikes Norway and kills two-thirds of the population.

1370 The Treaty of Stralsund gives the north German trading centers of the Hanseatic League free passage through Danish waters. German power increases throughout Scandinavia.

1397 The Kalmar Union is formed as a result of the dynastic ties between Sweden, Denmark, and Norway, the geographical position of the Scandinavian states, and the growing influence of Germans in the Baltic. Erik of Pomerania is crowned king of the Kalmar Union.

1520 Christian II, ruler of the Kalmar Union, executes 82 people who oppose the Scandinavian union, an event known as the "Stockholm blood bath." Sweden secedes from the Union three years later. Norway remains tied to Denmark and becomes a Danish province in 1536.

1536 The Reformation enters Scandinavia in the form of Lutheranism through the Hauseatic port of Bergen.

1559–1648 Norwegian trade flourishes.

1660 Peace of Copenhagen establishes modern boundaries of Denmark, Sweden, and Norway.

1814 Sweden, after Napoleon's defeat at the Battle of Leipzig, attacks Denmark and forces the Danish surrender of Norway. On 17 May, Norwegians adopt constitution at Eidsvoll. On 4 November, Norway is forced to accept Act of Union with Sweden.

1811 University of Oslo is established.

1884 A parliamentary system is established in Norway.

1903 Bjørnstjerne Bjørnson awarded Nobel Prize for literature.

1905 Norway's union with Sweden is dissolved.

1914 At the outbreak of World War I, Norway declares neutrality but is effectively blockaded.

1918 Norwegian women gain the right to vote.

1920 Norway joins the League of Nations. Novelist Knut Hansun receives Nobel Prize.

1928 Sigrid Undset receives Nobel Prize for literature.

1929–1937 Norway is ruled by a labor government.

1939 Norway declares neutrality in World War II.

1940 Germany occupies Norway.

1945 Norway joins the United Nations.

1946–1954 Norwegian statesman Trygve Lie presides as first Secretary-General of UN.

1949 Norway becomes a member of NATO.

1952 The Nordic Council, which promotes cooperation among the Nordic parliaments, is founded.

1968 Norway discovers oil in the North Sea.

1971 North Sea oil production begins, transforming the Norwegian economy.

1972 Norway declines membership in the EC.

1981 Gro Harlem Brundtland, a member of the Labor party, becomes Norway's first female prime minister.

1991 King Olav V dies. King Harald V ascends the throne. His wife, Queen Sonja, becomes first queen since the death of Maud in 1938.

1993 Norway applies for EC membership.

Norway's Minister of Foreign Affairs Thorvald Stoltenberg is appointed peace negotiator to Bosnia and Herzegovina.

1994 Norway hosts the XVII Olympic Winter Games at Lillehammer.

In Norway at Christmas

By Chunglu Tsen

Born in Shanghai, Chunglu Tsen grew up in Paris and received his education in England and the United States. Since 1974 he has worked as a translator for the United Nations in Geneva. This article appeared originally in the December 1990 issue of Wigwag.

Every culture reinvents the wheel. But every culture reinvents it slightly differently. In Norway, a traditional dining table may rest not on four legs, as tables usually do elsewhere, but on a cubic frame, like an imaginary cage that imprisons your feet while you eat.

I am a Chinese who has fallen in love with Norway. I was invited by my good friends Ole and Else to spend Christmas and New Year's with them in Oslo. It turned out to be the most marvelous Christmas of my fifty-two years.

It was one long feast, moving from household to household. On Christmas Eve we held hands and sang carols and danced ring-around-the-Christmas-tree. We skied at night on an illuminated track, whose lights switched off at ten, plunging us into obscurity on the downward slope. We played squash on the Norsk Hydro court and afterward relaxed in the sauna. We ushered in the New Year with fireworks on Oslo's frozen streets.

I am probably one of the few Chinese in two thousand years to have had such an intimate glimpse of Norwegian life. Of course, it is presumptuous of me to write about a people after an eight-day visit. Yet I have the feeling that Norwegians don't very much mind presumption (as long as it is straightforward and honest). Indeed, this exceptional tolerance of friendly rudeness bespeaks their generosity and is, to me, one of their most endearing qualities.

To begin with, to a Chinese who has seen something of the world, Norway is a most exotic country. Even ordinary, everyday things are done exotically here. For example, I saw my Norwegian friends: drink aquavit at breakfast; eat breakfast in the afternoon; turn on an electric switch to heat the sidewalk in front of their house; get a thrill out of driving their car like a bobsled; leave the house lights on day and night, when they went out and when they slept; wash their dishes with soap without rinsing them.

Norwegians also love to give gifts and make philosophical speeches at festive dinners. They decorate their Christmas trees not with angels but with strings of Norwegian flags. They don't find it necessary to have curtains around their showers, because it's simpler to build a drain on the bathroom floor. Cold dishes are de rigueur in the winter. There is a national horror of hot, spicy foods, and a national pact to ignore vegetables.

The Norwegians and the Chinese share certain cultural traits. The most striking is their common fondness for rituals. Confucius insisted on the importance of rituals as a collective code of behavior that gives order to life. The Master said, "To suppress the self and submit to ritual is to engage in Humanity." This precept might just as well apply to the Norwegians as to the Chinese.

At Christmas, all the traditional rituals are performed, some older than Christianity in Norway. A great deal of effort goes into making sure that they are done right. After each one—the baking of the gingerbread houses, the decorating of the tree—the excitement palpably mounts.

Christmas begins on the eve, with the hostess welcoming the guests to the dinner table. She assigns to each a specific seat according to a careful arrangement. The seating plan is the one touch of originality that marks the occasion. It is, in some ways, the hostess's signature for the evening. (You find seating charts of past banquets faithfully recorded in a family book.) It's quite touching to see a young hostess assign a seat to her own mother, who has undoubtedly done the same many times herself. It signals the passing of the torch from one generation of women to another.

Once the guests are seated and the candles lit, the feast begins. It begins with the dessert: rice pudding (reminiscent of the rice gruel that Chinese eat for breakfast and when ill, albeit without milk and butter). Toasts are offered, followed by a chorus of *skaals*.

Then comes raw fish of every kind—salmon, eel, herring, enough to send a sashimi-loving Japanese into ecstasy. From the sea, the food parade marches onto land. A whole side of roast pork, skin done to a golden crisp, is served with meatballs and sausage, and buried under potatoes. Throughout there is much toasting with aquavit.

Finally, after two hours the meal is done. You get up from the table and stagger into the living room. There, in a role reminiscent of her mother's, the little daughter of the house hands out the gifts—there is a mound of them under the tree—to each recipient with charming solemnity.

Great care is taken by each household to do everything the same way, so that, as with the retelling of a familiar tale, all expectations are happily satisfied. Once in a while, one may introduce an oddity, such as a Chinese guest from afar, to liven up the routine. But in general surprises tend to raise eyebrows.

If, for the Chinese, rituals recall the teachings of Confucius, for the Norwegians they go back to the pagans. In spite of the electric sidewalks, the past is very much alive in the modern Norwegian psyche. The feasting, the speech-making, the gift-giving, and especially the generous hospitality and the importance of friendship are all part of the Viking tradition. Yuletide was a pagan celebration of the winter solstice. The birth of Christ was a later liturgical imposition. In some families these days, it is celebrated almost as an afterthought.

The other thing that the Norwegians share with the Chinese is their strong attachment to the family. Like the Chinese, the Norwegians belong to extended families, practically clans. But what defines a family in Norway is not at all clear. The relations are so complex and intertwined that, rather than family trees, the Norwegians seem to have family bushes. To begin with, there is one's spouse and one's brothers and sisters and their spouses. And then there is one's former spouse and his or her present spouse. And then there is the former spouse of the present spouse of one's former spouse, who in some cases also happens to be one's present spouse. The children of the former spouse of one's spouse are somewhat like nephews and nieces. Beyond that, there are the living-together arrangements and the progeny thereof, which take on quasi-family status.

It's not unusual for people who are divorced to remain good friends. Their old pictures sometimes hang in each other's bedrooms. Christmastime finds them reunited with their old partners and all their children, old and new. At first, this kind of marital pluralism is slightly unsettling. What, no bad blood? No bitterness or jealousy?

I asked a young Norwegian if it upset him to be shuttling between his father's and his mother's separate households. He looked at me with astonishment. "But that's normal," he said. "Every kid in my class is in the same situation."

His guileless reaction gave me food for thought. "And indeed what's wrong with that?" I asked myself. Why try to stay with an unhappy relationship when one feels the need to change? And once changed, why not try to reconcile the past with the present?

The Chinese family is a vertical structure. Like the society itself, it is hierarchical, ruled from the top down. Confucius said, "Let the prince be prince, the minister be minister, the father be father, the son be son." Patriarchy and gerontocracy are the order of things: old men will rule, and the young will obey. Repression is inevitable under such a hierarchy. The collective always takes precedence over the individual; order always takes precedence over freedom. This denial of the self is responsible for much of the envy, backbiting, and hypocrisy common in Chinese communities.

The Norwegian family, on the other hand—or perhaps I should say the *new* Norwegian family—is horizontal. Like a strawberry plant, it spreads in all directions. Wherever it touches soil, it sprouts a new shoot. An obvious sign of this strawberry-patch kinship is the diminished importance of the family name. These days people are known mostly by first names. Children, too, often address their parents by their first names. As more and more households are headed by women, the old nuclear family is giving way to a fluid tribalism.

One way to understand the difference between the vertical and the horizontal cultures is to compare their concepts of space. To the Chinese, any space must have a center. The Chinese name for China, Zhongguo, means precisely Center Country. Every Chinese knows that the center of China is Beijing. Why? Because the vast expanse of China is not divided into time zones, and from the Pacific to Tibet every watch is set to Beijing time. Every Chinese also knows that the center of Beijing is the Forbidden City, the symbol of governmental power, and that inside the Forbidden City sits an old man whose word is law.

No one would dream of ordering Norway's space this way. Unlike elsewhere in Europe, you seldom see a square in a Norwegian town. People don't seem to feel the need to meet and sit in the sun and feed the pigeons. In some rural communities, the church stands not in the center of town but on a hill somewhere on the outskirts. The houses, in all forms and dispositions, are widely dispersed, disdaining to line up along a straight road. One gets the impression that zoning laws are not very strict in Norway.

The big question is, if the Norwegians are such confirmed individualists, how come they are so conformist? It's voluntary, true, they choose it, but it's conformity all the same. This is the question posed—but never answered—by Ibsen's plays.

For me, the key to understanding the Norwegians is to recognize that they are a nation of irreconciled opposites. They have taken on the contradiction of their seasons: the long happy summer days alternating with the gloomy nights of winter. They have inherited two pasts with totally different characters. For more than two hundred years, from the ninth to the eleventh centuries, they were the scourge of Europe. They raided Britain and discovered America; they ruled Kiev and besieged Paris; they served at the court of Byzantium, and—who knows?—maybe some of them even made it to China. Lusty, adventurous, destructive, and curious about the world, they were sea nomads, the maritime counterpart of the horsemen of Genghis Khan, who conquered Russia and China. Then, as suddenly as they burst upon the world in their splendid ships, they retreated, went back to their home in the north. They were converted to Christianity and not heard from again.

Why the seafaring Vikings turned into God-fearing Christians is one of those mysteries that history doesn't explain very well. What made them turn their gaze inward? Why did they change from thinking big to thinking small? What, finally, made them give up violence for peaceful ways? There is no satisfactory answer.

In any case, as the final image of Ingmar Bergman's *Fanny and Alexander* so powerfully shows, there are two ghosts walking beside the Scandinavian soul: the ghost of the hard-drinking father and the ghost of the psalm-singing stepfather. They walk beside the boy, each with a hand on his shoulder, never exchanging a word.

So the Norwegian labors under a double identity. In one ear, the Viking ghost tells him to leave Norway, this cold, homogeneous, incurious community, and discover the world. Go! The center is elsewhere! There are wonderful places to see and fabulous riches to be had!

In his other ear, the Christian ghost tells him Stay! Go back to your roots! Embrace the tradition and preserve the social order!

This ambivalence is at the heart of Norway itself. You see it reflected on canvas in the National Gallery in Oslo. Among the painters of the late nineteenth century, one finds two divergent sensibilities: the naturalists, who took as their subject the Norwegian folk, and the cosmopolitans, who, having spent time in Paris or Rome, insisted that art was not sociology or geography but, simply and purely, a composition of color and light.

For eight centuries, Christian ethics held sway in Norway as in the rest of Europe. But since 1945 something important has changed. There is a gap between the values of the prewar and the postwar generations. Between the threat of nuclear destruction and the temptation of America, the influence of the church waned. More and more, people have stopped practicing their faith. As they do so, they are reverting to their ancestral Viking instincts.

One clue to this reemergence of pagan consciousness is the marital pluralism that I observed. Another clue, probably closely related, is women's push for equality, a push that has been more forceful and more widely accepted in Scandinavia than anywhere else. A third indication of this new pagan way, I believe—and here I'm sticking my neck out—is the nation's collective decision, in the seventies, to turn Norway overnight into an oil economy.

There have been a lot of arguments about the reasoning behind this decision, but none of them address the Viking-versus-Christian dilemma. If Norway had listened to its Christian voice, it would have been content to remain a frugal, hard-working nation, tending the farm or the machine. Instead, after the oil crisis of 1973, Norway chose the Viking solution and went for broke. It decided to plunder the sea.

Agrarian people, like the Chinese, are naturally patient: it takes time to make things grow. The Vikings, on the other hand, never had patience. If they could survive by fishing and gathering berries, they would not care to cultivate. Whatever they could get by raiding, they would not care to make. It is still so today. Norwegians are willing to put all their ingenuity and technical skill into building gigantic derricks and drilling kilometers beneath the sea. They will do so in order to avoid making clothes and toys to compete with Hong Kong. This is the message I got from that magnificent Christmas feast: If it tastes good raw, *don't bother to cook it*. Take it raw. Don't transform. And nothing is rawer than oil.

In 1066, King Harald Hardraade left the shores of Norway to grab the big prize: the throne of England. At Stamford Bridge, he was offered by his enemy seven feet of English ground, "and more—if you are taller." Harald fought and lost. By nightfall, mortally wounded, he said, "I will accept that piece of kingdom that was offered me this morning."

I said to my friend Ole—who, as an oil engineer at Norsk Hydro, has staked his whole future on a challenge against the North Sea—"One day your oil will be depleted, and then where will you be?" He grinned and said, echoing King Harald's insouciance, "And then I will have nothing."

3 Oslo

So, you're getting away from it all.

Just make sure you can get back.

AT&T Access Numbers
Dial the number of the country you're in to reach AT&T.

*ANDORRA	19◊-0011	GERMANY**	0130-0010	*NETHERLANDS	06◊-022-9111
*AUSTRIA	022-903-011	*GREECE	00-800-1311	*NORWAY	050-12011
*BELGIUM	078-11-0010	*HUNGARY	00◊-800-01111	POLAND¹◆²	0◊010-480-0111
BULGARIA	00-1800-0010	*ICELAND	999-001	PORTUGAL¹	05017-1-288
CROATIA¹◆	99-38-0011	IRELAND	1-800-550-000	ROMANIA	01-800-4288
*CYPRUS	080-90010	ISRAEL	177-100-2727	*RUSSIA¹ (MOSCOW)	155-5042
CZECH REPUBLIC	00-420-00101	**ITALY**	172-1011	SLOVAKIA	00-420-00101
*DENMARK	8001-0010	KENYA¹	0800-10	SPAIN	900-99-00-11
*EGYPT¹ (CAIRO)	510-0200	*LIECHTENSTEIN	155-00-11	*SWEDEN	020-795-611
*FINLAND	9800-100-10	LITHUANIA◆	8◊196	*SWITZERLAND	155-00-11
FRANCE	19◊-0011	LUXEMBOURG	0-800-0111	*TURKEY	9◊9-8001-2277
*GAMBIA	00111	*MALTA	0800-890-110	UK	0800-89-0011

Countries in bold face permit country-to-country calling in addition to calls to the U.S. *Public phones require deposit of coin or phone card. **Western portion. Includes Berlin and Leipzig. ◊Await second dial tone. ¹May not be available from every phone. ◆ Not available from public phones. ¹Dial "02" first, outside Cairo. ²Dial 010-480-0111 from major Warsaw hotels. ©1993 AT&T.

Here's a travel tip that will make it easy to call back to the States. Dial the access number for the country you're visiting and connect right to AT&T **USADirect**® Service. It's the quick way to get English-speaking operators and can minimize hotel surcharges.

If all the countries you're visiting aren't listed above, call **1 800 241-5555** before you leave for a free wallet card with all AT&T access numbers. International calling made easy—it's all part of **The i Plan.**℠

THE **i** PLAN℠

AT&T

All The Best Trips Start with **Fodor's**

Fodor's Affordables

Titles in the series: Caribbean, Europe, Florida, France, Germany, Great Britain, Italy, London, Paris.

"Travelers with champagne tastes and beer budgets will welcome this series from Fodor's." — *Hartford Courant*

"These books succeed admirably; easy to follow and use, full of cost-related information, practical advice, and recommendations...maps are clear and easy to use." — *Travel Books Worldwide*

The Berkeley Guides

Titles in the series: California, Central America, Eastern Europe, France, Germany, Great Britain & Ireland, Mexico, The Pacific Northwest, San Francisco.

The best choice for budget travelers, from the Associated Students at the University of California at Berkeley.

"Berkeley's scribes put the funk back in travel." — *Time*

"Hip, blunt and lively."
— *Atlanta Journal Constitution*

"Fresh, funny and funky as well as useful." — *The Boston Globe*

Fodor's Bed & Breakfast and Country Inn Guides

Titles in the series: California, Canada, England & Wales, Mid-Atlantic, New England, The Pacific Northwest, The South, The Upper Great Lakes Region, The West Coast.

"In addition to information on each establishment, the books add notes on things to see and do in the vicinity. That alone propels these books to the top of the heap." — *San Diego Union-Tribune*

Exploring Guides

Titles in the series: Australia, California, Caribbean, Florida, France, Germany, Great Britain, Ireland, Italy, London, New York City, Paris, Rome, Singapore & Malaysia, Spain, Thailand.

"Authoritatively written and superbly presented, and makes worthy reading before, during or after a trip. "
— *The Philadelphia Inquirer*

"A handsome new series of guides, complete with lots of color photos, geared to the independent traveler."
— *The Boston Globe*

Visit your local bookstore or call 1-800-533-6478 24 hours a day.

Fodor's The name that means smart travel.

Although it is one of the world's largest capital cities in area, Oslo has only about 475,000 inhabitants. Nevertheless, in recent years the city has taken off: Shops are open late; pubs, cafés, and restaurants are crowded at all hours; and theaters play to full houses every night of the week.

Even without nightlife, Oslo has a lot to offer—parks, water, trees, hiking/skiing trails (2,600 kilometers/1,600 miles in greater Oslo), and above all, spectacular views. Starting at the docks opposite City Hall, right at the edge of the Oslo Fjord, the city extends in great sweeps up the sides of the mountains that surround it, providing panoramic vistas from almost any vantage point.

Oslo has been Norway's center of commerce for 1,000 years, and most major Norwegian companies are based in the capital. The sea has always been Norway's lifeline to the rest of the world: The Oslo Fjord teems with activity, from summer sailors and shrimpers to merchant ships and passenger ferries heading for Denmark and Germany.

Oslo is an old city, dating from the mid-11th century. All but destroyed by fire in 1624, it was redesigned with wide boulevards and renamed Christiania by Denmark's royal builder, King Christian IV. An act of Parliament finally changed the name back to Oslo, its original Viking name, in 1925.

Essential Information

Important Addresses and Numbers

Tourist Information The main tourist office (**Norway Information Center,** tel. 22/83–00–50), located in the old Vestbanen railway station, is open weekdays 9–6; weekends 9–4. The office at the main railway station, **Sentralstasjon** (Jernebanetorget, tel. 22/17–11–24) is open daily 8 AM–11 PM. Look for the big round blue-and-green signs marked with a white i. Information about the rest of the country can be obtained from **NORTRA** (Nortravel Marketing, Postboks 499, Sentrum, 0105 Oslo 1, tel. 22/42–70–44).

Embassies **U.S. Embassy,** Drammensvn. 18, tel. 22/44–85–50. **Canadian Embassy,** Oscarsgate 20, tel. 22/46–69–66. **U.K. Embassy,** Thomas Heftyesgate 8, tel. 22/55–24–00.

Emergencies **Police:** tel. 002 or 22/66–90–50. **Fire:** tel. 001 or 22/11–44–55. **Ambulance:** tel. 003 or 22/11–70–70. **Car Rescue:** tel. 22/23–20–85. After January 1, 1994, these numbers will change. **Police:** tel. 112 or 22/66–90–50. **Fire:** tel. 111 or 22/66–90–50. **Ambulance:** tel. 113 or 22/11–70–70. **Car Rescue:** tel. 22/23–20–85.

Hospital Emergency Rooms **Oslo Legevakt** (Storgt. 40, tel. 22/20–10–90), the city's public and thus less expensive hospital, is near the Oslo S Station and is open 24 hours.

Doctors **Volvat Medisinske Senter** (Borgenvn. 2A, tel. 22/95–75–00) is Norway's largest private clinic, located near the Borgen underground station. **Oslo Akutten** (N. Vollgt. 8, tel. 22/41–24–40) is an emergency clinic downtown, near Stortinget.

Dentists **Oslo Kommunale Tannlegevakt** (Kolstadgt. 18, tel. 22/67–30–00) is at Tøyen Senter. **Oslo Private Tannlegevakt** (Hansteens gt. 3, tel. 22/44–46–36) is a private clinic.

Late-night **Jernbanetorvets apotek** (Jernbanetorget 4B, tel. 22/41–24–
Pharmacies 82),across from Oslo S Station, is open 24 hours.

Where to After normal banking hours money can be changed at the fol-
Change Money lowing places: The bank at **Oslo S Station** is open June–Sept.,
daily 8 AM–11 PM; otherwise, weekdays 8 AM–8:30 PM, Saturday
8–2. The bank at **Oslo Fornebu Airport** is open weekdays 6:30
AM–9 PM, Saturday 7–5, Sunday 7 AM–8 PM. All post offices exchange money. **Oslo Central Post Office** (Dronningensgt. 15) is
open weekdays 8–8, Saturday 9–3.

English-language The best selection of English books can be found at **Tanum
Bookstores** **Libris** (Karl Johans Gate 37, tel. 22/42–93–10) and at **Erik Qvist**
(Drammensvn. 16, tel. 22/44–03–26 or 22/44–52–69).

Travel Agencies **American Express/Winge Reisebureau** (Karl Johans Gate 33/35,
tel. 22/41–20–30); **Bennett Reisebureau** (Pilestredet 35, tel. 22/
94–36–00); **Berg-Hansen** (agent for Thomas Cook, Arbiensgt.
3, tel. 22/55–19–01); and **Kilroy Travels Norway** (Universi-
tetssenteret, Blindern, tel. 22/85–32–00), for student travel.

Arriving and Departing by Plane

Airports and **Oslo Fornebu Airport,** 20 minutes west of the city, has interna-
Airlines tional and domestic services under the same roof. Nevertheless
the walks between international arrivals, baggage claim, and
passport control are long.

SAS (tel. 22/17–00–20) is the main carrier, with both international and domestic flights. **Braathens SAFE** (tel. 67/59–70–00)
and **Widerøe** (tel. 22/73–65–00) are the main domestic carriers.

Other major airlines serving Fornebu include **British Airways**
(tel. 22/33–16–00), **Air France** (tel. 22/83–56–30), **Delta Air
Lines** (tel. 22/41–56–00), **Finnair** (tel. 22/42–58–56), **Icelandair**
(tel. 22/42–39–75), **KLM** (tel. 67/58–38–00), and **Lufthansa**
(tel. 22/83–65–65).

Gardermoen Airport, 40 kilometers (25 miles) north of Oslo, is
the only one in the area that can handle 747s and DC10s. It is
used primarily for charter traffic.

Between the Oslo Fornebu Airport is a 10–15-minute ride from the center of
Airport and Oslo at off-peak hours. At rush hour (7:30–9 AM from the airport
Downtown and 3:30–5 PM to the airport), the trip can take more than twice as
long. None of the downtown hotels provide free shuttle service,
although some outside the city do.

By Bus **Flybussen** (tel. 67/59–62–20; tickets: NKr30 adults, children 15
and under free; weekdays 6 AM–9:45 PM, Sat. 6 AM–8:30 PM, Sun.
6 AM–9:45 PM) departs from its terminal under Galleri Oslo shopping center, three times per hour and reaches Fornebu approximately 20 minutes later. Another bus departs from the SAS
Scandinavia Hotel 10 minutes after and 20 minutes before the
hour and costs the same. Suburban bus No. 31, marked
"Snarøya," stops outside the Arrivals terminal. On the trip into
town, it stops on the main road opposite the entrance to the airport. The cost is NKr20.

By Taxi There is a taxi line to the right of the Arrivals exit. The fare to
town is about NKr100. All taxi reservations should be made
through the **Oslo Taxi Central** (tel. 22/38–80–80) no less than
one hour before pickup time.

Arriving and Departing by Car, Train, and Bus

By Car Route E18 connects Oslo with Göteborg, Sweden (by ferry between Sandefjord and Strömstad, Sweden), Copenhagen, Denmark (by ferry between Kristiansand and Hirtshals, Denmark), and Stockholm directly overland. The land route from Oslo to Göteborg is E6. An electronic ring around Oslo requires all vehicles entering the city to pay NKr11. If you have the correct amount in change, drive through one of the lanes marked "Mynt." If you don't, or if you need a receipt, use the "Manuell" lane.

By Train Long-distance trains arrive at and leave from **Oslo S** (tel. 22/17–40–00), while suburban commuter trains use **Nationaltheatret** or **Oslo S**. Commuter cars reserved for monthly pass holders are marked with a large black "M" on a yellow circle.

By Bus The terminal, **Bussterminalen** (tel. 22/17–01–66), is located under Galleri Oslo, across from the Oslo S Station. Tickets for **Nor-Way Bussekspress** (long-distance routes tel. 22/17–52–90, fax 22/17–59–22) can be purchased here or at travel agencies. Local bus tickets can be bought at the terminal or on the bus. For local traffic information, call 22/17–70–30.

Getting Around

The **Oslo Card** offers unlimited travel on all public transport in greater Oslo as well as free admission to museums, theaters, sightseeing attractions, the amusement park Tusenfryd, and racetracks, and discounts at various stores, cinemas (May, June, July), sports centers, and hotels. The three-day adult card gives a 30% discount for trains to and from Oslo. A one-day Oslo Card costs NKr95, a two-day card NKr140, and a three-day card NKr170.

Tickets on all public transportation within Oslo cost NKr15 without transfer, while tickets that cross communal boundaries have different rates. It pays to buy a pass or a multiple travel card, which includes transfers. A one-day pass costs NKr35 and a seven-day pass costs NKr130. A Flexicard is good for eight trips with free transfer within one hour and costs NKr 130. Children 15 and under and senior citizens pay half price. These cards can be purchased at any post office, at tourist information offices, at subway stations, and on some routes. **Trafikanten** (Jernbanetorget, tel. 22/17–70–30), the information office for public transportation, is open weekdays 7 AM–11 PM, weekends 8–11.

Most public transportation starts running by 5:30 AM, with the last run just after midnight. On weekends there is night service on certain routes.

By Subway Oslo has eight subway lines, which converge at **Stortinget** station. The four eastern lines all stop at **Tøyen** before branching off, while the four western lines run through **Majorstuen** before emerging aboveground for the rest of their routes to the northwestern suburbs. Tickets can be purchased at the stations.

By Bus About 20 bus lines, including four night buses on weekends, serve the city. Most stop at **Jernbanetorget** opposite Oslo S Station. Tickets can be purchased from the driver.

By Tram/Streetcar Five tram lines serve the city. All stop at **Jernbanetorget** opposite Oslo S Station. Tickets can be purchased from the driver.

By Ferry A ferry to **Hovedøya** and other islands in the harbor basin leaves from **Vippetangen**, behind Akershus castle (take bus No. 29 from Jernbanetorget). From April through September, ferries run between **Rådhusbrygge 3**, in front of City Hall, and **Bygdøy**, the western peninsula.

By Car **Oslo Card** holders can park for free at all parking places run by the city (P-lots), but pay careful attention to time limits. Handicapped travelers with valid parking permits from their home country are allowed to park free and with no time limit in spaces reserved for the handicapped.

If you plan to do any amount of driving in Oslo, buy a copy of the *Stor Oslo* map, available at book stores and gasoline stations.

By Taxi All city taxis are connected with the central dispatching office (tel. 22/38–80–90), which can take up to 30 minutes to send one during peak hours. Cabs can be ordered from 1 to 24 hours in advance (tel. 22/38–80–80). Special transport, including vans and cabs equipped for the handicapped, can also be ordered (tel. 22/38–80–70). Taxi stands are located all over town, usually alongside Narvesen kiosks, and are listed in the telephone directory under "Taxi" or "Drosjer."

It is possible to hail a cab on the street. A cab with its roof light on is available, but cabs are not allowed to pick up passengers within 100 meters of a stand. Rates start at NKr8 for hailed or rank cabs, NKr30 to NKr40 for ordered taxis, depending upon the time of day.

Guided Tours

Tickets for all tours are available from Tourist Information at Vestbanen and at the Oslo S Station. Tickets for bus tours can be purchased on the buses. All tours, except one, operate only during the summer.

Orientation All bus tours leave from the harborside entrance to the City Hall (**Rådhuset**), while combination boat-bus tours depart from Rådhusbrygge 3, the wharf in front of City Hall.

H.M.K. Sightseeing (Hegdehaugsvn. 4, tel. 22/20–82–06) offers three bus tours. **Båtservice Sightseeing** (Rådhusbrygge 3, tel. 22/20–07–15) offers one bus tour, five cruises, and one combination tour.

Special-interest Tourist Information at Vestbanen can arrange four- to eight-
Forest Tours hour motor safaris through the forests surrounding Oslo (tel. 22/83–00–50).

Sailing **Norway Yacht Charter** (H. Hyerdahls gt. 1, tel. 22/42–64–98) can arrange sailing or yacht tours for groups of 5 to 200 people.

Sleigh Rides During the winter it is possible to ride an old-fashioned sleigh through Oslomarka, the wooded area surrounding the city. **Vangen Skistue** (Laila and Jon Hamre, Fjell, 1404 Siggerud, tel. 64/86–54–81) or **Sørbråten Gård** (Helge Torp, Maridalen, tel. 22/42–35–79) can arrange this for you. In the summertime, they switch from sleighs to horses and buggies.

Dogsled Tours For a faster and more exciting experience, tour the *marka* by dogsled. Both lunch and evening tours are available. Contact

Norske Sledehundturer (Einar Kristen Aas, 1500 Moss, tel. 69/27–37–86).

Street Train   Starting at 11 AM and continuing at 45-minute intervals, the **Oslo Train** (tel. 22/42–23–64), which looks like a chain of dune buggies, leaves Aker Brygge for a 40-minute ride around the center of town.

Personal Guides   Tourist Information at Vestbanen can provide an authorized city guide for your own private tour. **OsloTaxi** (Trondheimsvn. 100, tel. 22/38–80–00) also offers private sightseeing.

Walking Tours   Organized walking tours are listed in *What's on in Oslo*, available from Tourist Information and at most hotels.

Highlights for First-time Visitors

Frogner Park (Vigeland sculpture park) (*see* Tour 3)
Holmenkollen (*see* Tour 3)
Kon-Tiki Museum (*see* Tour 4)
Munch Museum (*see* Tour 3)
Norsk Folkemuseum (*see* Tour 4)
Polar Ship *Fram* (*see* Tour 4)
Rådhus (*see* Tour 1)
Viking ships (*see* Tour 4)

Exploring Oslo

Karl Johans Gate, starting at Oslo S Station and ending at the Royal Palace, forms the backbone of downtown Oslo. Many of Oslo's museums and most of its historic buildings lie between the parallel streets of Grensen and Rådhusgata. Just north of the center of town is a historic area with a medieval church and old buildings. West of downtown is Frogner, the residential area closest to town, with embassies, fine restaurants, antiques shops, galleries, and the Vigeland sculpture park. Farther west is the Bygdøy Peninsula, with five museums and one castle. Northwest of town is Holmenkollen, with beautiful houses, a famous ski jump, and a restaurant. On the east side, where many new immigrants live, is the Munch Museum and the botanical gardens.

Numbers in the margin correspond to points of interest on the Oslo map.

Tour 1: Downtown, from the Royal Palace to the Harbor

Although the city is huge (454 square kilometers/175 square miles), downtown Oslo is compact, with shops, museums, historic sights, restaurants, and clubs concentrated in a small, walkable center—brightly illuminated at night.

Oslo's main promenade street, Karl Johans Gate, runs from **❶** **Slottet** (the Royal Palace). The neoclassical palace, completed in 1848, is closed to visitors, but the garden is open to the public. An equestrian statue of Karl Johan, king of Sweden and Norway, the street's namesake, stands in the square in front of the palace.

Down the incline and to the left are the three buildings of the **❷** old **Universitet** (university), which remains one of Norway's

Akershus Slott, **11**
Fram-museet, **23**
Gamle Aker Kirke, **14**
Historisk Museum, **4**
Holmenkollbakken, **18**
Kon-Tiki Museum, **24**
Kunstindustri-
museet, **13**
Munchmuseet, **19**
Museet for

Samtidskunst, **9**
Nasjonalgalleriet, **3**
Nationaltheatret, **5**
Norsk
Folkemuseum, **21**
Oscarshall Slott, **20**
Oslo Domkirke, **8**
Rådhus, **6**
Skogbrand
Insurance, **12**

Slottet, **1**
Stortinget, **7**
Teatermuseet, **10**
Tryvannstårnet, **17**
Universitet, **2**
Vigelands anlegget, **15**
Vigelandmuseet, **16**
Vikingskiphuset, **22**

Seildusgt.

Helgesens gt.

Grüners gt.

Helgesens gt.

Sofienberggt.

Akersbakken

Maridalsveien

Akerselva

Møllerveien   Nordregt.

Waldemar Thranes gt.

Colletts gt.

Parkveien

Pilestredet

Holbergs gate

Frederiks Gate

Ullevålsveien

Akersveien

Wessels gt.

Nordahl Bruns gt.

St. Olavsgt.

Hausmanns gt.

Trondheimsveien

Jens Bjelkes gt.

Drammensveien

Universitetsgt.

Henrik Ibsens gt.

Grubbe gt.

Møllergt.

Torggt.

Urtegt.

Norbygt.

Tøyengt.

Karl Johans gate

Rosenkrantz gt.

Akersgata

Grensen

Youngs-
torget

Storgate

Brugt.

Grønlandsleiret

Løkkegata

Munkedamsveien

R. Amundsens gt.

Stortingsgt.

Nedre Vollgt.

Stortorvet

Oslo
Spektrum

Oslo City

Schweigaards gt.

Nylandsveien

Dokkveien

Rådhusgt.

Slottsgt.

Prinsens gt.

Central
Station

Pipervika

Akershusstranda

Nedre Slottsgt.

Tollbugt.

Dronningens gt.

Skippergt.

Fred Olsens gt.

Strandgt.

Bispegate

Mynt gt.

Kirkegt.

Bjørvika

Akerselva

Bispevika

Kongens gate

Skippergt.

SØRENGA

Oslo gt.

Oslofjorden

Mosseveien

Ekebergsletta

premier educational centers. The great hall of the center building is decorated with murals by Norway's famed artist, Edvard Munch, and is often the site of the Nobel Peace Prize award ceremony. *Aulaen, Karl Johans Gate 47, tel. 22/85-93-00, ext. 756. Admission free. Open July, weekdays noon-2.*

❸ Around the corner from the university, with access from Universitetsgata, is the newly refurbished **Nasjonalgalleriet** (National Gallery). There are some excellent pieces in the 19th- and early 20th-century Norwegian rooms. Scandinavian impressionists, called the "Northern Light" artists, have recently been discovered by the rest of the world. The gallery also has an extensive Munch collection. *Universitetsgt. 13, tel. 22/20-04-04. Admission free. Open Mon., Wed., Fri., and Sat. 10-4; Thurs. 10-8; Sun. 11-3.*

❹ Back-to-back with the National Gallery, across a parking lot, is a big cream-brick Art Nouveau-style building housing the **Historisk Museum** (History Museum). In addition to Asian and African ethnographic displays, the museum features a collection of Viking and medieval artifacts, including many intricately carved stave church portals. *Frederiksgt. 2, tel. 22/41-63-00. Admission free. Open May 15-Sept. 14, Tues.-Sun. 11-3; Sept. 15-May 14, Tues.-Sun. noon-3.*

❺ Continue along Freriksgate to the university and cross Karl Johans Gate to **Nationaltheatret** (the National Theater) and **Studenterlunden Park,** a few steps from the train station. In front of the theater are statues of Norway's great playwrights, Bjørnstjerne Bjørnsen (who wrote the words to the national anthem and won a Nobel Prize for his plays) and Henrik Ibsen, who wrote *A Doll's House* and *Hedda Gabler.*

Across the street on the other side of the theater is the **Hotel Continental,** owned by the same family since it was built in 1900. Take a quick tour around the lobby bar to see the collection of Munch graphics. The hotel's Theatercafeen is one of Oslo's most fashionable restaurants.

❻ Turn right on Universitetsgata to reach the redbrick **Rådhus** (City Hall), dedicated during Oslo's 900-year jubilee celebrations in 1950 and a familiar landmark with its two block towers. It took 17 years to build because construction was interrupted by World War II. Many sculptures outside, as well as murals inside, reflect the artistic climate in Norway in the 1930s—socialist modernism in its highest form. *Rådhusplassen, tel. 22/86-16-00. Admission: NKr15 adults, Nkr5 children. Open May-Sept., Mon.-Wed. and Fri.-Sat. 9-3:30; Thurs. 9-7; Sun. noon-3.*

Return to Stortingsgata and walk past Tordenskioldsgate to Rosenkrantz' Gate, both lined with specialty shops. Cross over Stortingsgata and along the short end of the park back to Karl Johans Gate. On the left is a refurbished news kiosk from the early years of this century. Across the street is the **Grand Hotel,** where many Norwegians check in on Constitution Day, May 17, in order to have a room overlooking the parades. The Grand Café was a favorite with Ibsen, who began his mornings with a brisk walk followed by a stiff drink here, in the company of local journalists.

Time Out Inside the Grand Hotel, in the informal **Palmen,** salads and light meals are served, as well as pastries and cakes.

Walk past the Lille Grensen shopping area and once again **7** across Karl Johan to **Stortinget** (the Parliament), built in the middle of the 19th century. It's a classical building, magnificently perched on the top of the hill, and becomes a people-watching spot at night, with vendors, promenaders, and students. *Karl Johans Gate 22, tel. 22/31–30–50. Admission free. Open year-round when Parliament is not in session.*

Turn left on Kongens Gate from Karl Johans Gate to reach **8** **Stortorvet,** Oslo's main square. On its west side is **Oslo Domkirke** (cathedral), completed in 1697, which includes an intricately carved Baroque pulpit. *Stortorvet 1, tel. 22/41–27–93. Admission free. Open June 1–Aug. 31, weekdays 10–3, Sat. 10–1; Sept. 1–May 31, weekdays 10–1.*

Behind the cathedral is a semicircular arcade housing many small artisans' shops, called **Kirkeristen** or Basarhallene. The building was constructed in the middle of the 19th century but was inspired by medieval architecture.

Time Out Order a cup of hot, foamy **cappuccino** at the **café** of the same name in the inner arcade. A copy of the *International Herald-Tribune* hangs from a rod inside for anyone to read.

From the cathedral, follow Kirkegata left past Karl Johan to Bankplassen and the 1902 Bank of Norway building, since 1990 **9** **Museet for Samtidskunst** (the Museum of Contemporary Art). The building, a good example of geometric Norwegian Art Nouveau, houses a fine collection of international and Norwegian pieces, mostly in small rooms built around a large core. *Bankpl. 4, tel. 22/33–58–20. Admission free. Open Tues.–Fri. 11–7, weekends 11–4.*

Turn left onto Myntgata to reach Nedre Slottsgate, Oslo's oldest neighborhood, where the half-timber buildings on the left stable police horses. At the corner of Nedre Slottsgate and Rådhusgata is the old City Hall, housing **Gamle Rådhus** restaurant, which celebrates its 353rd anniversary this year. Upstairs **10** is **Teatermuseet** (the Theater Museum), a collection of old pictures and costumes, which sometimes holds an open house at which children can try on costumes and have makeup applied. The first public theater performance in Oslo took place here. *Nedre Slottsgt. 1, tel. 22/41–81–47. Admission: NKr10 adults, Nkr5 children. Open Wed. 11–3, Sun. noon–4.*

Diagonally across Rådhusgata are two 17th-century buildings that house art galleries and a café. Turn left on Rådhusgata and **11** walk over the grassy hill to the entrance of **Akershus Slott** (castle). It's a climb, but the views from the top are worth it. The oldest part of the castle was built around 1300 and includes an escape-proof room built for a thief named Ole Pedersen Høyland. In fact he broke out of this cell, robbed the Bank of Norway, was caught, and returned to jail. With no possibility of a second escape, he killed himself here. Today some of the building is used for state occasions, but a few rooms, including the recently restored chapel, are open to the public.

The castle became German headquarters during the occupation of Norway in World War II, and many members of the Resistance were executed on the castle grounds. Their memorial has been erected at the site, across the bridge at the harbor end of the castle precinct. In a building next to the castle, at the top of the hill, is **Norges Hjemmefrontmuseum** (the Norwegian Resistance Museum), which documents events that took place during the German occupation (1940–45). *Akershus Slott, Festningspl., tel. 22/41–25–21. Admission to castle grounds and concerts free. Open daily 6 AM–9 PM; concerts in chapel, May 20–Oct. 21, Sun. at 2. Admission to castle: NKr15 adults; NKr5 children, students, senior citizens. Open May 2–Sept. 15, Mon.– Sat. 10–4; year-round, Sun. 12:30–4. Norges Hjemmefrontmuseum, Akershus Festning, tel. 22/40–31–38. Admission: NKr15 adults; NKr5 children, students, senior citizens. Open Oct.–Apr. 14, Mon.–Sat. 10–3, Sun. 11–4; Apr. 15–June 14 and Sept., Mon.–Sat. 10–4 and Sun. 11–4; June 15–Aug., Mon.–Sat. 10–5, Sun. 11–5.*

Walk back to Rådhusgata to see another interesting building, Ⓓ **Skogbrand Insurance** (Rådhusgt. 23B), in the block above the retaining wall. Architects Jan Digerud and Jon Lundberg have won awards for their innovative 1985 vertical addition to this 1917 building. Continue along to the harborside, where you can buy shrimp from one of the boats docked opposite City Hall and enjoy them on a bench overlooking the water.

Tour 2: St. Olavs Gate to Damstredet

This quiet, old-fashioned district is particularly well preserved. It features artisans' shops and Oslo's most historic cemetery.

Ⓓ At the corner of St. Olavs Gate and Akersgata is **Kunstindustri-museet** (the Decorative Arts Museum), which houses a superb furniture collection as well as an entire floor of Norwegian decorative art. The most interesting collection is on the top floor— royal clothing, including Queen Maud's jewel-encrusted, wasp-waist coronation gown from 1904—clothes worthy of any fairy-tale. *St. Olavsgt. 1, tel. 22/20–35–78. Admission: NKr15 adults; NKr10 children, students, senior citizens. Open Tues.– Fri. 11–3, weekends noon–4.*

Across Akersgata is St. Olavs Kirke. Up the hill, on the right, is **Vår Frelsers Gravlund** (Our Savior's Cemetery), where many of Norway's famous, including Ibsen and Munch, are buried. Ⓓ At its northeastern corner is **Gamle Aker Kirke** (Old Aker Church), the city's only remaining medieval church, a stone basilica, which has undergone many changes since it was constructed around 1100. *Akersvn. 25, tel. 22/69–35–82. Admission free. Open Mon.–Sat. noon–2.*

Tour 3: Frogner, Holmenkollen, and the Munch Museum

Catch the No. 2 "Majorstuen og Frogner" streetcar, which stops on Stortingsgate at Nationaltheatret and runs along the Drammensveien side of the Royal Palace.

Opposite the southwestern end of the palace grounds is the triangular **U.S. Embassy**, designed by American architect Eero Saarinen and built in 1959. At Solli plass, the *trikk*, as Norwegians fondly call the streetcars, turns right onto Frognerveien.

Stay on the trikk and ride to Frogner Park or walk the seven short blocks, following Balders Gate to Arno Bergs plass with its central fountain. Turn left on Gyldenløves Gate (street of the golden lion) and walk through one of the city's most stylish neighborhoods. Most of the buildings were constructed in the early years of this century, and many have interesting sculptural decoration and wrought ironwork. Gyldenløves Gate ends at Kirkeveien. Turn right, past the Dutch Embassy, and cross the street at the light, which is next to the trikk stop. Frogner Park is just ahead.

⑮ There's nothing quite like **Vigelands anlegget** in Frogner Park anywhere else in the world. Sculptor Gustav Vigeland began his career as a wood-carver, and his talent was quickly appreciated and supported by the townspeople of Oslo. In 1921 they provided him with a free house and studio, in exchange for which, even during World War II and the German occupation, he began to chip away at his life's work, which he would ultimately donate to the city. After the war the work was unveiled, to the combined enchantment and horror of the townsfolk. Included was the 470-ton monolith that is now the highlight of the park, as well as hundreds of writhing, fighting, and loving sculptures representing the varied forms and stages of human life. The figures are nude, but they're more monumental than erotic—bullet-headed, muscular men and healthy, solid women with flowing hair.

Time Out Just before the sculpture bridge, on the left, is the park's outdoor restaurant, **Herregårdskroen,** where you can enjoy anything from a buffet lunch to a three-course dinner, depending on the time of day. It's a prime place for people-watching.

Frogner Park is a living part of the city—people walk dogs on the green and bathe chubby babies in the fountains, and they jog, ski, and sunbathe throughout. The park complex also includes the City Museum, a swimming pool, an ice rink and skating museum (tel. 22/46–68–50), several playgrounds, and a restaurant. *Kirkeveien. Admission free.*

⑯ **Vigelandmuseet** (the Vigeland Museum), across from the park, displays many of the plaster models for the sculptures, Vigeland's woodcuts and drawings, and mementoes of his life. *Nobelsgt. 32, tel. 22/44–23–06. Admission: NKr20 adults; NKr10 children, students, senior citizens. Open May 1–Sept. 30, Tues.–Sat. 10–6, Sun. noon–7; Oct. 1–Apr. 30, Tues.–Sat. noon–4, Sun. noon–6.*

Continue on Kirkeveien to Majorstuen underground station, up the steps on the left, and take the Holmenkollen line to Frognerseteren, a 15-minute ride.

Time Out **Frognerseteren Restaurant,** built in the national romantic style, dates from 1909, when newly independent Norway sought inspiration from its earlier history.

As if the view from Frognerseteren weren't spectacular enough, **Tryvannstårnet** TV tower, offering the best panoramic view of Oslo, is only a 15-minute, sign-posted walk away. *Voksenkollen, tel. 22/92–32–00. Admission: NKr50 adults; NKr25 children, students, senior citizens. Open July, daily 9*

AM–10 PM; June and Aug., daily 10–8; May and Sept., daily 10–5; Jan.–Apr., weekdays 10–3, weekends 11–4.

⑱ Downhill is **Holmenkollbakken** (the Holmenkollen Ski Museum and Ski Jump). The jump was built for the 1952 Winter Olympics and can be seen from many points in the city. At the base of the jump, turn right, past the statue of the late King Olav V on skis, to enter the museum. In addition to a collection of skis, the oldest dating from pre-Viking times, it displays equipment from the Nansen and Amundsen polar voyages and a model of a ski-maker's workshop. You can also climb (or ride the elevator) to the top of the jump tower. It's intimidating enough with a firm grip on the rail, but on skis and snow, it's mind-boggling. *Kongevn. 5, tel. 22/92–32–00. Admission: NKr50 adults; NKr25 children, students, senior citizens. Open July, daily 9 AM–10 PM; June and Aug., daily 10–8; May and Sept., daily 10–5; Jan.–Apr., weekdays 10–3, weekends 11–4.*

To catch the train back to town, walk downhill to Holmen Kollen Station, less than a mile away. Leave the train at Majorstuen, cross the street, and catch the No. 20 bus, marked **⑲** "Galgeberg," which runs east to **Munchmuseet** (the Munch Museum). Edvard Munch, one of Scandinavia's leading artists, bequeathed an enormous collection of his work (about 1,200 paintings, 4,500 drawings, and 18,000 graphic works) to the city when he died in 1944. It languished in warehouses for nearly 20 years, until the city built a museum to house it in 1963. For much of his life Munch was a troubled man, and his major works, dating from the 1890s, with such titles as *The Scream* and *Vampire*, reveal his angst, but he was not without humor. His extraordinary talent as a graphic artist emerges in the print room, with its displays of lithographic stones and wood blocks. *Tøyengt. 53, tel. 22/67–37–74. Admission: NKr40 adults; NKr15 children, students, senior citizens. Open June 1–Sept. 15, Mon.–Sat. 10–6, Sun. noon–6; Sept. 16–May 31, Tues.–Sat. 10–4, Sun. noon–4.*

You can walk downhill from the Munch Museum to Tøyen Senter shopping area to catch the subway back downtown.

Tour 4: Bygdøy

Oslo's most important historical sights are concentrated on Bygdøy Peninsula. Take bus No. 30, marked "Bygdøy," from Stortingsgate at Nationaltheatret along Drammensveien to Bygdøy Allé, a wide avenue lined with chestnut trees. The bus passes Frogner Church and several embassies on its way to Olav Kyrres plass, where it turns left, and soon left again, onto the peninsula. If you see some horses on the left, they come from the king's stables (the dark red building with the monogram); the royal family's current summer palace, actually just a big white frame house, is on the right. Get off at the next stop, "Norsk Folkemuseum." Backtrack until you come to the nar- **⑳** row Oscarshallveien, which leads to **Oscarshall Slott**, an eccentric neo-Gothic palace built in 1852 for King Oscar I as a site for picnics and other summer pursuits. *Oscarshallvn., tel. 22/43–77–49. Admission: NKr15 adults, NKr5 children. Open June 1–Sept. 30, Sun. 11–4.*

㉑ Next is the **Norsk Folkemuseum** (Norwegian Folk Museum), which consists of some 140 structures from all over the country that have been reconstructed on site. The best-known and most important building is **Gol Stavkirke** (Gol Stave Church), constructed around 1200. During summer and on weekends, guides in the buildings demonstrate various home crafts, such as weaving tapestries, sewing national costumes, and baking flatbread. On one side of the museum is a reconstructed 19th-century village, with shops and houses. Among its exhibits are a pharmaceutical museum and a dentist's office, complete with turn-of-the-century braces—a real mouthful of springs and bands. Indoor collections in the main building include toys, dolls and dollhouses, a Sami (Lapp) collection, national costumes, and Ibsen's actual study. The museum puts on a special summer calendar of events, including daily activities from folk dancing to concerts with instruments from the museum's collection. *Museumsvn. 10, tel. 22/43–70–20. Summer admission: NKr35 adults, NKr25 students and senior citizens, NKr10 children. Winter: NKr20, NKr15, and NKr5. Open May 15–Sept. 14, daily 10–6; Sept. 15–May 14, daily noon–4.*

㉒ Around the corner to the right is **Vikingskiphuset** (the Viking Ship Museum), one of Norway's best-known attractions. It looks like a cathedral from the outside, and inside the feeling of reverence is very real. It's hard to imagine that the three ships on display, all found buried along the Oslo Fjord, are nearly 1,200 years old. The richly carved *Oseberg* ship, thought to have been the burial chamber for Queen Åse, is the most decorative, while the *Gokstad* ship is a functional longboat, devoid of ornament. The small *Tune* ship has been left unrestored. Items found with the ships, including sleds with intricately carved decoration, tools, household goods, and a tapestry, are also on view. *Huk aveny 35, tel. 22/43–83–79. Admission: NKr20 adults; NKr10 students, senior citizens, children. Open May 2–Aug. 31, daily 9–6; Sept., daily 11–5; Apr. and Oct., daily 11–4; Nov. 1–Mar. 31, daily 11–3.*

Time Out Besides a collection of model ships and small boats, the nearby **Maritime Museum** has an outdoor café, **Najaden,** overlooking the Oslo Fjord.

㉓ Just beyond the Maritime Museum is the **Fram-museet,** an A-frame structure in the shape of a traditional Viking boathouse. This museum, with its matter-of-fact displays of life on board ship, vividly depicts the history of polar exploration. The *Fram* was constructed in 1892 by Scottish-Norwegian shipbuilder Colin Archer. Fridtjof Nansen led the first *Fram* expedition across the ice surrounding the North Pole; its most famous voyage took Roald Amundsen to Antarctica, the first leg of his successful expedition to the South Pole in 1911. Visitors board the ship by gangplank and are allowed to walk all over the vessel. *Bygdøynes, tel. 22/43–83–70. Admission: NKr15 adults; NKr8 students, children, senior citizens. Open May 16–Aug. 31, daily 9–5:45; May 1–15 and Sept., daily 10–4:45; Apr. and Oct., daily 11–2:45; Mar., weekends 11–2:45; closed Dec.–Feb.*

㉔ Across the parking lot from the *Fram* is the older **Kon-Tiki Museum,** which houses the famous raft, along with the papyrus boat, *Ra II.* Thor Heyerdahl continued the Norwegian tradition of exploration in his 1947 voyage from Peru to Polynesia on the *Kon-Tiki,* a balsa raft, to confirm his theory that the first Polynesians originally came from Peru. The *Kon-Tiki,* now showing its age, is suspended on a plastic sea. The *Ra II* sailed from Morocco to the Caribbean in 1970. *Bygdøynesvn. 36,* *tel. 22/43–80–50. Admission: NKr20 adults; NKr10 students, children, senior citizens. Open May 18–Aug. 31, daily 10–6; Apr. 1–May 16 and Sept., daily 10:30–5; Oct. 1–Mar. 31, daily 10:30–4.*

From May to September 30, you can take a 15-minute ferry ride from the dock in front of the *Fram* to the City Hall docks.

Short Excursions from Oslo

Numbers in the margin correspond to points of interest on the Oslo Excursions map.

The Henie-Onstad Center It's been more than 20 years since Sonja Henie died, but she still skates her way through many a late-night movie. The three-time Olympic gold medal winner was the first to realize the potential of the ice show, and her technical assistant, Frank Zamboni, has been immortalized in skating rinks around the world by the ice-finishing machine he developed just for her, the Zamboni. Henie had a shrewd head for money and marriage, and her third, to Norwegian shipping magnate Niels Onstad, resulted in the **Henie-Onstad Center,** about 12 kilometers (7 miles) from Oslo. They put together a fine collection of early 20th-century art, with important works by Leger, Munch, Picasso, Bonnard, and Matisse.

Bus Nos. 151, 153, 161, 162, 251, and 252 from the old university on Karl Johans Gate stop at the entrance to the museum grounds. To drive, follow E18 (toward Drammen) 12 kilometers (about 7 miles) from Oslo. *1311 Høvikodden, tel. 67/54–30–50. Admission: NKr30 adults, NKr20 students and senior citizens, and NKr10 children. Open Mon. 11–5, Tues.–Fri. 9–7; also June–Aug., weekends 11–7 and Sept.–May, weekends 11–5.*

The Cobalt Works **Blaafarveværket** (the Cobalt Works), founded in 1776 to extract cobalt from the Modum mines, is about 70 kilometers (45 miles) from Oslo, in Åmot i Modum. The mineral was used to make dyes for the world's glass and porcelain industries. Today the complex is a museum and a national park. The main building houses a one-man/woman show of works by a different Scandinavian artist every year. There is also a permanent collection of old cobalt-blue glass and porcelain. For the children, there's a petting farm. Up the hill from the art complex is **Haugfossen,** the highest waterfall in eastern Norway. Beside the falls is an old-fashioned country store. Restaurants serve Norwegian country dishes. Outdoor concerts are held on the grounds throughout the summer.

Take E18 to Drammen, then Route 11 west to Hokksund, and Route 35 to Åmot, turning onto Route 287 to Sigdal. The bus to Modum leaves from the old university on Karl Johan at 9:45 AM on Tuesday, Thursday, and Saturday. *Tel. 32/78–28–00. Admission to special exhibitions: NKr35 adults, NKr10 children; cobalt works: NKr60 adults, children free with adults. Open May 28–Aug. 29, daily 10–8; Aug. 29–Sept. 30, daily 10–4.*

Hadeland A day trip to **Hadeland** combines a drive along the Tyrifjord, where you can see some of the best fjord views in eastern Norway, with a visit to a glass factory that has been in operation since 1762. **Hadeland Glassverk** (Rte. 241, toward Jevnaker, tel. 61/31–10–00) produces both practical table crystal and one-of-a-kind art glass. You can watch artisans blowing glass and

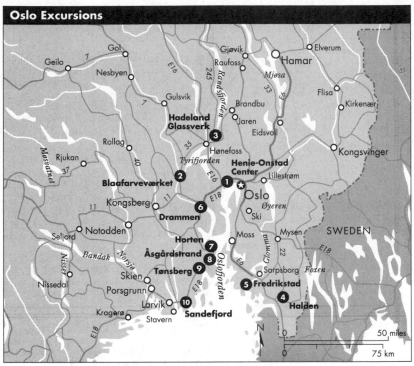

Oslo Excursions

buy their handiwork (first quality and seconds) at the gift shop. The museum and gallery have a collection of 15,000 items, with about 800 on display. Take E18 west to Sandvika, turn right onto E16 and follow the signs to Hønefoss. At the Route 241 intersection, take the road to Jevnaker, which passes the glass factory. You can also take bus No. 71, marked Hønefoss, which leaves the old university on Karl Johan at seven minutes after the hour. Change in Hønefoss for the Jevnaker bus (no number). The total trip takes about two hours.

What to See and Do with Children

Bygdøy (*see* Tour 4, *above*) is a good place to take children. The Viking Ship, *Fram*, and *Kon-Tiki* museums are also good choices; the **Norsk Folkmuseum** has special exhibitions of old toys and doll houses. Live events, changing daily all summer, include old-fashioned bicycle races and sheep shearing.

The **Barnekunst** (Children's Art) **Museum** was the brainchild of Rafael Goldin, a Russian immigrant, who has collected children's drawings from more than 150 countries. Materials are provided for children to create on the spot. *Lille Frøensvn. 4, tel. 22/46–85–73. Admission: NKr30 adults; NKr15 children, students, senior citizens. Open June 25–Aug. 15, Tues.– Thurs., Sun. 11–4; Sept. 10–Dec. 15, Jan. 1–June 23, Tues.– Thurs. 9:30–2, Sun. 11–4.*

One stop closer to town on the subway is **Sporveismuseet** (the Transport Museum), with old buses and trains, including a horse-drawn streetcar. Take the subway to Majorstuen.

Gardevn. 15, tel. 22/60-94-09. Admission: NKr10 adults, NKr5 children. Open Apr.-Sept., weekends noon-3; Oct.-Aug., Sun. noon-3.

Oslo is proud of its **Teknisk** (Technical) **Museum,** located about 20 minutes north of the city. Exhibits include the first airplane to fly over the North Sea, classic cars and motorcycles, and the development of computers, waterpower, and communication, all accompanied by demonstrations and films. *Kjelsåsvn. 143, tel. 22/22-25-50. Admission: NKr30 adults, NKr15 children. Open June-Aug., Tues.-Sun. 10-7; Sept.-May, Tues. 10-9, Wed.-Sat. 10-4, Sun. 10-5.*

Everyone enjoys **Tusenfryd,** Oslo's amusement park, a 20-minute ride east of the city. There are carnival rides, such as a merry-go-round, a Ferris wheel, and a roller coaster with a loop, and a water slide. *Vinterbro, tel. 64/94-63-63. Admission: NKr50. Open June 1-Aug. 20, daily 10:30-8; May and Aug. 21-Sept. 15, weekends 10-7:30.*

Off the Beaten Track

Oslo was founded by Harald Hårdråde (hard ruler) in 1048, and the earliest settlements were near what is now Bispegata, a few blocks behind Oslo S Station. The ruins at **Minneparken** are all that is left of the city's former spiritual center: **Korskirken** (Cross Church; Egedes Gate 2), a small stone church dating from the end of the 13th century; **Olavs kloster** (cloister; St. Halvards plass 3), built around 1240 by Dominican monks; and the foundations of **St. Halvards Kirke,** named for the patron saint of the city and dating from the early 12th century. The latter remained the city's cathedral until 1660. Stones from its walls were used to build Akershus Slott. Take trikk 9, marked "Ljabru," to Bispegata, where signs point to the various ruins.

Once you have your fill of history, you can get in touch with something a bit more corporeal at the **Emanuel Vigeland Museum.** Although he never gained the fame of his brother Gustav, the creator of Vigeland Park, the younger Emanuel is an artist of some notoriety. His alternately saucy, natural, and downright erotic frescoes make even the sexually liberated Norwegians blush. Take commuter train 15 to Slendal. *Grimelundsveien 8, tel. 22/14-23-28. Admission free. Open Sun. noon-3.*

Shopping

Oslo is the best place to buy anything Norwegian. Prices of handmade articles, such as knitwear, are controlled, making comparison shopping unnecessary. Otherwise, shops have both sales and specials—look for the words *salg* and *tilbud.* Sales of seasonal merchandise, combined with the value-added tax refund, can save you more than half the original price. Norwegians do like au courant skiwear so there are plenty of bargains in last season's winter sportswear.

Two shopping districts stand out—downtown, in the area around **Karl Johans Gate;** and **Majorstuen,** starting at the subway station with the same name and proceeding down Bogstadveien to the Royal Palace.

Shopping Centers **Aker Brygge,** Norway's first major shopping center, is right on the water across from the Tourist Information office at Vestbanen. Shops are open until 8 most days, and some even on Sundays. **Oslo City,** at the other end of downtown, with access to the street from Oslo S station (Stenersgt. 1E, tel. 22/44–44–44), is the largest indoor mall, but the shops are run-of-the-mill, and the food is mostly fast. **Paleet Karl Johan** (Karl Johans Gate 39–41, between Universitetsgt. and Rosenkrantz Gate), the newest downtown development, opens up into a grand atrium lined with supports of various shades of black and gray marble. Upstairs are familiar chain stores and specialty shops, while in the basement is a food court.

Department Stores **Christiania GlasMagasin** (Stortorvet 9, tel. 22/11–63–50) is not a true department store, but it has a much more extensive selection of merchandise than a specialty shop. The best buys are glass and porcelain: Hadeland, Magnor, Randsfjord, and Severin glass, and Porsgrunn and Figgjo porcelain and stoneware. Christmas decorations reflecting Norway's rural heritage are easily packed. There is also a wide selection of pewter ware. **Steen & Strøm** (Kongensgt. 23, tel. 22/41–68–00) consists of several individually organized shops, including **Årstidene,** which offers a fine selection of Norwegian souvenirs.

Street Markets The best flea market is on Saturday at **Vestkanttorvet,** near Frogner Park. Check the local paper for others.

Specialty Stores Norwegian rustic antiques cannot be taken out of the country, *Antiques* but just about anything else can with no problem. **Kaare Berntsen** (Universitetsgt. 12, tel. 22/20–34–29) sells paintings, furniture, and small items, all very exclusive, and priced accordingly. **Blomqvist Kunsthandel** (Tordenskiolds Gate 5, tel. 22/41–26–31) has a good selection of small items and paintings, with auctions six times a year. **West Sølv og Mynt** (Niels Juels Gate 27, tel. 22/55–75–83) has the largest selection of silver, both old and antique, in town. The Frogner district is dotted with antiques shops, especially Skovveien and Thomas Heftyes Gate between Bygdøy Allé and Frogner Plass. **Esaias Solberg** (Dronningens Gate 27, tel. 22/42–41–08), behind Oslo Cathedral, has exceptional small antiques.

Books **Tanum Libris** (Karl Johans Gate 37, tel. 22/42–93–10) and **Erik Qvist** (Drammensveien 16, tel. 22/44–52–69) have the best selections of English books in Oslo. **Bjørn Ringstrøms Antikvariat** (Ullevålsvn. 1, tel. 22/20–78–05), across the street from the Museum of Decorative Art, has a wide selection of used books and records. For new and used paperbacks, go to **Pocketboka** (Ole Vigs Gate 25, tel. 22/69–00–18), at Majorstuen.

Embroidery **Husfliden** (*see* Handicrafts, *below*) sells embroidery kits, including do-it-yourself *bunader* (national costumes), while traditional yarn shops also sell embroidery. **Randi Mangen** (Jac Aalls Gate 17, tel. 22/60–50–59), near Majorstuen, sells only embroidery.

Food Take back a smoked salmon or trout for a special treat. Most grocery stores sell vacuum-packed fish. **W. Køltzow,** at Aker Brygge (Stranden 3, tel. 22/83–00–70), specializes in fish and can arrange for just about anything to be packed for export.

Fur Look for the Saga label for the best-quality farmed Arctic fox and mink. The most exclusive designs are found at **Studio H. Olesen** (Karl Johans Gate 31, enter at Rosenkrantz Gate, tel.

22/33–37–50, and Universitetsgt. 20, tel. 22/42–99–49). Another shop with an excellent selection is **Hansson Pels** (Kirkevn. 54, tel. 22/69–64–20), near Majorstuen.

Furniture Norway is well known for both rustic furniture and orthopedic, yet well-designed, chairs. Starting at **Tannum** (Stortingsgt. 28, tel. 22/83–42–95), Drammensveien and Bygdøy allé have a wide selection of interior-design stores.

Glass, Ceramics, If there's no time to visit a glass factory (*see* Short Excursions
and Pewter from Oslo, *above*), go to **Christiania GlasMagasin** (Stortorvet 9, tel. 22/11–63–50) or to **Norway Designs** (Stortingsgt. 28, tel. 22/83–11–00) for the best items. The shops at Basarhallene behind the cathedral also sell glass and ceramics. Behind the Royal Palace is **Abelson Brukskunst** (Skovvn. 27, tel. 22/55–55–94), with a shop crammed with the best modern designs.

Handicrafts **Heimen** (Rosenkrantz Gate 8, tel. 22/41–40–50) has small souvenir items and a specialized department for Norwegian *bunader* (national costumes). **Husfliden** (Møllergt. 4, tel. 22/42–10–75), has an even larger selection, including pewter, ceramics, knits, handwoven textiles, furniture, handmade felt boots and slippers, hand-sewn loafers, sweaters, national costumes, wrought-iron accessories, and Christmas ornaments, all made in Norway. For individual pieces, visit **Format Kunsthandverk** (Vestbanepl. 1, tel. 22/83–73–12) or **Basarhallene**, the arcade behind the cathedral.

Jewelry Gold and precious stones are no bargain, but silver and enamel jewelry, along with reproductions of Viking pieces, are. Some silver pieces are made with Norwegian stones, particularly pink thulite. **David-Andersen** (Karl Johans Gate 20, tel. 22/41–69–55), Norway's best-known goldsmith, has the widest selection in Oslo. Other good jewelers are **Heyerdahl** (Stortingsgt. 18, tel. 22/41–59–18), near City Hall, and **Expo-Arte** (Drammensvn. 40, tel. 22/55–93–90), who specialize in custom pieces. (*See also* Antiques, *above*.)

Knitwear and Norway is famous for its handmade multicolored ski sweaters,
Clothing but even mass-produced models are of top quality. The prices are regulated, so buy what you like when you see it. Sweaters are sold at **Heimen** and **Husfliden** (*see* Handicrafts, *above*) and at special sweater shops. **Maurtua** (Fr. Nansens pl. 9, tel. 22/41–31–64), near City Hall, has a huge selection of both sweaters and blanket coats. **Oslo Sweater Shop** (SAS Scandinavia Hotel, Tullinsgt. 5, tel. 22/11–29–22) has one of the city's widest selections. **Siril** (Rosenkrantz Gate 23, tel. 22/41–01–80), near City Hall, is a small shop that offers personal service. **Rein og Rose** (Ruseløkkvn. 3, tel. 22/83–21–39) has a good selection of knitwear, yarn, and textiles. **William Schmidt** (Karl Johans Gate 41, tel. 22/42–02–88), founded in 1853, is Oslo's oldest shop specializing in sweaters and souvenirs.

Sportswear Look for the Helly-Hansen brand. The company makes everything from insulated underwear to rainwear, snow gear, and great insulated mittens. **Sportshuset** (Ullevålsvn. 11, tel. 22/20–11–21, and Frognervn. 9C, tel. 22/55–29–57) has the best prices; **Gresvig** (Storgt. 20, tel. 22/17–39–80) and **Sigmund Ruud** (Kirkevn. 57, tel. 22/69–43–90) have the best selections.

Watches For some reason, Swiss watches are much cheaper in Norway than in many other countries. **Bjerke** (Karl Johans Gate 31, tel.

22/42–20–44, and Prinsensgt. 21, tel. 22/42–60–50) has the
largest selection in town.

Sports and the Outdoors

Surrounding Oslo's compact center are a variety of lovely and
unspoiled landscapes, including forests, countrysides, and, of
course, the fjord. Just 15 minutes north of the city center by
tram is the **Oslomarka,** where locals ski in winter and hike in
summer. The area is dotted with 27 small cottages, or *hytter,*
which can be reserved through **Den Norske Turistforening**
(Stortingsgt. 28, tel. 22/83–25–50), which has maps of the
marka as well. The **Oslo Archipelago** is also a favorite with sun-
bathing urbanites, who hop ferries to their favorite isles.

Bicycling **Den Rustne Eike** (The Rusty Spoke, Enga 2, tel. 22/83–72–31)
rents bikes and equipment, including helmets (required by
law). **Sykkeldelisk** (Fridtjof Nansens pl. 7, tel. 22/42–60–20)
and **Oslo Sykkelutleie** (Kjelsåsvn. 145, tel. 22/22–13–46) also
rent a full range of bikes. The latter are located just on the edge
of Oslomarka, and they specialize in arranging routes covering
that territory. **Syklistenes Landsforening** (National Organization of Cyclists; Maridalsvn. 60, tel. 22/71–92–93) sells books
and maps for cycling holidays in Norway and abroad and provides friendly, free advice.

Fishing A national fishing license (NKr60, available in post offices) and
a local fee (NKr60 from local sports shops) are required in order
to fish in the Oslo Fjord and the surrounding lakes. Ice fishing
is also popular in the winter, but you'll have a hard time finding
an ice drill—truly, you may want to bring one from home.

Golf Oslo's international-level golf course, **Oslo Golfklubb** (Bogstad,
tel. 22/50–44–02) is private, and heavily booked, but will admit
members of other golf clubs if the space is available. There are
also one 18-hole and several nine-hole courses, with expansions
planned.

Hiking and Jogging Head for the woods surrounding Oslo, the **marka,** for jogging or
walking; there are thousands of kilometers of trails, hundreds
of them lit. Frogner Park has many paths, and you can jog or
hike along the Aker River, but a few unsavory types may be
about late at night or early in the morning. Or you can take the
Sognsvann tram to the end of the line and walk or jog along the
Sognsvann stream. Den Norske Turist forening (*see above*) has
many maps of trails around Oslo and can recommend individual
routes.

Skiing The **Skiforeningen** (Storgt. 20, tel. 22/92–32–00) can provide
tips on the multitude of cross-country trails. Among the flood-
lighted trails in the Oslomarka are the **Bogstad** (3.5 kilometers/
2.1 miles, marked for the disabled and blind), the **Lillomarka**
(about 25 kilometers/15.6 miles), and the **Østmarken** (33 kilom-
eters/20.6 miles).

For downhill, which usually lasts from mid-December to March,
there are 15 local city slopes, and organized trips to several outside slopes, including **Norefjell** (tel. 32/14–92–79), 110 kilometers (69 miles) north of the city, are also available.

The Skiforeningen also offers cross-country classes for young
children (3- to 7-year-olds), downhill for older children (7- to 12-

year-olds) and both, in addition to Telemark-style and racing-techniques for adults. For details, call the Skiforeningen.

Swimming **Tøyenbadet** (Helgesensgt. 90, tel. 22/68–24–23) and **Frogner Park** have large outdoor swimming pools that are open from May 18 through August 25 (open weekdays 7–7 and 10–7, weekends 10–5). Tøyenbadet also has an indoor pool (open weekdays 7–7 and 10–7, weekends 10–2:30). All pools cost NKr35 adults, NKr15 children.

Dining

Food once was an afterthought in Oslo, but no longer. Its chefs are winning contests all over the world, and Norwegian cuisine, based on the products of its pristine waters and countryside, is firmly in the culinary spotlight. Eating out is a luxury for many Norwegians. Oslo is also a place where bad food is expensive and good food doesn't necessarily cost more—it's just a matter of knowing where to go.

Highly recommended restaurants are indicated by a star ★.

Very Expensive

★ **Bagatelle.** Oslo's best restaurant is a short walk from downtown. Paintings by contemporary Norwegian artists accent the otherwise subdued interior. Internationally known chef/owner Eyvind Hellstrøm's cuisine is modern Norwegian with French overtones. His grilled scallops with a saffron-parsley sauce, and the marinated salmon tartare with an herbed *crème fraîche* sauce are extraordinary. Bagatelle has a wine cellar to match its food. *Bygdøy allé 3/5, tel. 22/44–63–97. Reservations advised. Jacket and tie required. AE, DC, MC, V. Closed Sun., 1 week at Christmas and Easter. Dinner only.*

D'Artagnan. Freddie Nielsen's restaurant, right off Karl Johan, recently underwent a facade refurbishment, but inside it's still the same. The stairs lead to a comfortable lounge, while another floor up is the dining room. The decor is eclectic, but the food is classic and pure. The saffron-poached pike with asparagus is a good way to start a meal, while the boned fillet of salmon with lobster-cream sauce seasoned with dill is attractive and flavorful. The dessert cart is loaded with jars of fruit preserved in liqueurs, which are served with various sorbets and ice creams. *Øvre Slottsgt. 16, tel. 22/41–74–04. Reservations advised. Jacket and tie required. AE, DC, MC, V. Closed weekends and July. No lunch.*

De Fem Stuer. Located near the famous Holmenkollen ski jump, in the historic Holmenkollen Park Hotel, this restaurant has first-rate views and food. Bent Stiansen has won an assortment of prizes for his cooking, the latest, the 1993 Bocuse d'Or medal. His modern Norwegian dishes have strong classic roots. Well worth trying is the three-course "A Taste of Norway," with salmon, reindeer, and cloudberries. *Holmenkollen Park Hotel, Kongevn. 26, tel. 22/92–20–00. Reservations advised. Jacket and tie required. AE, DC, MC, V.*

★ **Feinschmecker.** The name is German, but the food is modern Scandinavian. The atmosphere is friendly and intimate, with green rattan chairs, yellow tablecloths, and floral draperies. The owners are Lars Erik Underthun, one of Oslo's foremost chefs, and Bengt Wilson, one of Scandinavia's leading food photographers, so the food at Feinschmecker looks as good as it tastes. The roast rack of lamb with crunchy fried sweetbreads on tagliatelle and the chocolate-caramel teardrop with passionfruit sauce are two choices on a menu that also makes fascinating reading. *Balchensgt. 5, tel. 22/44–17–77. Reservations advised. Dress: casual but neat. AE, DC, MC, V. Closed Sun., 1 week Christmas and Easter, last 3 weeks of July. No lunch.*

Expensive

Ambassadeur. This cozy restaurant serving modern Scandinavian food is in the cellar of the Ambassadeur Hotel. It has one of the best bars in town, comfortable and well stocked. Huge swaths of fabric, dark colors, and baroque-style paintings of food create a plush, cocoonlike ambience. The food itself stands in contrast to the decor—it's light, in both concept and color. The seafood salad in a light vinaigrette with plump mussels and shrimp is a winner, while the scallops in lemon buerre blanc are delicate and subtle. *Hotel Ambassadeur, Camilla Collets vei 15, tel. 22/55–25–31. Reservations advised. Dress: casual but neat. AE, DC, MC, V. Closed Sat., Sun., and July. No lunch.*

Babette's Gjesthus. This tiny restaurant is hidden in the shopping arcade by City Hall. The atmosphere is warm and intimate. Bright blue walls, starched white tablecloths, and lace curtains against paned windows create a rustic, homey feel. The food is Scandinavian with a French touch. The dishes vary according to season but are always well prepared. Chef Ortwin Kulmus and his friendly staff know how to make their guests feel at home. *Rådhuspassasjen, Olav Vs Gate 6, tel. 22/41–64–64. Reservations required. Dress: casual but neat. AE, DC, MC, V. Closed Sun. No lunch.*

Hos Thea. This gem has only 36 seats. It's located at the beginning of Embassy Row, a short distance from downtown. The decor is beige and blue, with a homey, old-fashioned look. The small menu offers four or five choices in each category, but every dish is superbly prepared, from the venison in a sauce of mixed berries to the orange-flavored crème caramel. Owner Sergio Barcilon, originally from Spain, is one of the pioneers of the new Scandinavian cooking. The noise and smoke levels can be high late in the evening. *Gabelsgt. 11, entrance on Drammensvn., tel. 22/44–68–74. Reservations required. Dress: casual but neat. AE, DC, MC, V. Closed 1 week at Christmas and Easter. No lunch.*

Le Canard. This oasis in Frogner is furnished with antiques and Oriental rugs; fresh, white crocheted tablecloths and silver candlesticks contrast with the somber stone walls. The specialty is, of course, duck, but Chef Lucien Mares is known to conjure up sumptuous treats for his guests. The wine list is extensive. *Oscars Gate 81, tel. 22/43–40–28. Reservations advised. Dress: casual but neat. AE, DC, MC, V. Closed Sun., Christmas, Easter. No lunch.*

Moderate

★ **Dinner.** Though its name is not the best for a restaurant specializing in Szechuan-style cuisine, this is the only place for Chinese food, both hot and not so pungent. The mango pudding for dessert is wonderful. Don't bother with the other Chinese restaurants. *Arbeidergt. 2, tel. 22/42–68–90. Reservations advised. Dress: casual. AE, DC, MC, V. No lunch.*

Oslo Dining and Lodging

KEY

AE American Express Office

ℹ Tourist Information

—— Rail Lines

(Map of Oslo showing Frogner Park, Bygdøy, Frognerkilen, Langvikbukta, with numbered dining and lodging locations and street names including Drammensveien, Bygdøy allé, Sólli Plass, U.S. Embassy, etc.)

0 ——— 1 mile

0 ——— 1 km

N ↑

Dining

A Touch of France, **26**
Ambassadeur, **11**
Babette's Gjestehus, **14**
Bagatelle, **10**
D'Artagnan, **26**
De Fem Stuer, **2**
Den Grimme Ælling, **16**
Dinner, **24**
Dionysos Taverna, **29**

Feinschmecker, **4**
Gamle Rådhus, **25**
Hos Thea, **8**
Kaffistova, **22**
Kastanjen, **5**
Le Canard, **9**
Lofotstua, **3**
Quatro Amigos, **13**
Shalimar, **32**
Theatercafeen, **15**
Tysk City Grill, **28**

Lodging

Ambassadeur, **11**
Bondeheimen, **22**
Bristol, **20**
Cecil, **19**
Gabelshus, **7**
Grand Hotel, **23**
Gyldenløve, **6**
Haraldsheim, **31**
Holmenkollen Park Hotel Rica, **2**
Hotel Continental, **15**

Munch, **17**
Oslo Plaza, **30**
Rica Victoria, **18**
Royal Christiania, **27**
SAS Park Royal, **1**
SAS Scandinavia Hotel, **12**
Stefan, **21**

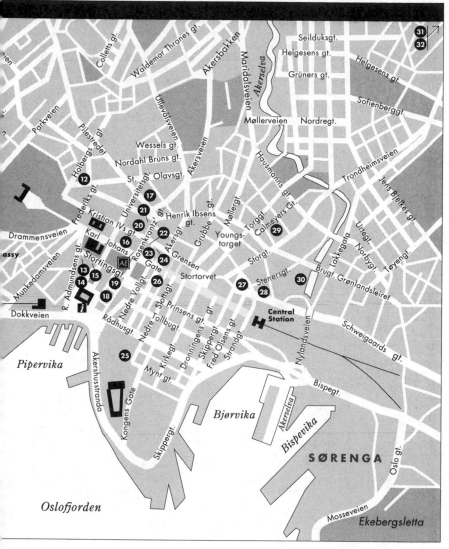

Seilduksgt.
Helgesens gt.
Grüners gt.
Helgesens gt.
31
32
Collets gt.
Waldemar Thranes gt.
Akersbakken
Maridalsveien
Akerselva
Sofienberggt.
Møllerveien
Nordregt.
Parkveien
Pilestredet
Ullevålsveien
Akersveien
Hausmanns gt.
Trondheimsveien
Jens Bjelkes gt.
Holbergs gt.
Wessels gt.
Nordahl Bruns gt.
St. Olavsgt.
12
Universitetsgt.
17
Kristian IVs gt.
21
Henrik Ibsens gt.
Møllergt.
Torggt.
Calmeyers Gt.
Urtegt.
Norbygt.
Tøyengt.
Frederiks gt.
20
Grubbe gt.
Youngs-torget
29
Drammensveien
Karl Johans
16
Rosenkrantz'
22
Akersgt.
Grensen
Storgt.
Takkegata
Brugt. Grønlandsleiret
Munkedamsveien
R. Admundsens gt.
Stortingsgt.
23
24
Stortorvet
assy
13
15
19
26
27
Stenersgt.
28
30
14
18
Slottsgt.
Prinsens gt.
Schweigaards gt.
Dokkveien
Rådhusgt.
Nedre Vollgt.
Nedre Slottsgt.
Tollbugt.
Dronningens gt.
Skippergt.
Fred Olsens gt.
Strandgt.
Central Station
Nylandsveien
Pipervika
Akershusstranda
25
Kirkegt.
Mynt gt.
Bispegt.
Kongens Gate
Skippergt.
Bjørvika
Akerselva
Bispevika
SØRENGA
Oslo gt.
Oslofjorden
Mosseveien
Ekebergsletta

★ **Dionysos Taverna.** Nicola Murati gives his guests a warm welcome in this unpretentious little Greek restaurant. The hors d'oeuvre platter, which includes stuffed vine leaves, meatballs, feta cheese, tzatziki, tomatoes, and cucumbers, is a meal in itself. The souvlaki and moussaka are authentically prepared, as are the more unusual casserole dishes. A bouzouki duo provides live music on Friday and Saturday. *Calmeyersgt. 11, tel. 22/60–78–64. Dress: casual. AE, MC, V. No lunch.*

Gamle Rådhus. Oslo's oldest restaurant, which celebrated its 350th birthday in 1991, is in the old City Hall. Don't let the beer signs and dirty windows put you off. The dining room is straight out of Ibsen, with dark brown wainscoting, deep-yellow painted walls, old prints, and heavy red curtains. Famous for its *lutefisk*, a Scandinavian specialty made from dried fish that has been soaked in lye and then poached, the restaurant's menu allows ample choice for the less daring. Try the fresh cod in season. *Nedre Slottsgt. 1, tel. 22/42–01–07. Dinner reservations advised. Dress: casual but neat. AE, DC, MC, V.*

★ **Kastanjen.** This casual Frogner bistro is the kind every neighborhood needs. The style of food is new traditional, with modern interpretations of classic Norwegian dishes. The three-course meal is good value for the money, but check out the "dish of the day" (*husmannskost*) at an unbeatable price. *Bygdøy allé 18, tel. 22/43–44–67. Reservations advised. Dress: casual. AE, DC, MC, V. Closed Sun., 1 week at Christmas and Easter.*

Shalimar. This Pakistani restaurant is off the beaten track but worth the trip, for the food, prepared by chefs imported from Karachi, is delectable. Try the tandoori mixed grill, which includes chicken, lamb, and kebab, or the chicken biryani with aromatic rice. Vegetarians have ample choices, and the naan bread is addictive. *Konghellegt. 5, tel. 22/37–47–68. Dress: casual. AE, DC, MC, V. No lunch.*

★ **Theatercafeen.** This Oslo institution, on the ground floor of the Hotel Continental, is jammed day and night. Built in 1900, the last Viennese-style café in northern Europe retains its Art Nouveau character. The menu is small and jumbled, with starters and main dishes interspersed; the only hint of the serving size is the price column. From 1 to 7, there's a reasonably priced two-course "family dinner." Pastry chef Robert Bruun's *konfektkake* (a rich chocolate cake) and apple tart served with homemade ice cream are reasons enough to visit. *Stortingsgt. 24–26, tel. 22/33–32–00. Reservations advised. Dress: casual but neat. AE, DC, MC, V.*

A Touch of France At this clean, inviting brasserie where the tables sit close together, the French ambience is further accented by the waiters' long, white aprons. The tempting menu includes a steaming hot bouillabaisse. *Øvre Slottsgt. 16, tel. 22/42–56–97. Reservations advised weekends. Dress: casual but neat. AE, DC, MC, V.*

Inexpensive

Den Grimme Ælling. Dane Bjarne Hvid Pedersen is well established with his popular Copenhagen restaurant in the food court at Paleet. His *smørbrød* are the best buy in town: lots of meat, fish, or cheese on a small piece of bread. He also has daily dinner specials, such as *hakkebøf* (Danish Salisbury steak) with gravy, onions, and potatoes, or *frikadeller* (Danish meat cakes), all homemade. *Paleet, Karl Johans Gate 41B, tel. 22/42–47–83. Dress: casual. No credit cards.*

★ **Kaffistova.** Norwegian country cooking is served, cafeteria style, at this downtown restaurant. Everyday specials include soup and a selection of entrées, including a vegetarian dish. *Kjøttkaker* (meat cakes rather like Salisbury steak) served with creamed cabbage is a Norwegian staple, and the steamed salmon with Sandefjord butter is as good here as in places where it costs three times as much. Low-alcohol beer is the strongest drink served. *Rosenkrantz' Gate 8, tel. 22/42–99–74. Dress: casual. AE, DC, MC, V.*

Lofotstua. This rustic fish restaurant has a cozy atmosphere and personal service right out of Norway's far north. Good, moderately priced food includes fresh cod and seafood from Lofoten. *Kirkevn. 40, tel. 22/46–93–96. Reservations advised. Dress: casual. AE, DC, MC, V. Closed Sat.*

Quatro Amigos. A favorite among young Oslonians, this simple restaurant is the place to hit when you crave spicy Mexican fare and big portions. The menu has all the standards, including enchiladas, tacos, and burritos, which are served alongside rice, black beans, and salad. *Stortingsgt. 16, tel. 22/42–48–30. Dress: casual. AE, MC, V.*

★ **Tysk City Grill.** In the midst of the Oslo City shopping mall's food court is a tiny, authentic German restaurant, complete with oompah music. The grilled bratwurst (with real German mustard and curry ketchup) with homemade potato salad is the best cheap meal in town, while the eisbein and the pea soup, both homemade, are hearty fare. *Stenersgt. 1, tel. 22/17–05–12. Dress: casual. No credit cards.*

Lodging

Most hotels are centrally located, a short walk from the top of Karl Johans Gate, the main street. The newest hotels are in the area around Oslo S Station, at the bottom end of Karl Johan. For a quiet stay, choose a hotel in Frogner, the elegant residential neighborhood just minutes from downtown.

Lodging in the capital is expensive. Prices for downtown accommodations are high, even for bed-and-breakfasts, although just about all hotels have weekend, holiday, and summer rates (25% to 50% reductions). Taxes, service charges, and, unless otherwise noted, a buffet breakfast are included.

Oslo usually has enough hotel rooms to go around, but it's always a good idea to reserve a room at least for the first night of your stay, especially if you arrive late. The hotel accommodations office at Oslo S Station is open from 8 AM to 11 PM and can book you in anything from a luxury hotel to a room in a private home for a fee of NKr20 adults, NKr10 children, plus 10% of the room rate, which is refunded when you check in.

If you are interested in renting an apartment, contact **Bed & Breakfast** (Stasjonsvn. 13, Blommenholm, 1300 Sandvika, tel. 67/54–06–80, fax 67/54–09–70; open weekdays 8:30–4). Most are located in Bærum, 15 to 20 minutes from downtown Oslo. All addresses provided by the group are no more than a 10-minute walk from public transport.

Highly recommended lodgings are indicated by a star ★.

Very Expensive

★ **Grand Hotel.** Located right in the center of Karl Johan, the Grand has been the premier hotel since it opened in 1874. Ibsen and Munch were regular guests, and since their time, the Grand has hosted many famous people and all recipients of the Nobel Peace Prize. The lobby gives no idea of the style and flair of the redecorated (1989–90) rooms. Even standard rooms are large, looking more like guest quarters in an elegant home than hotel rooms. Those in the new wing are smaller, cheaper, and not as nice. *Karl Johans Gate 31, 0159, tel. 22/42–93–90, fax 22/42–12–25. 270 rooms with bath, 60 suites. Facilities: 3 restaurants, 2 bars, health club, pool, conference center, newsstand. AE, DC, MC, V.*

Hotel Continental. The Brockmann family, owners since 1900, have succeeded in combining the rich elegance of the Old World with modern, comfortable living. The Theatercafeen (*see* Dining, *above*) is a landmark, and the newest addition, LPP, a restaurant, café, and bar in one, is among Oslo's "in" places. The newly refurbished Dagligstuen (The Sitting Room) is a wonderful place in which to start or end the evening with an appetizer or nightcap. Munch graphics from the family's own collection adorn the walls. *Stortingsgt. 24–26, 0156, tel. 22/41–90–60, fax 22/42–96–89. 169 rooms with bath, 12 suites. Facilities: 3 restaurants, 2 bars, nightclub. AE, DC, MC, V.*

Oslo Plaza. Northern Europe's largest hotel, built in 1990, is a three-minute walk from Karl Johans Gate (not a safe place to walk to at night). Modern, decorated in Scandinavian style, it is favored by business travelers, who tend toward the pricier, deluxe suites in the tower. Below the 27th floor the standard rooms are decorated in red tones and have ample marble baths. The hotel has one of the city's best Japanese restaurants, and the wild rooftop nightclub offers spectacular views of the city. *Sonja Henies pl. 3, 0107, tel. 22/17–10–00, fax 22/17–73–00. 685 rooms with bath, 20 suites. Facilities: 3 restaurants, 2 bars, nightclub, health club, pool, business/conference center, shops. AE, DC, MC, V.*

Royal Christiania. It started out as bare-bones housing for 1952 Olympians. The original exterior has been retained, but inside it's a whole new hotel, remodeled in 1990 and built around a central atrium. The rooms, decorated in soft colors with light furniture, are large. The California-style restaurant serves tasty, colorful food. *Biskop Gunnerus' Gate 3, 0106, tel. 22/42–94–10, fax 22/42–46–22. 451 rooms with bath, 100 suites. Facilities: 3 restaurants, 3 bars, nightclub, health club, pool, business/conference center, newsstand. AE, DC, MC, V.*

SAS Scandinavia Hotel. Oslo's only downtown business hotel, built in 1974, is getting some competition, but it still can hold its own: There's a business-class check-in in the lobby; the lower-level shopping arcade features high-fashion clothing and leather goods shops. Most of the rooms were modernized in 1991 in four different styles, from high-tech to Oriental. Standard rooms are spacious and light. The SAS is across the street from the palace grounds (but don't walk through them at night). *Holbergs Gate 30, 0166, tel. 22/11–30–00, fax 22/11–30–17. 500 rooms with bath, 15 suites. Facilities: 2 restaurants, 2 bars, nightclub, health club, pool, business center, shopping arcade. AE, DC, MC, V.*

Expensive

★ **Ambassadeur.** This comfortable and elegant hotel hides behind a pale pink facade with wrought-iron balconies in a stylish residential area behind the Royal Palace, a few minutes from downtown. Originally built in 1889 as an apartment hotel, the Ambassadeur has practically no lobby, but the rooms make up for that. Apart from several singles, each room is individually furnished with thematic decors and good Norwegian art. The small, professional staff don't bother with titles because everyone does whatever task presents itself, from laundering a shirt on short notice to delivering room service. *Camilla Colletts vei 15, 0258, tel. 22/44–18–35, fax 22/44–47–91. 42 rooms with bath, 8 suites. Facilities: restaurant, bar, pool, conference room. AE, DC, MC, V.*

Bristol. In the past few years, the Bristol has begun catering to people who want a classy but quiet hotel in the center of town. The lobby, decorated in the 1920s with a Moorish theme, is a tribute to style, and the library bar is Oslo's most comfortable. Some of the newly refurbished rooms are decorated with lightly colored painted Scandinavian furniture, while others have a Regency theme. The banquet rooms have true Old World elegance, and at the restaurant, the Bristol Grill, red meat has not gone out of style. *Kristian IV's Gate 7, 0130, tel. 22/41–58–40, fax 22/42–86–51. 141 rooms with bath, 4 suites. Facilities: 2 restaurants, 2 bars, nightclub, conference center, newsstand. AE, DC, MC, V.*

Holmenkollen Park Hotel Rica. The magnificent 1894 building in the national romantic style commands an unequaled panorama of the city and is worth a visit even if you don't lodge there. The rather ordinary guest rooms are in a newer structure (1982) behind it. The ice-covered snowflake sculpture in the lobby is appropriate for a hotel that's a stone's throw from Holmenkollen ski jump. Ski and walking trails are just outside. *Kongevn. 26, 0390, tel. 22/92–20–00, fax 22/14–61–92. 191 rooms with bath. Facilities: 2 restaurants, bar, nightclub, pool, business/conference center. AE, DC, MC, V.*

Rica Victoria. Opened in May 1991, the hotel occupies a contemporary structure built around a center atrium. The rooms are furnished with Biedermeier reproductions and textiles in bold reds and dark blues, elegant and very stylish. Rooms with windows on the atrium may be claustrophobic for some. *Rosenkrantz' Gate 13, 0160, tel. 22/42–99–40, fax 22/42–99–43. 161 rooms with bath or shower, 5 suites. Facilities: restaurant, bar. AE, DC, MC, V.*

SAS Park Royal. Oslo Fornebu Airport's only hotel is somewhat anonymous, with long, narrow corridors and standard American-style motel rooms. The restaurant serves modern Scandinavian food. There are excellent business facilities, including a business-class check-in, and the airport bus stops outside. *Fornebuparken, 1324 Lysaker, tel. 67/12–02–20, fax 67/12–00–11. 254 rooms with bath, 14 suites. Facilities: restaurant, bar, health club, tennis court, newsstand. AE, DC, MC, V.*

Stefan. This hotel makes every aspect of a stay a positive experience, from hot welcome drinks for late arrivals to breakfast tables complete with juice boxes and plastic bags for packing a lunch. The top-floor lounge has books and magazines in English. The Stefan's kitchen still creates the best buffet lunch in town—but it's only open to guests. *Rosenkrantz' Gate 1, 0159, tel. 22/42–92–50, fax 22/33–70–22. 130 rooms with bath or* *shower. Facilities: restaurant, conference center. AE, DC, MC, V.*

Moderate

Bondeheimen. Founded in 1913 for country folk visiting the city, Bondeheimen, which means "farmers' home," still gives discounts to members of agricultural associations. The lobby and rooms are decorated with pine furniture, handwoven rag rugs, soft blue textiles, and modern Norwegian graphics, just the way a Norwegian country home should look. Bondeheimen serves no alcohol, and the staff of country girls has a squeaky-clean look. *Rosenkrantz' Gate 8, 0159, tel. 22/42–95–30, fax 22/41–94–37. 76 rooms with shower. Facilities: restaurant, conference room. AE, DC, MC, V.*

★ **Cecil.** This bed-and-breakfast one block from Parliament was built in 1989. The second floor opens onto an atrium: the hotel's activity center. In the morning it's a breakfast room, with one of Oslo's best buffets, while in the afternoon it becomes a lounge, serving coffee, juice, and fresh fruit, plus newspapers in many languages. The single rooms have double beds, while doubles have queen-size beds. *Stortingsgt. 8, 0130, tel. 22/42–70–00, fax 22/42–26–70. 110 rooms with bath, 2 suites. AE, DC, MC, V.*

Gabelshus. With only a discreet sign above the door, this ivy-covered brick house in an international residential area is one of Oslo's most personal hotels. It has been owned by the same family for 45 years. The lounges are filled with antiques, some in the national romantic style, but the rooms, renovated in 1989, are plain. It's a short walk to several of Oslo's best restaurants, and a short streetcar ride to the center of town. The Ritz Hotel, across the parking lot, is owned by the same family and takes the overflow. *Gabels Gate 16, 0272, tel. 22/55–22–60, fax 22/44–27–30. 45 rooms with bath (plus 42 rooms with bath in Ritz). Facilities: restaurant. AE, DC, MC, V.*

Inexpensive

Gyldenløve. Located in the heart of a busy shopping area, this hotel, modernized in 1992, is one of the city's most reasonable bed-and-breakfast establishments. It is within walking distance of Vigeland park, and the streetcar stops just outside the door. Reproductions of city scenes from old Christiania (Oslo) hang in every room. *Bogstadvn. 20, 0355, tel. 22/60–10–90, fax 22/60–33–90. 156 rooms with shower. AE, DC, MC, V.*

Haraldsheim. Oslo's youth hostel is one of Europe's largest. Most of the rooms have four beds, and those in the new wing all have showers. Nonmembers of the International Youth Hostel organization pay a surcharge. Bring your own sheet sleeping bag or rent one here. It is 4 kilometers (2½ miles) from city center. *Haraldsheimvn. 4, tel. 22/15–50–43, fax 22/34–71–97. 270 beds. Breakfast. No credit cards.*

Munch. This modern bed-and-breakfast, about a 10-minute walk from Karl Johans Gate, is unpretentious, well run, clean, and functional. The rooms are of a decent size and are under renovation in 1994. The lobby, with Chinese rugs and leather couches, contrasts markedly with the rest of the hotel. *Munchsgt. 5, 0165, tel. 22/42–42–75, fax 22/20–64–69. 180 rooms with shower. Facilities: breakfast room. AE, DC, MC, V.*

The Arts and Nightlife

The Arts

The monthly *Oslo Guide* lists cultural events, as does section four of *Aftenposten,* Oslo's (and Norway's) leading newspaper. The information number at **Oslo Spektrum** congress and concert complex (tel. 22/17–80–10) gives a rundown of all scheduled events. Tickets to virtually all performances in Norway, from classical or rock concerts to a hockey games, can be purchased at any post office.

Nationaltheatret (Stortingsgt. 15, tel. 22/41–27–10.) performances are in Norwegian: bring along a copy of the play in translation, and you're all set.

Det Norske Teatret (Kristian IV's Gate 8, tel. 22/42–43–44) is a showcase for pieces in Nynorsk, musicals, and guest artists from abroad. **Bryggeteatret** (Aker Brygge, tel. 22/83–88–20), Oslo's newest theater, features musicals and dance events.

The **Norwegian Philharmonic Orchestra,** under the direction of Mariss Janssons, is among Europe's leading ensembles. Its house, **Konserthuset** (Munkedamsvn. 14, tel. 22/83–32–00), was built in 1977 in marble, metal, and rosewood. **Den Norske Opera** *(Storgt. 23, tel. 22/42–77–24)* and the ballet perform at Youngstorvet.

Oslo Spektrum *(Sonja Henies pl. 2, tel. 22/17–80–10),* a rounded brick building sprinkled with vignettes of glazed tile, is the most interesting piece of architecture in the area around Oslo S Station. The Spektrum is used as a congress/conference complex, a sports stadium, and a concert hall.

All **films** are shown in the original language with subtitles, except for some children's films, which are dubbed. If you plan to take children to see a film, check the age limits first. The Norwegian film censors set high and strictly enforced age limits on films they consider to be violent.

Nightlife

For the past few years Oslo been the nightlife capital of Scandinavia. At any time of the day or night, people are out on Karl Johan, and many clubs and restaurants in the central area stay open until 4 or 5 AM. Night-lifers can pick up a copy of the free monthly paper *Natt og Dag,* which lists rock, pop, and jazz venues and contains a "barometer" listing the city's cheapest and most expensive places for a beer—a necessary column in a city where a draft, on the average, costs NKr33.

Bars and Lounges   **Churchill Wine Bar** (Fr. Nansens pl. 6, tel. 22/33–53–43) and **Fridtjof's** (Fr. Nansens pl. 7, tel. 22/33–40–88) are yuppie favorites for pricey after-work imbibing. Both are near City Hall. For the serious beer connoisseur, **Oslo Mikrobryggeri** (Bogstadvn. 6, tel. 22/56–97–76) is the place, with beer brewed on the premises; for variety, go to **Lorry** (Parkvn. 12, tel. 22/69–69–04). Filled with a cast of grizzled old artists, the place advertises 81 brews. **Eilefs Landhandleri** (Kristian IV's gt. 1, tel. 22/42–53–47) is a pub cum disco, with a piano player and a dance floor. For a more refined venue, go to **3 Brødre** (Øvre Slottsgt. 14, tel. 22/42–39–00), with a beer and wine bar at street level and 1890s-style wall paintings of forest maidens and cherubs on the ceiling. If you're more partial to lounging than drinking, try the English-style bar at the **Bristol Hotel** (Kristian IV's gt. 7, tel. 22/41–58–40).

Cafés For cappuccino and a quiet conversation, many cafés are open practically around the clock, and they're the cheapest eateries as well. In the trendy area around Frogner and Homansbyen, try **Onkel Oswald** (Hegdehaugsvn. 34, tel. 22/69–62–50) and **Clodion Art Café** (Bygdøy allé 63, tel. 22/44–97–26). Downtown, **Kafe Celsius** (Rådhusgt. 19, 22/42–45–39) in a half-timber building from 1626, attracts an arty crowd, while **Sjakk Matt** (Haakon VII's Gate, tel. 22/83–41–56) appeals to a very hip set. If you prefer the '50s, go to **Teddy's Soft Bar** (Brugt. 3, tel. 22/17–71–83), complete with vinyl stools.

Discos and Most discos open late, and the beat doesn't really start until
Nightclubs near midnight. There's usually an age limit, and the cover charge is around NKr50. Thursday is student disco night at **Snorre-Kompagniet** (Rosenkrantz' Gate 11, tel. 22/33–46–40). Oslo's beautiful people congregate at **Barock** (Universitetsgt. 26, tel. 22/42–44–20) and **Lipp** (Olav Vs Gate 2, tel. 22/41–44–00), a restaurant, nightclub, and bar. Most of the big hotels have discos that appeal to the over-30 crowd. **Sky Bar,** on the top floor of the Oslo Plaza (Sonja Henies pl. 3, tel. 22/17–10–00), is the most bizarre, accessible only from the glass elevator outside. **Grotten** (Wergelandsvn. 5, tel. 22/20–96–04) is popular with well-heeled and well-dressed singles over 30.

Jazz Clubs Norwegians love jazz, and every summer the Oslo Jazz Festival, with a list of major international artists, attracts big crowds. **Oslo Jazzhus** (Toftesgt. 69, tel. 22/38–59–63) is in an out-of-the-way location, but the music is worth it. **Stortorvets Gjæstgiveri** (Grensen 1, tel. 22/42–88–63) often presents New Orleans and ragtime bands. **Gamle Christiania** (Grensen 1, tel. 22/42–74–93) features the New Orleans Jazz Workshop. **Smuget** (Rosenkrantz' Gate 22, tel. 22/42–52–62) has live jazz, blues, and rock every evening.

Rock Clubs At Oslo's numerous rock clubs, the cover charges are low, the crowds young, and the music loud. **Rockefeller** (Torggt. 16, tel. 22/20–32–32) presents a good mix of musical styles, from avant-garde to Third World; Thursday is student disco night. Its only real competitor is **Sentrum Scene** (Arbeidersamfunnets pl. 2, tel. 22/20–60–40). There's always music at **Cruise Cafe** (Aker Brygge, tel. 22/83–64–30). If your taste leans toward reggae and calypso, the **Afro International Night Club** (Brennerivn. 5, tel. 22/36–07–53) has frequent Caribbean evenings.

Gay Bars For information about gay activities in Oslo, call **Homo-guiden** (tel. 02/07–80–46) or the information telephone (tel. 22/11–36–60), or read *Blikk,* the gay newsletter. **LLH** (The Union for Lesbian and Gay Liberation), the nationwide gay association, has offices at St. Olavs Pl. 2, and operates **Molina Pub and Eatery** at the same address. **Andy Capp Pub** (Fridtjof Nansens pl. 4, tel. 22/41–41–65) is popular with gays (later at night), but it reeks of old smoke. **London Bar og Pub** (C. J. Hambros pl. 5, tel. 22/41–41–26) is packed on weekends. **Den Sorte Enke** (The Black Widow, Møllergt. 23, tel. 22/11–05–60), **Coco Chalet** (Øvre Slottsgt. 8, tel. 22/33–32–66), and **Recepten Bar** (Prinsensgt. 22, tel. 22/42–65–00) are also popular meeting places for lesbians and gays.

Excursions from Oslo

Halden and Fredrikstad

Tourist Information **Fredrikstad:** Fredrikstad turistkontor (Turistsentret v/Østre Brohode, N–1632 Gamle Fredrikstad, tel. 69/32–03–30). **Halden:** Halden Reiselivskontor (Box 167, N–1751 Halden, tel. 69/18–24–87). **Moss:** Moss Turistkontor (Chrystiesgt. 3, N–1530 Moss, tel. 69/25–54–51).

Getting There **By Car** Follow the E18 southeastward from Oslo and turn south at Mysen to reach Halden. E6 takes you north to Sarpsborg, where you can turn left to Fredrikstad.

By Train Trains for Halden leave from Oslo S Station and take two hours to make the 136-kilometer (85-mile) trip. There are regular train connections between Halden and Fredrikstad.

Exploring Halden and Fredrikstad *Numbers in the margin correspond to points of interest on the Oslo Excursions map.*

❹ Halden is practically at the Swedish border, a good enough reason to fortify the town; **Fredriksten Festning** (fort), built on a French star-shaped plan in the late 17th century, is perched on the city's highest point. Norwegians and Swedes had ongoing border disputes, and the most famous skirmish at Fredriksten resulted in the death of King Karl XII in 1718. Few people realize that slavery existed in Scandinavia, but until 1845 there were up to 200 slaves at Fredriksten, mostly workers incarcerated and sentenced to a lifetime of hard labor for trivial offenses. Inside the fort itself is **Fredriksten Kro,** a good, old-fashioned inn, with outdoor seating. *Tel. 69/18–24–87. Admission: NKr15 adults, NKr5 children.*

❺ North of Halden is **Fredrikstad,** at the mouth of the Glomma, Norway's longest river. The country's oldest fortified city, it has bastions and a moat that date from the 1600s. The old town has been preserved and offers museums, art galleries, cafés, artisans' workshops, antiques shops, and old bookstores, as well as the **Fredrikstad Museum,** which documents town history. *Tel. 69/32–09–01. Admission NKr20 adults, children free with an adult. Open June–Aug., Mon.–Sat. 11–5, Sun. noon–5.*

Just east is **Kongsten Festning** (fort), which mounted 200 cannons and could muster 2,000 men at the peak of its glory. *Tel. 69/34–20–62. Admission free. Open 24 hours. Guided tours.*

A 5-kilometer (3-mile) ride outside **Moss,** at **Jeløy,** is **Galleri F15,** an art center set in an old farm. *Tel. 69/27–10–33. Admission free. Open daily 11–7.*

Dining and Lodging **★** **Refsnes Gods.** The main building dates from 1770, when it was a family estate, but it did not become a hotel until 1938. In the back is a long, tree-lined promenade extending to the shores of the Oslo Fjord. Refsnes has one of Norway's best kitchens and a wine cellar with some of the oldest bottles of Madeira in the country. Chef Frank Baer, a member of Norway's Culinary Olympic team, makes a meal here a memorable experience. *Jeløy, 1500 Moss, tel. 69/27–04–11, fax 69/27–25–42. 60 rooms. Facilities: restaurant, sauna, pool, beach, boats, function rooms. AE, DC, MC, V. Expensive.*

Drammen, Tønsberg, and Sandefjord

The towns lining the western side of the Oslo Fjord are among Norway's oldest and wealthiest, their fortunes derived from whaling and lumbering. Although these areas no longer dominate, their influence remains in the monuments and in the wood architecture. This is summer-vacation country for many Norwegians, who retreat to cabins on the water during July.

Tourist　**Drammen:** Drammen Kommunale Turistinformasjonskontor
Information　(Rådhuset, N–3017 Drammen, tel. 32/80–62–10). **Sandefjord:** Sandefjord Reiselivsforening (Torvet, N–3200, tel. 33/46–05–90). **Tønsberg:** Tønsberg og Omland Reiselivslag (Storgt. 55, N–3100, tel. 33/31–02–20).

Getting There　Route E18 south from Oslo follows the coast to within reach of
By Car　the towns of this region. Sandefjord is 125 kilometers (78 miles) south of Oslo.

By Train　Drammen is about 40 kilometers (25 miles) from Oslo. Take a suburban train from Nationaltheatret or trains from Oslo S to reach Horten, Tønsberg, and Sandefjord.

By Bus　Because train service to these towns is infrequent, bus travel is the best alternative to cars. Check with Nor-Way Bussekspress (tel. 22/33–01–91) for schedules.

By Boat　The most luxurious and scenic way to see the region is by boat: There are guest marinas at just about every port.

Exploring　**Drammen,** an industrial city of 50,000 situated on the Simoa
Drammen,　River at its outlet to a fjord, was a timber town and port for 500
Tønsberg, and　years, the main harbor for silver exported from the Kongsberg
Sandefjord　mines. Today cars are imported into Norway through Dram-
❻　men. The city's main attraction, **Spiralen** (The Spiral), is a corkscrew road tunnel that makes six complete turns before emerging about 600 feet above, on Skansen Plateau. It's open year-round and is free. The entrance is behind the hospital by way of a well-marked road.

Drammens Museum, on the grounds of Marienlyst manor (which dates from 1750), is across the river. Its new addition looks like a small temple set in the manor garden. Displays include glass from the Nøstetangen factory and a collection of rustic painted pieces. *Konnerudgt. 7, tel. 32/83–89–48. Admission: NKr20 adults, NKr10 senior citizens and students, NKr5 children. Open May–Oct., Tues. 11–7, Wed.–Sat. 11–3, Sun. 11–5; Nov.–Apr., Tues.–Sat, 11–5, Sun. 11–3.*

❼ Off the main route south, toward the coast, is **Horten,** which has some distinctive museums. The town was once an important naval station and still retains the officers' candidates school. **Marinemuseet** (the Royal Norwegian Navy Museum), built in 1853 as a munitions warehouse, has displays of relics from the nation's naval history. Outside is the world's first torpedo boat, from 1872, plus some one-man submarines from World War II. Mistletoe thrives in the trees, but don't pick it: It's protected by law. *Karl Johans Vern, tel. 33/34–20–81, ext. 452. Admission free. Open June–Sept., weekdays 10–3, weekends noon–4; Oct.–May, weekdays 10–3, Sun. noon–4.*

Redningsselskapets Museum (Museum of the Sea Rescue Association) traces the history of ship-rescue operations. The organization has rescued more than 320,000 people since it was

We can wire money to every major city in Europe almost as fast as you can say, "Zut alors! J'ai perdu mes valises".

How fast? We can send money in 10 minutes or less, to 13,500 locations in over 68 countries worldwide. That's faster than any other international money transfer service. And when you're *sans* luggage, every minute counts.

MoneyGram from American Express® is available throughout Europe. For more information please contact your local American Express Travel Service Office or call: 44-71-839-7541 in England; 33-1-47777000 in France; or 49-69-21050 in Germany. In the U.S. call 1-800-MONEYGRAM.

MoneyGram
INTERNATIONAL MONEY TRANSFERS.

519 M.P.H.

190 M.P.H.

75 M.P.H.

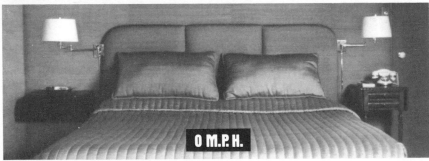

0 M.P.H.

WE LET YOU SEE EUROPE AT YOUR OWN PACE.

Regardless of your personal speed limits, Rail Europe offers everything to get you over, around and through anywhere you want in Europe. For more information, call your travel agent or 1-800-4-EURAIL.

founded more than 100 years ago. *Strandpromenaden 8, tel. 33/ 34–70–66. Admission: NKr10 adults, NKr5 children. Open Apr. 1–Sept. 30, Fri.–Sun. noon–4.*

Preus Fotomuseum houses one of the world's largest photographic collections. Exhibits include a turn-of-the-century photographer's studio and a tiny camera that was strapped to a pigeon for early aerial photography. *Langgt. 82, tel. 33/04–27– 37. Admission: NKr10 adults, NKr5 children. Open weekdays 10–2, Sun. noon–2.*

Just beyond the town, between the road and the sea, is a Viking grave site, **Borrehaugene,** with five earth and two stone mounds. Continue past the 12th-century Borre church to **⑧ Åsgårdstrand,** which was an artists' colony for outdoor painting at the turn of the century. Edvard Munch painted *Girls on the Bridge* here and earned a reputation as a ladies' man. He spent seven summers at **Munchs lille hus** (little house), now a museum. *Munchs gt., no tel. Admission: NKr5. Open June–Aug., Tues.–Sun. 1–7; May and Sept., weekends 1–7.*

Continuing south, you'll pass the site where the Oseberg Viking ship, dating from around AD 800 and on display in Oslo, was found at **Slagen,** on the road to Tønsberg, 105 kilometers (64 miles) from Oslo. Look for a mound where it was buried as you pass Slagen's church.

⑨ According to the sagas, **Tønsberg** is Norway's oldest settlement, founded in 871. Little remains of its early structures, although the ruins at **Slottsfjellet** (Castle Hill), by the train station, include parts of the city wall, the remains of a church from around 1150, and a 13th-century brick citadel. Other medieval remains are below the cathedral and near Storgata 17. Tønsberg lay dormant from the Reformation to the end of the 18th century, when shipping and later whaling brought it into prominence again.

Vestfold Fylkesmuseum (county museum), north of the railroad station, houses a small Viking ship, several whale skeletons, and some inventions. There's an open-air section, too. *Farmannsvn. 30, tel. 33/31–29–19. Admission: NKr15 adults, NKr8 groups over 10, NKr2 children. Open mid-May–mid-Sept., weekdays 10–5, Sun. noon–5; mid-Sept.–mid-May, weekdays 10–3:30.*

Time Out Take a break at **Seterkafe,** the museum's restaurant. Try *spekemat* (dried cured meats) served with sour cream and/or potato salad.

⑩ Continue 25 kilometers (16 miles) south of Tønsberg to **Sandefjord,** which, in 1900, was the whaling capital of the world and possibly Norway's wealthiest city. Now the whales are gone and all that remains of that trade is a monument to it. Thanks to shipping and other industries, however, the city is still rich.

Kommandør Christensens Hvalfangstmuseum (Commander Christensen's Whaling Museum) traces the development of the industry from small primitive boats to huge floating factories. An especially arresting display chronicles whaling in the Antarctic. *Museumsgt. 39, tel. 33/16–32–51. Admission: NKr10 adults, NKr5 children and senior citizens. Open May–Sept., Mon.–Sat. 11–4, Sun. 11–5, Thurs. also 4–7; Oct.–Apr., Sun. noon–4, Thurs. 4–7.*

Dining
★

Edgar Ludl's Gourmet. It took an Austrian chef to show the Norwegians that there's more in the sea than cod and salmon. Ludl is a champion of the local cuisine, and a "catch of the day" platter may include salmon, ocean catfish, stuffed sole, a fish roulade, and lobster. Ludl's desserts are equally good, especially the cloudberry marzipan basket. *Rådhusgt. 7, Sandefjord, tel. 33/16–27–41. Reservations advised. Dress: casual but neat. AE, DC, MC, V. Moderate–Expensive.*

Lodging

Rica Park Hotel. It *looks* formal for a hotel built right on the water in a resort town, but there's no dress code. The older rooms are nicer than the new ones. The decor is 1960s style, but it doesn't look passé. Summer rates make the Park more affordable. *Strandpromenaden 9, 3200 Sandefjord, tel. 33/16–55–50, fax 33/16– 79–00. 174 rooms with bath, 6 suites. Facilities: 2 restaurants, 4 bars, 2 nightclubs, pool, health club, marina, business/ conference center. AE, DC, MC, V. Moderate–Very Expensive.*

Atlantic. The Atlantic was built in 1914, when Sandefjord was a whaling center, and remodeled in 1990. The history of whaling is traced in exhibits in glass cases and in pictures throughout the hotel. There's no restaurant, but the hotel provides *aftens*, a supper consisting of bread and cold cuts plus a hot dish, as part of the room rate. *Jernbanealleen 33, 3200 Sandefjord, tel. 33/16–31–05, fax 33/16–80–20. 77 rooms with bath. Facilities: supper. AE, DC, MC, V. Inexpensive–Expensive.*

4   Sørlandet

The coast bordering the Skagerrak is lined with small communities as far as Lindesnes, which is at the southernmost tip. Sørlandet (Southland) towns are often called "pearls on a string," and in the dusk of a summer evening, reflections of the white painted houses on the water have a silvery translucence.

This is a land of wide beaches toasted by the greatest number of sunny days in Norway, waters warmed by the Gulf Stream, and long, fertile tracts of flatland. Not a people to pass up a minute of sunshine, the Norwegians have sprinkled the south with their hytter and made it their number-one domestic holiday spot. Nonetheless, even at the height of summer, you can sail to a quiet skerry or take a solitary walk through the forest.

The two chief cities of Norway's south, Kristiansand on the east coast and Stavanger on the west coast, differ sharply. Kristiansand is a resort town, scenic and relaxed, while Stavanger, once a fishing center, is now the hub of the oil industry and Norway's most cosmopolitan city. Between the two is the coastal plain of Jæren, dotted with prehistoric burial sites and the setting for the works of some of the country's foremost painters.

Essential Information

Important Addresses and Numbers

Tourist Information The tourist information office in **Kristiansand** is at Dronningensgt. 2, Box 592, 4601, tel. 38/02–60–65, fax 38/02–52–55. **Stavanger's** is at Stavanger Kulturhus, Sølveberget, tel. 51/53–51–00.

Other tourist offices in the region are in **Horten** (Torget 6A, 3190, tel. 33/04–33–90), **Kvinesdal** (Vestre Vest-Agder Reiselivslag, N–4480, tel. 38/35–00–42), **Larvik** (Storgt. 3250, tel. 33/13–01–00), **Mandal** (Mandalsregionens Reiselivslag, Bryggegt., N–4500, tel. 38/26–08–20), **Sandefjord** (Torvet, 3200, tel. 33/46–05–90), and **Tønsberg** (Storgt. 55, 3100, tel. 33/31–02–20).

Emergencies **Police:** tel. 112. **Fire:** tel. 111. **Ambulance:** tel. 113. **Car Rescue:** in Kristiansand, tel. 38/02–60–00, in Stavanger, tel. 51/58–29–00.

Hospital Emergency Rooms In Kristiansand, **Røde Kors** (Red Cross) **Legevakt** (Kirkegt. 3, tel. 38/02–52–20) is open weekdays 4 PM–8 AM *and* weekends 24 hours. In Stavanger, call **Rogaland Sentralsykehus** (tel. 51/51–80–00).

Doctors In Kristiansand, **Kvadraturen Legesenter** (Vestre Strandgt. 22, tel. 38/02–66–11) is open 8–4.

Dentists In Kristiansand, **Sentraltannklinikken** (Festningsgt. 40, tel. 38/02–19–71) is open 7–3. In Stavanger, the tourist office has a list of dentists available for emergencies.

Pharmacies **Elefantapoteket** (Gyldenløvesgt. 13, Kristiansand, tel. 38/02–20–12) is open Monday through Saturday 8:20–8 and Sunday 4–8. **Løveapoteket** (Olav V's gt. 11, Stavanger, tel. 51/52–06–07) is open daily 8 AM–11 PM.

Arriving and Departing by Plane

Kristiansand Kjevik Airport, 16 kilometers (10 miles) outside town, is served by **Braathens SAFE** (tel. 38/02–14–10), with nonstop flights from Oslo, Bergen, and Stavanger, and **SAS** (tel. 38/06–30–33) with nonstop flights to Copenhagen. **MUK Air** serves Aalborg, Denmark, while **Agder Fly** serves Göteborg, Sweden, and Billund, Denmark. Tickets on the latter two can be booked with Braathen or SAS.

The airport bus (tel. 94/67–22–42) departs from the Braathens SAFE office, Vestre Strandgate, approximately one hour before every departure and proceeds, via downtown hotels, directly to Kjevik. Tickets cost NKr30 for adults, NKr15 for children.

Stavanger **Sola Airport** is 14 kilometers (9 miles) from downtown. **Braathens SAFE** (tel. 51/51–10–00) has nonstop flights from Oslo, Sandefjord, Kristiansand, Haugesund, Bergen, and Trondheim. **SAS** (tel. 51/63–89–00) has nonstop flights from Bergen, Oslo, Copenhagen, Aberdeen, Göteborg, and London. **KLM** (tel. 51/65–10–22), and **British Airways** (tel. 51/65–15–33) have nonstop flights to Stavanger from Billund and London, respectively.

The **Flybussen** to town takes 15 minutes and stops at hotels and outside the railroad station. Tickets cost NKr30.

Arriving and Departing by Car, Train, Bus, and Boat

By Car From Oslo, it is 329 kilometers (203 miles) to Kristiansand and 574 kilometers (352 miles) to Stavanger. E18 parallels the coastline but stays slightly inland on the eastern side of the country and farther inland in the western part. Although seldom wider than two lanes, it is easy driving because it is so flat.

By Train The **Sørlandsbanen** leaves Oslo S Station four times daily for the approximately five-hour journey to Kristiansand and three times daily for the 8½- to nine-hour journey to Stavanger. Two more trains travel the 3½-hour Kristiansand–Stavanger route. Kristiansand's train station is at V. Strandgata (tel. 38/02–27–00). For information on trains from Stavanger call 51/52–61–37.

By Bus **Aust-Agder Trafikkselskap** (tel. 37/02–65–00), based in Arendal, has two departures daily in each direction for the 5½- to six-hour journey between Oslo and Kristiansand.

Sørlandsruta (38/02–43–80), based in Mandal, has two departures in each direction for the 4½-hour trip from Kristiansand (Strandgt. 33) to Stavanger.

For information about both long-distance and local bus services in Stavanger, call 51/52–26–00; the bus terminal is outside the train station.

By Boat **Color Line** (Strandkaien, Stavanger, tel. 51/52–45–45) has four ships weekly on the Stavanger–Newcastle route. High-speed boats to Bergen are based in Stavanger at **Hurtigbåtterminalen** (tel. 51/52–20–90). There is also a car ferry from Hirtshals, in northern Denmark, that takes about four hours to make the crossing. Another connects Larvik to Frederikshavn, on Denmark's west coast. In Denmark contact DSB (tel. 33/14–17–01); in Norway contact **Color Line** (tel. 51/52–45–45).

Getting Around

By Car Sørlandet is flat, so it's easy driving throughout. All the water makes the center of **Stavanger** difficult to maneuver by car. One-way streets are the norm downtown. Parking is limited, and streets are very crowded on Saturday.

By Bus Bus connections in Sørlandet are infrequent; the tourist office can provide a comprehensive schedule. Tickets on **Stavanger's** excellent bus network cost NKr12.

By Taxi All **Kristiansand** taxis are connected with a central dispatching office (tel. 38/03–27–00). Journeys are charged by the taximeter within the city, otherwise by the kilometer.

Stavanger taxis are also connected to a central dispatching office (tel. 51/52–60–40). The initial charge is NKr19, with NKr9 per kilometer during the day and NKr11 at night.

Passes A **Sommerpass Kristiansand,** which costs NKr50 for adults and
Kristiansand NKr30 for children, gives free admission to many sights and a 25% discount on tickets to the zoo and the M/S *Maarten*. It can be purchased at the tourist office, the zoo, and at all hotels. If you stay at any hotel in the city for four nights, the pass is free.

Stavanger The **Stavanger card,** sold at hotels, post offices in the region, and Stavanger Tourist Information, gives discounts of up to 50% on sightseeing tours, museums, buses, car rentals, and other services and attractions.

Guided Tours

Kristiansand Tours of Kristiansand run only in the summer. The **City Train** (Rådhusgt. 11, tel. 38/03–05–24) runs a 15-minute tour of the center. The M/S *Maarten* (Pier 6 by Fiskebrygga, tel. 30/02–60–65) offers two-hour tours of the eastern archipelago (mid-June–mid-Aug.) and a three-hour tour of the western archipelago (July).

Stavanger A two-hour bus tour leaves from the Marina at **Vågen** daily at 1 between June and August. **Rødne Clipperkontoret** (Skagenkaien 18, tel. 51/89–52–70) offers three different tours, including an eye-popping fjord tour of the Lysefjord and Pulpit Rock. **Rogaland Trafikkselskap** (tel. 51/51–65–90) does the same, in either high-speed boats or ferries.

Exploring Sørlandet

Numbers in the margin correspond to points of interest on the Sørlandet map.

Tour 1: The Coast

1 **Larvik** is the last of the big whaling towns, 19 kilometers (12 miles) south of Sandefjord. It's still a port, but now the traffic is made up of passengers to Fredrikshavn, Denmark. Near the ferry quays is **Kong Haakon VIIs kilde** (King Haakon VII's spring), also called Farris kilde (Farris spring), Norway's only natural source of mineral water. A spa was built here in 1880,

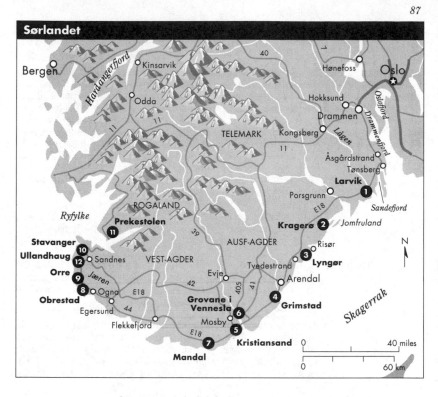

Sørlandet

but now people drink the water rather than bathe in it. *Fjellvn. Guided tours in summer.*

Larvik is the site of **Herregården,** a large estate once owned by the noble Gyldenløve family. The main building was finished in 1677. Inside, the furnishings are masterful examples of trompe l'oeil: Scandinavian nobility had to make do with furniture painted to look like marble or carving rather than the real thing. *Herregaardssletta 1, tel. 33/13–04–04. Admission: NKr15 adults, NKr5 children. Open mid-June–Aug., daily 1–5; May 27–Sept. 2, Sun 1–5; Apr.–Oct., open on request. Call to confirm times.*

From Larvik, it's only 8 kilometers (5 miles) along the coast to **Stavern,** a popular sailing center. On the water east of town is **Fredriksvern,** which was Norway's main naval station between 1750 and 1850, named for King Fredrik V. The church is a fine example of Scandinavian Rococo. Its pews were designed so their backs could be folded down to make beds in case the church had to be used as a field hospital in time of war. *Stavern Church, tel. 33/19–91–78. Guided tours.*

Farther down the coast about 35 kilometers (22 miles) comes **Kragerø,** a picturesque town with its own small archipelago. **Theodor Kittelsen** (1857–1914), famous for his drawings of trolls and illustrations of Norwegian fairy tales, lived in Kragerø, and his birthplace is now a museum. *Th. Kittelsens v. 5. Admission: NKr20 adults, NKr10 children. Open June 15–Aug. 15, weekdays 11–3.*

The next pearl on the southern string is **Risør**, east from E18 on the coast. On the first weekend in August the town holds a festival that fills the harbor with beautiful antique boats.

③ **Lyngør**, on four tiny rocky islands off the coast, was recently chosen Europe's best-preserved village. In winter the population is 110, but every summer thousands descend upon it. Hardly changed since the days of sailing ships, it's idyllic and carless, lined with rows of white-painted houses and window boxes full of pink and red flowers. You'll find white houses all along the southern coast, a tradition that began about 100 years ago, when Dutch sailors traded white paint for wood. Up until that time, only red paint was available in Norway. To get to Lyngør follow E18 to the sign for Sørlandsporten (Gateway to the South). Turn off just after the sign and drive 26 kilometers (16 miles) to Lyngørfjorden Marina, where you can take a five-minute watertaxi (tel. 37/16–68–00) ride to the island. The only hotel books most of its rooms by the year to large firms, so don't count on staying overnight.

Time Out In a historic 100-year-old white house with blue trim, **Den Blå Lanterne** (tel. 37/16–64–80, reservations advised) is Lyngør's only restaurant. Although it's pricey, you can eat as much of their famous fish soup as you like, and there's often live music.

Arendal, a little farther south, has more tidy white houses. On the island of **Merdøy**, a 30-minute boat ride from Arendal's Langbrygga (wharf), is an early 18th-century sea-captain's home, now a museum, **Merdøgaard**. *Tel. 37/02–24–22. Admission: NKr10 adults, NKr5 children. Open June 15–Aug. 20, 11–4.*

④ To the south is **Grimstad**. Its glory was also in the days of sailing ships—about the same time the 15-year-old Henrik Ibsen worked as an apprentice at the local apothecary shop. Grimstad Apotek is now a part of the **Ibsenhus** (Ibsen House) and has been preserved with its 1837 interior intact. Ibsen wrote his first play, *Catlina,* here. *Henrik Ibsensgt. 14, tel. 37/14–46–53. Admission: NKr15 adults, NKr5 children and senior citizens. Open May 15–Sept. 15, Mon.–Sat. 11–5, Sun. 1–5.*

Tour 2: Kristiansand

⑤ **Kristiansand,** with 65,000 inhabitants, is one of Sørlandet's leading cities and the domestic summer-vacation capital of Norway. According to legend, King Christian IV in 1641 marked the four corners of the city with his walking stick, and within that framework the grid of wide streets was drawn. The center of the city, called the **Kvadrat,** still retains the grid, even after numerous fires.

Start at **Fisketorvet** (the fish market) at the southern corner of the grid right on the sea. Follow Strandpromenaden (the Beach Walk), and past Norwegian artist Kjell Nupen's interpretation of Kristiansand's roots more than 350 years ago to **Christiansholm Festning** (fortress), on a promontory opposite Festningsgata. Completed in 1672, the circular building with 15-foot-thick walls, has played more a decorative than a defensive role; it was used once, in 1807, to defend the city against British invasion. Now it contains art exhibits.

Six blocks inland is the Gothic Revival **Cathedral** from 1885. The third-largest church in Norway, it often hosts summer-time concerts in addition to an annual week-long International Church Music Festival (beginning May 10) that includes organ, chamber, and gospel music. *Kirkegt., tel. 38/02–11–88. Admission free. Open May–Aug., Sun.–Fri. 10–2.*

Next, head north, across the Otra River, on bus No. 22, or drive to Route E18 and cross the bridge over the Otra to Parkveien. Turn left onto Ryttergangen and drive to Gimleveien, where you'll turn right to **Gimle Gård** (Gimle Manor). Built by a wealthy merchant/shipowner around 1800 in the Empire style, it boasts period furnishings, paintings, silver, and decoration, including hand-blocked wallpaper. *Gimlevn. 23, tel. 38/09–21–32. Admission: NKr10 adults, NKr5 children (free with Summerpass). Open July 1–Aug. 15, Tues.–Sun. noon–3; May 1–June 30, Aug. 16–Nov. 1, Sun. noon–5.*

Eastward on Gimleveien is **Odderness Church,** one of the oldest churches in Norway dedicated to St. Olav. The runestone in the cemetery tells that Øyvind, godson of St. Olav, built this church on property he inherited from his father. The altar and the pulpit are both in the Baroque style, and richly gilded. *Oddernesvn., tel. 38/09–01–87. Admission free. Open May–Aug., Sun.–Fri. 10–4.*

Continue to **Vest-Agder Fylkesmuseum** (County Museum), just south of Vigeveien. Here you can visit two *tun* (farm buildings traditionally set in clusters around a common area, which suited the extended families). A reconstructed city street features dwellings and workshops. *Vigevn., Kongsgård, tel. 38/09–02–28. Admission: NKr20 adults, NKr10 children (free with Summerpass). Open June 20–Aug. 20, Tues.–Sat. 10–6, Sun. noon–6; May 24–Sept. 13, Sun. noon–6.*

Once you've had your fill of museums, head back across the river and northwest of town to **Ravnedalen** (the Raven Valley), a lush park, filled in spring with flowers. It's a favorite with hikers and strolling nannies. Wear comfortable shoes and you can hike the narrow, winding paths up the hills and climb 200 steps up to a 100-meter (304-foot) lookout.

East of town 11 kilometers (6 miles) is one of Norway's most popular attractions. **Kristiansand Dyrepark** is five separate parks, including a water park (bring bathing suits and towels), a forested park, an entertainment park, and a zoo, which contains an enclosure for Scandinavian wolves and Europe's (possibly the world's) largest breeding ground for Bactrian camels. Finally, the park contains **Kardemomme By** (Cardamom Town), named for a book by Norwegian illustrator and writer Thorbjørn Egner. His story comes alive here in a precisely replicated village, with actors playing townsfolk, shopkeepers, pirates, and a delightful trio of robbers. Families who get hooked can even stay overnight in one of the village's cozy apartments or nearby cottages (reserve at least a year in advance). *Kristiansand Dyrepark, 4609 Kardemomme by, tel. 38/04–97–00. Admission: NKr130 adults, NKr110 children; includes admission to all parks and rides. Open late May–mid-June, daily 10–3; mid-June–mid-Aug., daily 9–7; mid-Aug.–mid-Sept., daily 10-6.*

Excursions from Kristiansand

6 **Setesdalsbanen** (the Setesdal Railway) at **Grovane i Vennesla,** 20 kilometers (13 miles) north of Kristiansand, is a 4.7-kilometer- (3-mile-) long stretch of narrow-gauge track featuring a steam locomotive from 1894 and carriages from the early 1900s. Follow Route 39 to Mosby, veer right onto 405, and continue to Grovane. *Grovane, tel. 38/15–64–82. Fare: NKr40 adults, NKr20 children (50% discount with Summerpass). Open June 9–Aug. 25, Sun. at 11:30, 1, 2:30; July, Wed. at 6.*

Many rockhounds head for **Evje,** about 60 kilometers (36 miles) north of Kristiansand, to look for semiprecious stones. At **Evje Mineralsti,** you can hunt for blue-green amazonite. *No tel. Admission: NKr35, NKr70 family. Open daily 10–5:30. At other times, visitors pay by honor system.*

You can also visit **Fennefoss Museum** just south of Evje in Hornnes and look at the mineral collection. *No tel. Admission: NKr15 adults, NKr5 children. Open daily 10–2.*

Tour 3: The South

7 From Kristiansand you can go 28 kilometers (17 miles) southwest to **Mandal,** with its historic core of well-preserved wood houses and its beautiful long beach, Sjøsanden.

Lindesnes Fyr, Norway's oldest lighthouse, was built on the southernmost point of the country. The old coal-fired light dates from 1822.

8 Route E18 continues northward now along the rich agricultural coastal plain of **Jæren,** painted by many Norwegian artists. Ancient monuments are still visible here, notably the **Hå gravesite** below the Hå parsonage near **Obrestad** light on coastal Route 44, which connects with Route E18 by way of Route 504. It consists of about 60 mounds, including two star-shaped and one boat-shaped, dating from around AD 500, all marked with stones. **Hå parsonage,** built in the 1780s, is now a cultural center. *Admission: NKr15. Open May 1–Sept. 30, Sun.–Fri. noon–7, Sat. noon–5; Oct. 1–Apr. 30., Sat. noon–5, Sun. noon–7.*

9 Continue northward on Route 507 to **Orre,** site of a medieval stone church. Near Orre pond, slightly inland, is a bird-watching station.

Tour 4: Stavanger

10 **Stavanger** has always prospered from the riches of the sea. During the 19th century, huge harvests of brisling and herring established it as the sardine capital of the world. A resident is still called a Siddis, from S(tavanger) plus *iddis,* which means "sardine label," and the city symbol, fittingly enough, is the key of a sardine can.

During the past two decades, a different product from the sea has been Stavanger's lifeblood—oil. Since its discovery in the late 1960s, North Sea oil has transformed both the economy and the lifestyle of the city. In the early days of drilling, expertise was imported from abroad, chiefly from the United States. Although Norwegians have now taken over most of the projects, foreigners constitute almost a tenth of the inhabitants, making

Stavanger the country's most cosmopolitan city. Though the population hovers around 100,000, the city has all the agreeable bustle of one many times its size.

In the center, next to a small pond called Breiavatnet, is **Stavanger Domkirke** (the cathedral), a large, well-preserved medieval church. Construction was begun about 1100 by Bishop Reinald of Winchester, probably assisted by English craftsmen. Largely destroyed by fire in 1125, it was rebuilt to include a Gothic chancery, the result of which is that its once elegant lines are now festooned with macabre death symbols and airborne cupids. The cathedral often hosts organ recitals, with coffee served afterward in the crypt. *Admission free. Open mid-May–mid-Sept., Mon.–Sat. 9–8, Sun. 1–6; mid-Sept.–mid-May, Mon.–Sat. 9–2.*

Next to the cathedral is the **Kongsgård,** former residence of bishops and kings, but now a school and not open to visitors. A few streets to the left, on Eiganesveien, is an old patrician residential district. As the road angles to the left, it's only one long block to **Breidablikk** manor house, built by a Norwegian shipping magnate. An outstanding example of what the Norwegians call "Swiss style" architecture, it has been perfectly preserved since the '60s and feels as if the owner has only momentarily slipped away. In spite of its foreign label, the house is uniquely Norwegian, inspired by national romanticism. *Eiganesvn. 40A, tel. 51/52–60–35. Admission: NKr20 adults, NKr10 children. Open mid-June–mid-Aug., Tues.–Sun. 11–3; mid-Aug.–mid-June, Sun. 11–4.*

Across the road and through the park is **Ledaal,** a stately house built by the Kielland family in 1799 but now the residence of the royal family when they visit Stavanger. The second-floor library is dedicated to the writer Alexander Kielland, a social critic and satirist. *Eiganesvn. 45, tel. 51/52–60–35. Admission: NKr20 adults, NKr10 children. Open mid-June–mid-Aug., Tues.–Sun. 11–3; mid-Aug.–mid-June, Sun. 11–4.*

Exit toward Alexander Kiellands Gate, turn right, and walk around the stadium complex and several blocks farther, until you reach Øvre Strandgate. Along with Nedre Strandgate, this forms the periphery of old Stavanger, where you can wind down narrow cobblestoned streets, past small, white houses with many-paned windows and terra-cotta roof tiles.

Tucked between the neighborhood and the harbor is the fascinating, albeit obscure, **Norsk Hermetikkmuseum** (Canning Museum), housed in a former canning factory. Exhibits document the production of brisling and sardines—the city's most important industry for nearly 100 years, thanks greatly to savvy turn-of-the-century packaging (naturally, the inventor of the sardine-can key was from Stavanger). Sundays between August and April, the museum hosts an iddis, or sardine-label, swap meet that draws a local crowd, many of whom have collected thousands of labels. *Øvre Strandgt. 88A, tel. 51/52–60–35. Admission: NKr20 adults, NKr10 children. Open June–Aug., Wed.–Sun. 11–3; Sept.–May, Sun. 11–4.*

Walk along Strandkaien to **Sjøfartsmuseet** (the Maritime Museum), in the only two shipping merchants' houses that remain completely intact. The warehouses face the wharf, while the shops, offices, and apartments face the street on the other side. Inside, the house is just as it was a century ago, complete with office furniture, files, and posters, while the apartments show the standard of living for the mercantile class at that time. *Nedre Strandgt. 17–19, tel. 51/52–60–35. Admission: NKr20 adults, NKr10 children. Open mid-June–mid-Aug., Tues.– Sun. 11–3; mid-Aug.–mid-June, Sun. 11–4.*

From all along the quay you can see **Valbergtårnet** (Valberget 4, tel. 51/52–21–95), built on the highest point of the old city. Once a fire watchtower, it is now a craft center.

If you are of Norwegian stock, you can trace your roots at **Det Norske Utvandrersenteret** (The Norwegian Emigrant Center). Bring along any information you have, especially where your ancestors came from in Norway and when they arrived in the United Kingdom, North America, or elsewhere. *Bergjelandsgt. 30, 4012 Stavanger, tel. 51/50–12–67. Admission is free, but each written request costs NKr180. Open weekdays 9–3.*

Excursions from Stavanger

⑪ Not a good choice if you suffer from vertigo, but great for a heart-stopping view is **Prekestolen** (Pulpit Rock), a huge cube of rock with a vertical drop of 600 meters (2,000 feet). You can take a tour there (*see* Guided Tours, *above*) or you can do it on your own from June 16 to August 25 by taking the ferry from Fiskepiren to Tau. It takes 1½ to two hours to walk to the rock—the well-marked trail crosses some uneven terrain, so good walking shoes or boots are vital. Food and lodging are near the trail. The rock can also be reached by sightseeing boat.

⑫ About 5 kilometers (3 miles) west of Stavanger is **Ullandhaug**, a reconstruction of an Iron-Age farm. Three houses have been built around a central garden, and guides wearing period clothing demonstrate the daily activities of 1,500 years ago, spinning thread on a spindle, weaving, and cooking over an open hearth. *Ullandhaug, tel. 51/53–41–40. Admission: NKr10 adults, NKr5 children. Open June 15–Aug. 15, daily noon–5; May 8–June 14 and Aug. 16–Sept. 16, Sun. noon–5.*

What to See and Do with Children

Kristiansand   **Kardemomme by** (Cardamom Town) and **Dyrehaven** (*see* Tour 2, *above*) are the big draws in Kristiansand.

Stavanger   At the **Canning Museum** (*see* Tour 4, *above*), children can collect sardine-can labels and play marbles. **Kongeparken Amusement Park** has an 85-meter (281-foot) -long figure of Gulliver as its main attraction, and plenty of rides. *4330 Ålgård, tel. 51/61–71–11. Admission: NKr25; rides and activities, NKr5–20. Open mid-June–mid Aug., daily 11–7. Other spring and summer hours vary. Call the park for specific times.*

Shopping

Porsgrunn   Outside Porsgrunn, 27 kilometers (17 miles) west of Larvik, is **Porsgrunn Porselænfabrik** (porcelain factory) (Porselensgt. 12, tel. 35/55–00–40), where you can take a factory tour and visit the seconds shop.

Stavanger   Outside of town are a ceramics factory and an outlet store: **Figgjo Ceramics** (Rte. E18, 4333 Figgjo, tel. 51/67–00–00) was started during World War II, when Norway was occupied by German forces. A museum traces the history of the factory; the seconds shop has discounts of around 50%. **Skjæveland Strikkevarefabrikk** (4330 Ålgård, tel. 51/61–85–06) has a huge selection of men's and women's sweaters in both Norwegian patterns and other designs for around NKr200 less than prices found in the shops.

Sports and Fitness

Southern Norway is an outdoor paradise, with a mild summer climate and terrain varying from coastal flatland to inland mountains and forests. There's plenty of fish in the rivers and lakes, as well as along the coast. The region is particularly well suited to canoeing, kayaking, and rafting, as well as hiking. Southern Norway is home to beavers, deer, fox, and forest birds, so bring binoculars if you like to see them more closely.

Bicycling **Kristiansand** has 70 kilometers (43 miles) of bike trails around the city. The tourist office can recommend routes and rentals.

From Stavanger you can take your bike onto the ferry that departs for Finnøy, one of the larger islands of the Ryfylke Archipelago. Spend the day or longer: Week-long cottage rentals are available from **Finnøy Fjordsenter** (N–4160, Judaberg, tel. 51/71–26–46). For more information about cottages in the archipelago and maps, contact the Stavanger Tourist Board. The Department of the Environment can also provide information; call their **Cycle Projects** (Sadnes Turistinformajon, Langgt. 8, N–4300 Sadnes, Stavanger, tel. 51/65–03–19).

Bird-watching The **Jaerstrendene** in Jaeren, from Randabergvika in the north to Ogna in the south, is a protected national park—and a good area for spotting puffins, cormorants, and black guillemots, as well as such waders as dunlins, little stints, and ringed plovers. Some areas of the park are closed to visitors, and it is forbidden to pick flowers, or for that matter, disturb anything.

Fishing Both Sørlandet, around Kristiansand, and Rogaland, around the Stavanger area, are famed for their fishing waters. For details on fishing holidays, contact the regional tourist boards.

Kristiansand Just north of Kristiansand there is excellent trout, perch, and eel fishing at Lillesand's **Vestre Grimevann** lake. You can get a permit at any sports store or at the tourist office (tel. 37/27–21–30). South of Kristiansand, in Mandal, sea trout run from mid-May to mid-September. The daily fishing fee is NKr30. For details, contact the tourist office (tel. 38/26–08–20).

Stavanger Three of the 10 best fishing rivers in Norway, the **Ognaelva, Håelva,** and **Figgjo,** are located in Jæren, just south of Stavanger. Fishing licenses, which are sold in groceries and gas stations, are required at all of them.

The longest salmon river in western Norway, the **Suldalslågen,** is also nearby, made popular 100 years ago by a Scottish aristocrat, who built a fishing lodge there. **Lindum** still has cabins and camping facilities, as well as a dining room. Contact the **Lindum Ferie- og Kurssenter** (N–4240 Suldalsosen, tel. 52/79–91–61). The main salmon season is July through September (*see* also Water Sports, Stavanger, *below*).

Golf At Randesund, southeast of **Kristiansand**, is a nine-hole golf course. Contact **Kristiansand Golfklubb's** secretary (tel. 38/04–58–63) for details. The **Stavanger Golf klubb** (tel. 51/55–54–31) offers a lush, 18-hole, international-championship course and equipment rental.

Hiking In addition to the gardens and steep hills of **Ravnedalen** (*see*
Kristiansand Tour 2, *above*), the **Baneheia** forest, just a 15-minute walk north from the city center, is full of evergreens, small lakes, and paths that are ideal for a lazy walk or a challenging run.

Stavanger **Stavanger Turistforening** (Postboks 239, 4001 Stavanger, tel. 51/52–75–66) can plan a hike through the area, particularly in the rolling **Setesdalsheiene** and the thousands of islands and skerries of the **Ryfylke Archipelago.** The tourist board oversees 33 cabins for members (you can join on the spot) for overnighting along the way. Also in the Ryfylke area, thrill seekers can hike up to the **Kjerag**, a sheet of granite mountain that soars 3,555 feet, at the Lysefjord, near Forsand.

Hunting Throughout the Kristiansand and Stavanger areas, hunting laws are similar to those in the rest of Norway. For larger game, including elk, you must literally purchase a Norwegian's right, thereby ensuring that there is no overhunting. Beavers in the Kristiansand area and hare around Stavanger are numerous but still require the purchase of a permit. For information, contact **Info Sø** (Info South, Brokelandsheia, 4993 Sundrebru, tel. 37/15–85–60).

Water Sports **Kuholmen Marina** (Roligheden Camping, tel. 38/09–67–22) ar-
Kristiansand ranges rentals of boats, water skis, and water scooters. **Sail Scandinavia** (Tollbodgt. 8, tel. 38/07–07–49) rents sailboats by the day, weekend or week, with or without captain, while **Hamresanden Båtutleie** (Kirsti Stabel, Moneheia 4, tel. 38/04–68–25) rents out kayaks and rowboats. **Anker Dykkersenter** (Randesundsgt. 2, Kuholmen, tel. 38/09–79–09) rents scuba equipment, and **Blomberg Sport** (Skansen 24, tel. 38/02–98–08) rents windsurfers and holds classes.

Combining history and sailing, the magnificent full-rig, square-sail school ship *Sørlandet* (Gravene 2, N–4610 Kristiansand, tel. 38/02–98–90, fax 38/02–93–34) built in 1927 takes on passengers ranging from senior citizens to college students and younger for two weeks, usually stopping for several days in a northern European port. Prices range from NKr6,500 for adults to NKr5,500 for students.

Stavanger Diving is excellent all along the coast—although Norwegian law requires all foreigners to dive with a Norwegian in order to ensure that wrecks are left undisturbed. Contact **Dive In** (Bergjelandsgt. 11, tel. 51/52–89–36), in the Ryfilke Archipelago, which rents equipment and offers a weekend rate. In Kristiansand contact the **Kristiansand Diving Club** (Myrbakken 3, tel. 38/01–03–32) between 6 PM and 9 PM.

On the island of **Kvitsøy**, in the archipelago just west of Stavanger, you can rent an apartment, complete with fish-smoking and -freezing facilities, and arrange to use a small sail- or motorboat. Contact **Kvitsøy Maritime Senter** (Box 35, N–4090 Kvitsøy, tel. 51/73–51–88).

Dining and Lodging

Dining   Coastal Sørlandet is seafood country. Restaurants in this resort area are casual and unpretentious, and the cooking is simple. Better restaurants can usually be found in the hotels, especially in small towns.

Stavanger has many more good restaurants than other cities of comparable size, thanks to the influx of both foreigners and money to the city.

Lodging   Hotels in the small towns along the coast are either modern and practical—suited for business guests—or quaint and old-fashioned. Prices are about the same regardless of style and are quite competitive during the low-season summer months.

Highly recommended establishments are indicated by a star ★.

Bryne   **Time Station.** It's a 40-minute train ride from Stavanger to
Dining   Bryne and the restaurant is next to the station. The specialty of the house is a seafood platter with salmon, monkfish, ocean catfish, mussels, and ocean crayfish in a beurre-blanc sauce. For dessert, try the *krumkake*, a cookie baked on an iron, wafer thin, and filled with blackberry cream. *4340 Bryne, tel. 51/48-22-56. Reservations required. Dress: casual but neat. AE, DC, MC, V. No weekday lunch. Closed Sun. Moderate.*

Kristiansand   **Sjøhuset.** Built in 1892 as a salt warehouse, this white-trimmed
Dining   red building is furnished with comfortable leather chairs and accented with maritime antiques. The specialty is seafood, and the monkfish with Newburg sauce on green fettuccine is both colorful and delicious. *Østre Strangt. 12, tel. 38/02-62-60. Reservations advised. Dress: casual but neat. AE, DC, MC, V. Moderate-Expensive.*

Restaurant Bakgården. At this small and intimate restaurant the menu varies from day to day, but the seafood platter and rack of lamb are standard items. The staff is especially attentive to guests' wishes. *Tollbodgt. 5, tel. 38/02-79-55. Dress: casual but neat. AE, DC, MC, V. No lunch. Moderate-Expensive.*

Mållaget Kafeteria. At this cafeteria everything is homemade (except for the gelatin dessert). That includes such dishes as meatballs, brisket of beef with onion sauce, and trout in sour-cream sauce. It's the best deal in town, but it closes right around the time most people think about eating dinner. *Gyldenløves Gate 11, tel. 38/02-22-93. Reservations advised. Dress: casual. No credit cards. Inexpensive.*

Lodging   **Ernst Park.** It was modernized in 1988, but a few clusters of chairs and sofas are left in nooks and crannies. The rooms are decorated in light furniture, with chintz bedspreads and drapes. The corner rooms have a tower nook at one end. On Saturday the atrium restaurant is the local spot for a civilized tea and lovely cakes. *Rådhusgt. 2, 4611, tel. 38/02-14-00, fax 38/02-03-07. 113 rooms with bath or shower, 3 suites. Facilities: 3 restaurants, 2 bars, nightclub, conference rooms. AE, DC, MC, V. Moderate-Expensive.*

Hotel Norge. This recently refurbished hotel in the heart of town has an entrance more modern than that of the Ernst Park, but upstairs, the difference is negligible. Here the rooms are furnished in bright colors and dark woods. Get up for breakfast to taste the homemade breads and rolls. *Dronningens Gate 5,*

4610, tel. 38/02-00-00, fax 38/02-35-30. 115 rooms with bath or shower. Facilities: restaurant, conference rooms; no alcohol. AE, DC, MC, V. Inexpensive-Moderate.

Stavanger
Dining
★

Jans Mat & Vinhus. The cellar setting is rustic, with old stone walls and robust sideboards providing a nice counterpoint to the refined menu. Saddle of Rogaland county lamb is boned and rolled around a thyme-flavored stuffing, and the fillet is topped with a crunchy mustard crust. For dessert, there's a nougat parfait dusted with cocoa. *Breitorget, tel. 51/52-45-02. Reservations required. Jacket and tie required. AE, DC, MC, V. No lunch. Closed Sun. Expensive.*

Straen Fiskerestaurant. The city's chief fish restaurant, right on the quay, has two old-fashioned dining rooms. The three-course dinner of the day is always the best value. The house fish soup and the tournedos of monkfish with lobster sauce and a garnish of mussels and shrimp are excellent. *Strandkaien, tel. 51/52-62-30. Reservations advised. Dress: neat but casual. AE, DC, MC, V. Dinner only. Closed Sun. Expensive.*

City Bistro. This turn-of-the-century frame house with a tiled roof is furnished with massive oak tables and benches. Choose from reindeer medallions with rowanberry jelly, deer fillet with lingonberries and pears, or halibut poached in cream with saffron, garnished with shrimp, crayfish, and mussels. The dish of the day is served from 5 to 6. *Madlavn. 18-20, tel. 51/53-31-81. Reservations required. Dress: casual but neat. AE, DC, MC, V. No lunch. Moderate.*

Galeien Bistro. It used to be a sardine cannery, and the pictures on its wall illustrate the early history of the building. Ask for a window table overlooking the sea. Back in the kitchen, which you can visit, there are tanks filled with cod, flounder, oysters, mussels, crabs, and lobster. Simple preparations emphasize the natural flavor of the fish. *Hundvågvn. 27, tel. 51/54-91-44. Reservations advised. Dress: casual but neat. V. Moderate.*

Café Sting. It's a restaurant-gallery-concert hall-meeting place day and night. All food is made in-house and is less stodgy than most inexpensive fare in Norway. There's a skillet dish with crisp fried potatoes and bacon, flavored with leek and topped with melted cheese; and a meat loaf with mashed potatoes and sprinkled with cheese. The chocolate and almond cakes are good. *Valberggt. 3, tel. 51/53-24-40. Dress: casual. AE, DC, V. Inexpensive.*

Lodging

SAS Royal. Room styles include Scandinavian, American, Japanese, and Italian and lots of fashionable furniture that provides more good looks than real comfort. The Chicago Bar & Grill serves prime steaks. *Løkkevn. 26, 4008 Stavanger, tel. 51/56-70-00, fax 51/56-74-60. 204 rooms with bath, 8 suites. Facilities: 2 restaurants, bar, 24-hour room service, pool, fitness center, business/conference center. AE, DC, MC, V. Moderate-Very Expensive.*

Skagen Brygge. This hotel incorporates three rehabilitated old sea houses. Almost all rooms are different, from modern to old-fashioned maritime with exposed beams and brick and wood walls; many have harbor views. The hotel has an arrangement with 15 restaurants in the area—they make the reservations and the tab ends up on your hotel bill. *Skagenkaien 30, 4006, tel. 51/53-03-50, fax 51/89-58-83. 110 rooms with bath, 2 suites. Facilities: bar, pool, fitness center, conference center. AE, DC, MC, V. Moderate-Expensive.*

Grand Hotel. This hotel on the edge of the town center doesn't aim to be fancy; rooms are comfortable and bright, done in light pastels and white. In summer the rates drop significantly. *Klubbgt. 3, Boks 80, 4001 Stavanger, tel. 51/53–30–20, fax 51/ 56–19–42. 92 rooms with bath. Facilities: restaurant, bar. AE, DC, MC, V. Inexpensive–Moderate.*

Hummeren. Built in 1986 in the style of old harborside buildings, Hummeren (The Lobster) is 15 kilometers (9 miles) from Stavanger, at Tananger Harbor. Boats dock immediately outside, and it even has showers for people who otherwise live on their boats. Many of the large rooms face the harbor, and some have balconies. The restaurant serves fine, old-fashioned fare. *4056 Tananger, tel. 51/69–04–33. 32 rooms with shower or tub. Facilities: restaurant, bar, conference rooms. AE, DC, MC, V. Inexpensive–Moderate.*

The Arts and Nightlife

The Arts
Stavanger

Stavanger Konserthus (Concert Hall, Bjergsted, tel. 51/56–17–16) features local artists and hosts free summertime foyer concerts. Built on an island in the archipelago in the Middle Ages, today **Ulstein Kloster** is used for its superior acoustics and hosts classical and jazz concerts on some weekday afternoons from June to August.

Nightlife
Kristiansand

As in most smaller cities, Kristiansand's nightlife centers around hotels.

Stavanger

In summer people are out at all hours, and sidewalk restaurants stay open until the sun comes up. Walk along **Skagenkaien** and **Strandkaien** for a choice of pubs and nightclubs. Among media junkies the place for a beer and a bit of CNN is the **Newsman** (Skagen 14, tel. 51/53–57–09). The **Amadeus Disco,** at the Atlantik Hotel (Olav V's gt. 3, tel. 51/52–75–20) is for the mid-twenties crowd.

5 Bergen

People from Bergen like to say they do not come from Norway but from Bergen. Enfolded at the crook of seven mountains and fish-boned by seven fjords, Bergen does seem far from the rest of Norway.

Hanseatic merchants from northern Germany settled in Bergen during the 14th century and made it one of their four major overseas trading centers. The surviving Hanseatic buildings on Bryggen (the quay) are neatly topped with triangular cookie-cutter roofs and scrupulously painted red, blue, yellow, and green. A monument in themselves (they are on the UNESCO World Heritage List), they now house boutiques, restaurants, and museums. In the evening, when the harborside is illuminated, these modest buildings, together with the stocky Rosencrantz Tower, are reflected in the water—and provide one of the loveliest cityscapes in northern Europe.

During the Hanseatic period, this active port was Norway's capital and largest city. Boats from northern Norway brought dried fish to Bergen to be shipped abroad by the Dutch, English, Scottish, and German merchants who had settled here. By the time the Hansa lost power, the city had an ample supply of wealthy local merchants and shipowners to replace them. For years Bergen was the capital of shipping, and until well into the 19th century, it remained the country's major city.

Culturally, Bergen has also had its luminaries, including dramatist Ludvig Holberg, Scandinavia's answer to Molière—whom the Danes claim as their own. Bergensers know better. Norway's musical geniuses Ole Bull and Edvard Grieg also came from the city of the seven hills. In fact, once you've visited Troldhaugen, Greig's "Hill of Trolls," it's not difficult to see the source of his inspiration.

About 217,000 people live in the greater metropolitan area now, compared with nearly 500,000 in Oslo. Even though the balance of power has shifted to the capital, Bergen remains a strong commercial force, thanks to shipping and oil, and is a cultural center, with an international music and arts festival every spring. Although it's true that an umbrella and slicker are necessary in this town, the raindrops—actually 219 days per year of them—never obstruct the lovely views.

Essential Information

Important Addresses and Numbers

Tourist Information The **tourist information office** at Bryggen (tel. 55/32–14–80), by the wharf, has brochures and maps and can arrange for accommodations and sightseeing. There is also a currency exchange.

Emergencies Police: tel. 002. Fire: tel. 001. **Ambulance:** tel. 003. **Car Rescue:** tel. 55/29–22–22. After January 1, 1994, these numbers will change. **Police:** tel. 112. **Fire:** tel. 111. **Ambulance:** tel. 113.

Hospital Emergency Rooms The outpatient center at Lars Hillesgate 30 (tel. 55/32–11–20), near Grieghallen, is open 24 hours.

Dentists The dental emergency center, also at Lars Hillesgate 30 (tel. 55/32–11–20), is open daily 10–11 AM and 7–9 PM.

Pharmacies **Apotek Nordstjernen** (tel. 55/31–68–40), by the bus station, is open daily from 8:30 AM to midnight.

Where to Outside normal banking hours, the tourist information office
Change Money on Bryggen can change money. Post offices exchange money and are open Monday through Wednesday 8 to 4:30, Thursday and Friday 8–6, and Saturday 9 to 2.

Arriving and Departing by Plane

Flesland Airport is 20 kilometers (12 miles) south of Bergen. SAS (tel. 55/99–76–10) and **Braathens SAFE** (tel. 55/23–23–25) are the main domestic carriers. **British Airways** and **Lufthansa** also serve Flesland.

Between the Flesland is a 30-minute ride from the center of Bergen at off-
Airport and peak hours. The **airport bus** departs three times per hour (less
Downtown frequently on weekends) from the SAS Royal Hotel via
By Bus Braathen SAFE's office at the Hotel Norge and from the bus station. Pickup prior to departure can be arranged. Tickets cost NKr36.

By Taxi A taxi rank is outside the Arrivals exit. The trip into the city costs around NKr200.

By Car Driving from Flesland to Bergen is simple, and the road is well marked. Bergen has an electronic ring surrounding it, so any vehicle entering the city weekdays between 6 AM and 10 PM has to pay NKr5. There is no toll in the other direction.

Arriving and Departing by Car, Train, Bus, and Boat

By Car Bergen is 485 kilometers (300 miles) from Oslo. Route 7 is good almost as far as Eidfjord at the eastern edge of the Hardangerfjord, but then deteriorates considerably. The ferry along the way, crossing the Hardanger Fjord from Main to Bruravik, runs continually 5 AM to midnight and takes 10 minutes. Route 7 from Kvanndal to Bergen hugs the fjord part of the way, making for spectacular scenery.

Driving from Stavanger to Bergen involves from two to four ferries and a long journey packed with breathtaking scenery. The Stavanger tourist information office can help plan the trip and reserve ferry space.

By Train The *Bergensbanen* has four departures daily, plus one more on Friday and two on Sunday, in both directions on the Oslo–Bergen route; it is widely acknowledged as one of the most beautiful train rides in the world. Trains leave from Oslo S Station for the 7½- to 8½-hour journey. For information about trains out of Bergen, call 55/96–60–50.

By Bus The summer-only bus from Oslo to Bergen, **Geiteryggekspressen** (literally, "Goat-Back Express"—does it refer to speed, comfort, or terrain?) leaves the Nor-Way bus terminal (Galleri Oslo, tel. 22/17–52–90) at 8 AM and arrives in Bergen 12½ hours later. Buses also connect Bergen with Trondheim and Ålesund. Western Norway is served by several bus companies, which use the station at Strømgaten 8 (tel. 55/32–67–80).

By Boat Boats have always been Bergen's lifeline to the world. **Color Line** (Skuteviksboder 1–2, 5023, tel. 55/56–86–60) ferries serve Newcastle. Others connect with the Shetland and Faroe islands, Denmark, Scotland, and Iceland. All dock at Skoltegrunnskaien.

Express boats between Bergen and Stavanger run three times daily on weekdays, twice daily on weekends, for the four-hour trip. All arrive and depart from **Munkebryggen**.

Getting Around

The best way to see the small center of Bergen is on foot. Most sights are within walking distance of the marketplace.

By Bus Tourist tickets for 48 hours of unlimited travel within the town boundaries cost NKr60, payable on the yellow city buses. All buses serving the Bergen region depart from the central bus station at Strømgaten 8 (tel. 55/32–67–80).

By Taxi Taxi ranks are located in strategic places downtown. All taxis are connected to the central dispatching office (tel. 55/99–09–90) and can be booked in advance (tel. 55/99–13–00).

By Car Downtown Bergen is enclosed by an inner ring road. The area within is divided into three zones, which are separated by ONE-WAY and DO-NOT-ENTER signs. To get from one zone to another, return to the ring road and drive to an entry point into the desired zone. It's best to leave your car at a parking garage (the Birkebeiner Senter is on Rosenkrantz Gata, and there is a lot near the train station) and walk. You pay an NKr5 toll every time you drive into the city—but driving out is free.

Opening and Closing Times

Shops are open Monday–Wednesday and Friday 9–4:30. On Thursday, as well as Friday for some shops, the hours are 9–7. On Saturday shops are open 9–2. The shopping centers are open weekdays 9–8 and Saturday 9–4.

Guided Tours

Bergen is the guided-tour capital of Norway because it is the starting point for most fjord tours. Tickets for all tours are available from the tourist information office.

Orientation HSD Busstrafikk (tel. 55/23–87–00) offers two tours departing from Hotel Norge; one on Bergen sights, the other to Edvard Grieg's Home and the Fantoft Stave Church. **De Gule Bussene** (yellow buses, tel. 55/28–13–30) offers three tours departing from Torggaten by the Hotel Norge. The excellent **Bryggen Guiding** (1½ hours, June 1–Aug. 31) offers a historic tour of the buildings at Bryggen, as well as entrance to Bryggens Museum, the Hanseatic Museum, and Schøtstuene after the tour, conducted by knowledgeable guides. **Bergens-Expressen** (tel. 55/18–10–19), a "train on tires," leaves from Torgalmenningen for a one-hour ride around the center of town.

Fjord Tours Bergen is the much-acclaimed "Gateway to the Fjords," with dozens of fjord-tour possibilities. The following is only meant as a sampling. The ambitious all-day **"Norway-in-a-Nutshell"** bus/train tour (NSB, Strømgata 2, 50 15 Bergen, tel. 55/96–60–50) goes through Voss, Flåm, Myrdal, and Gudvangen—truly a breathtaking trip, especially if you're pressed for time.

Traveling by boat is an advantage because the contrasts between the fjords and mountains are greatest at water level, and
the boats are comfortable and stable (the water is practically
still), so seasickness is rare. Stops are frequent, and all sights
are explained. *The White Lady* (tel. 55/31–43–20) offers a four-
hour local fjord tour. **Fylkesbaatane** (County Boats) **i Sogn og
Fjordane** (tel. 55/32–40–15) has several combination tours.
Tickets are sold at the tourist information center (tel. 55/32–
14–80) and at the quay. Students receive a 25% discount for
most tours.

There are other combinations of tours through the Hardanger
and Sogne fjords that include the surrounding countryside;
some tours include options to fish or visit local villages or islands. The three-day **Panorama Fjord Cruise** plies the Hardanger and Sognefjords but includes overnights in hotels.
Fjord Sightseeing (tel. 55/31–43–20), offers boat tours leaving
from Fisketorget. Both of these lines are operated by **Winge of
Scandinavia** (Karl Johans Gate 35, Box 1705, Vika, N–0121
Oslo, tel. 02/41–20–20).

Highlights for First-time Visitors

Bryggen (*see* Tour 1)
Bryggens Museum (*see* Tour 1)
Fantoft Stave Church (*see* Tour 3)
Fisketorget (*see* Tour 1)
Fløybanen (*see* Tour 1)
Hanseatisk Museum (*see* Tour 1)
Lysøen (*see* Tour 4)
Troldhaugen (Edvard Grieg's home) (*see* Tour 3)

Exploring Bergen

*Numbers in the margin correspond to points of interest on the
Bergen map.*

Many of Bergen's sights are concentrated in a small area, so
walking tours are the best way to see the city.

Tour 1: Historic Bergen

❶ Start at **Torget,** Bergen's marketplace, also called **Fisketorget**
(fish market). At the turn of the century, pictures of this active
and pungent square, with fishermen in Wellington boots and
mackintoshes and women in long aprons, were popular post-
card subjects. Times haven't changed, and it remains just as
picturesque: Bring your camera. *Open Mon.–Sat. 8–3.*

❷ Look over toward **Bryggen,** the row of 14th-century painted
wood buildings with pointed gables facing the harbor, built by
Hansa merchants. The buildings, which are on the UNESCO
World Heritage List, are mostly reconstructions, with the oldest dating from 1702. Several fires, the latest in 1955, destroyed the original structures.

❸ Follow the pier to the **Hanseatisk** (Hanseatic) **Museum** at
Finnegården, which was office and home to an affluent German
merchant. Apprentices lived upstairs, in boxed-in beds with
windows cut into the wall, so the tiny cells could be made up
from the hall. Although claustrophobic, they retained body

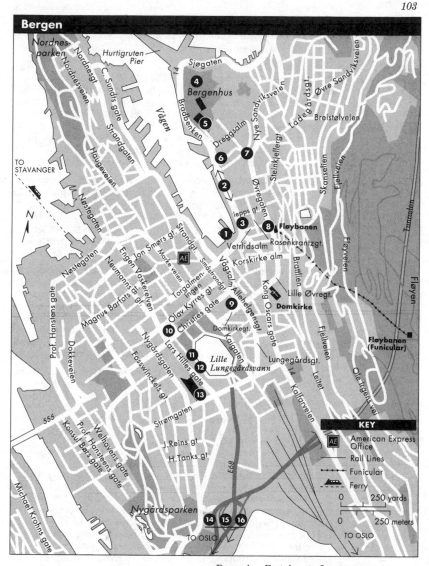

Bergenhus Festning, **4**

Bryggen, **2**

Bryggen Museum, **6**

Fantoft Stavkirke, **15**

Fløybanen, **8**

Gamle Rådhuset, **9**

Grieghallen, **13**

Hanseatisk Museum, **3**

Lysøen, **16**

Mariakirken, **7**

Rasmus Meyers
Samlinger, **12**

Rosenkrantztårnet, **5**

Stenersen
Collection, **11**

Torget, **1**

Troldhaugen, **14**

Vestlandske
Kunstindustri-
museum, **10**

heat, practical in these unheated buildings. *Bryggen, tel. 55/ 31–41–89. Admission: NKr15 adults, NKr8 children. Open June–Aug., daily 9–5; May and Sept., daily 11–2; Oct.–Apr., Sun., Mon., Wed., and Fri. 11–2.*

4 Past the historic buildings, at the end of the Holmen promontory, is **Bergenhus Festning** (fort), dating from the mid-13th century. **Håkonshallen,** a royal ceremonial hall used as early as 1261, was badly damaged by the explosion of a Dutch ship in 1944 but was restored by 1961. *Bergenhus, tel. 55/31–60–67. Admission: NKr10 adults, NKr5 children. Open May 15–Sept. 14, daily 10–4; Sept. 15–May 14, daily noon–3, also Thurs. 3–6. Closed during Bergen International Music Festival.*

5 Nearby, **Rosenkrantztårnet** (Rosenkrantz tower), damaged in the same explosion that rocked Håkonshallen, was built in the 1560s by the Danish governor of Bergenhus, Erik Rosenkrantz, as a fortified official residence. It is furnished in the same formal, austere style as the hall. *Bergenhus, tel. 55/31– 43–80. Admission: NKr10 adults, NKr5 children. Open May 15–Sept. 14, daily 10–4; Sept. 15–May 14, Sun. noon–3.*

6 Retrace your steps to the SAS Royal Hotel. Nearby is **Bryggen Museum,** which houses artifacts found during excavations on Bryggen, including 12th-century buildings constructed on site from the original foundations. The collection provides a good picture of daily life before and during the heyday of the Hansa, down to a two-seater outhouse. *Bryggen, tel. 55/31–67–10. Admission: NKr15. Open May 1–Aug. 31, daily 10–5; Sept. 1–Apr. 30, weekdays 11–3, Sat. noon–3, Sun. noon–4.*

7 The 12th-century **Mariakirken** (St. Mary's Church) is just up the street. Bergen's oldest building began as a Romanesque church but has gained a Gothic choir, richly decorated portals, and a splendid Baroque pulpit, much of it added by the Hanseatic merchants, who owned it from the 15th century. Organ recitals are held Tuesday and Thursday June 15 to August 26. *Dreggen, tel. 55/31–59–60. Admission: NKr10. Open May– Aug., weekdays 11–4; Sept.–Apr., Tues.–Fri. noon–1:30.*

From Øvregaten, the back boundary of Bryggen, you can look down toward the wharf along the narrow passages where the citizens of the city lived. Walk about four blocks to the popular
8 **Fløybanen,** the funicular (a cable car that runs on tracks on the ground) to **Fløyen,** a lookout point 326 meters (1,050 feet) above the sea. Several marked trails lead from Fløyen into the surrounding wooded area, or you can walk back to town on Fjellveien. *Admission: NKr28 adults, NKr14 children; one-way tickets are half price. Rides every half hour 8 AM–11 PM.*

On Lille Øvregaten, and the area of crooked streets and hodge-podge architecture nearby, you'll find most of Bergen's antiques shops. On your left at the intersection with King Oscars Gate is Bergen **Domkirke** (the cathedral), another building constructed in a profusion of styles. The oldest parts, the choir and lower portion of the tower, date from the late 12th century. *Tel. 55/31–05–70. Open weekdays 11–2.*

9 Walk down Domkirkegaten to Allehelgensgate, past the police station, and turn right. Across the street is **Gamle Rådhuset** (the old City Hall), built in the 16th century as the residence of the governor. The city council still meets there.

Tour 2: For Art Lovers

From Torgalmeningen, walk to Nordahl Bruns Gate and turn left for the **Vestlandske Kunstindustrimuseum** (West Norway Museum of Decorative Arts). Seventeenth- and 18th-century Bergen silversmiths were renowned throughout Scandinavia for their heavy, elaborate Baroque designs. Tankards embossed with flower motifs or inlaid with coins form a rich display. The museum reopens in 1994 after major restoration. *Permanenten, Nordahl Bruns Gate 9, tel. 55/32–51–08.*

Follow Christies Gate along the park and turn left to reach the **Stenersen Collection,** which concentrates on Norwegian art since the mid-18th century but also houses an impressive collection of modern art, including works by Max Ernst, Paul Klee, Vassily Kandinsky, and Joan Miró, as well as Edvard Munch. *Rasmus Meyers allé, tel. 55/32–14–60. Admission: NKr15 adults, NKr8 children. Open May 15–Sept. 15, Mon.–Sat. 11–4, Sun. noon–3; Sept. 16–May 14, Tues.–Sun. noon–3.*

Just beyond is **Rasmus Meyers Samlinger** (collections). Meyer, a businessman who lived from 1858 to 1916, assembled a superb collection, with many names that are famous today but were unknown when he acquired them. You'll see the best Munchs outside Oslo, as well as major works by Scandinavian impressionists. The gallery also hosts summertime Grieg concerts. *Rasmus Meyers allé 7, tel. 55/97–80–00. Admission: NKr15 adults, NKr8 children. Open May 15–Sept. 15, Mon.–Sat. 11–4, Sun. noon–3; Sept. 16–May 14, Tues.–Sun., noon–3.*

Next is **Grieghallen** (the concert hall), named for the city's famous son, composer Edvard Grieg (1843–1907). Built in 1978, this home of the Bergen Philharmonic Orchestra is a conspicuous slab of glass and concrete, but the acoustics are marvelous. It is the stage for the annual International Music Festival.

Tour 3: Troldhaugen and Fantoft

Follow Route 1 (Nesttun/Voss) out of town about 5 kilometers (3 miles). Composer Edvard Grieg began his musical career under the tutelage of his mother, then went on to study music in Leipzig and Denmark, where he met his wife Nina, a Danish soprano. Even in his early compositions, his own unusual chord progressions fused with elements of Norwegian folk music.

Norway and its landscape were always an inspiration to him, and nowhere is this more clear than at his villa, **Troldhaugen** (Troll Hill) by Nordåsvannet, where he and Nina lived from about 1885. An enchanting white clapboard house, with restrained green gingerbread trim, it served as a salon and gathering place for many Scandinavian artists, and brims with paintings, prints, and memorabilia. On Grieg's desk you'll see a small red troll—which, it is said, he religiously bid good night before he went to sleep. The house also contains his Steinway piano, which is still used for special concerts. Behind the grounds, at the edge of the fjord, you'll find a sheer rock face that was blasted open to provide a burial place for the couple. In 1985 **Troldsalen** (Troll Hall), which can seat 200 people, was built for concerts. *Tel. 55/91–17–91. Admission: NKr15 adults, NKr8 children. Open May 2–Oct. 1, daily 9:30–5:30.*

⑮ On the return trip, visit **Fantoft Stavkirke** (Stave Church), which was completely rebuilt after a fire in 1992. It was originally built in the early 12th century in Sognefjord but was later moved to its present site. Stave churches are unique to Norway, a sort of first step, spiritually and architecturally, into Christianity, without complete relinquishment of pagan beliefs. They also parallel Viking ships, as they are built of strips of wood laid edge to edge rather than in log-cabin style. Peaked with what appears to be Oriental decoration, the Fantoft church is pure black, the result of ancient pitch waterproofing. You'll also see a hole at one end of the church that was used by lepers, who watched the service from outside. *Paradis, tel. 55/ 28–07–10. Admission: NKr10. Open May 15–Sept. 15, daily 10:30–1:30 and 2:20–5:30.*

Tour 4: Lysøen

Ole Bull, not as well known as some of Norway's other cultural luminaries, was a virtuoso violinist and patron of visionary dimension. In 1850, after failing to establish a "New Norwegian Theater" in America, he founded the National Theater in Norway. He then chose the young, unknown playwright Henrik Ibsen to write full-time for the theater and later encouraged and promoted another neophyte—15-year-old Edvard Grieg.

⑯ Getting to his villa, **Lysøen,** is a trek, but it's worth the effort. Take Route 1 or Route 553 to Fana, over Fanafjell to Sørestraumen. Follow signs to Buena Kai. The ferry, *Ole Bull,* leaves on the hour (Mon.–Sat. noon–3 and Sun. 11–4; last ferry leaves Lysøen Mon.–Sat. 4, Sun. 5; return fare is NKr30 adults, NKr15 children).

This Victorian dream castle, built in 1873, complete with an onion dome, gingerbread gables, curved staircase, and cutwork trim just about everywhere, has to be seen to be believed. Inside, the music room is a frenzy of filigree carving, fretwork, braided and twisted columns, and gables with intricate openwork in the supports, all done in knotty pine. Bull's descendants donated the house to the national preservation trust in 1973. *Tel. 56/30–90–77. Admission: NKr20 adults, NKr5 children. Open May 19–Aug. 29, Mon.–Sat. noon–4, Sun. 11–5.*

What to See and Do with Children

Akvariet (the aquarium) has 50 tanks with a wide variety of fish, but the main attractions are penguins—several kinds, one of which has a platinum feather "hairdo," strangely appropriate in this land of blonds. There are also several seals. It's on Nordnes Peninsula, a 15-minute walk from downtown, or take bus No. 4. *Nordnes, tel. 55/32–04–52. Admission: Nkr30 adults, Nkr15 children. Open May–Sept., daily 9–8; Oct.– Apr., daily 10–6. Feeding times: 11, 2, and 6.*

Off the Beaten Track

Drum and crossbow drill teams are unique to Bergen. **Buekorpsmuseet** (the Crossbow Drill Corps Museum) is at "Muren," built in 1562. The exhibits include medals, banners, drums, and pictures. *Wall Gate. Admission free. Consult the tourist office for opening times, which vary.*

Shopping

Sundt City (Torgalmenningen 14, tel. 56/38–80–20) and **Kløverhuset** (Strandkaien 10, tel. 55/32–17–20) are traditional **department stores** with a wide selection of Norwegian sweaters and gifts. **Galleriet,** on Torgalmenningen, and **Bystasjonen,** by the bus terminal, are downtown **malls** with small shops. Shops specializing in Norwegian **crafts** are either near Torgalmenningen, on Bryggen, or just behind it. **Antiques** shops are concentrated in the area around Fløybanen.

Sports and Outdoor Activities

Below is a sampling of activities for the Bergen area, but outdoors lovers should be aware that the city is within easy reach of the Hardangervidda, the country's great plateau, which offers limitless outdoor possibilities (*see* Sports and Outdoor Activities in Mountains and Valleys of the Interior, *below*).

Fishing The **Bergen Angling Association** (Fosswinckelsgt. 37, tel. 55/ 32–11–64, closed July) can provide tips and information on permits. Among the many charters in the area, the *Fiskestrilen* (tel. 56/33-75–00 or 56/33–87–40) offers evening fishing tours from Glesvaer on the island of Sotra, about an hour's drive from Bergen, where you can catch coal fish, cod, mackerel, or haddock. On the sail home, they'll cook part of the catch.

Golf There is a nine-hole golf course at Åstveit (tel. 55/18–20–77), 15 minutes north of the city on E16. Or you can take the Åsane bus from the bus station.

Hiking Take the funicular up **Fløyen,** and minutes later you'll be in the midst of a forest. For a simple map of the mountain, ask at the tourist information office for the cartoon **"Gledeskartet"** map, which outlines 1.5- to 5-kilometer (1- to 3-mile) hikes. **Mount Ulriken** is also popular with walkers and can be best reached near the Montana Youth Hostel (bus No. 4). Maps of the many walking-tour opportunities around Bergen are available from bookstores and from **Bergens Turlag** (touring club; Tverrgata 2–4, 5017-Bergen, tel. 55/32-22-30), which arranges hikes and maintains cabins for hikers.

The archipelago to the west of Bergen also offers many hiking options, ranging from the simple path between Morland and Fjell to the more rugged mountain climb at Haganes. For details, contact the Sund Cultural Office (tel. 56/33–75–00).

Skiing When there is snow on the ground, you can take the funicular up to the mountains for nearby cross-country skiing. Otherwise, Bergen is close to the major skiing center of Voss (*see* Sports under Central Fjord Country, *below*).

Yachting The **Bergen Yachting Club** (55/22–65–45) has its harbor at Hjellestad, about a half-hour bus ride from the city bus station. If you want to do more than ogle the boats, however, the 100-year-old Hardanger yacht, *Mathilde* (Stiftinga Hardangerjekt, Box 46, N–5601 Nordheimsund, tel. 56/55–22–77), with the world's largest authentic yacht rigging, does both one- and several-day trips, as well as coastal safaris.

Dining

Among the most characteristic of Bergen dishes is a fresh, perfectly poached, whole salmon, served with new potatoes and parsley-butter sauce. Then again, stroll among the stalls at Fisketorvet (the fish market), and you can munch bagsful of pink shrimp, heart-shaped fish cakes, and round buns topped with salmon—a typical Bergen repast, without the typical bill. Top it off with another local specialty, a *skillingsbolle*, a big cinnamon roll, sometimes with a custard center, but most authentic without.

Highly recommended restaurants are indicated by a star ★.

Very Expensive

Bellevue. Established in 1899, this restaurant is on a hill overlooking the city; it has an elegant and formal dining room, with 18th-century-style furnishings. Poached salmon in the traditional manner is a specialty, along with fillet of venison with chanterelle mushrooms, but more modern dishes are also on the menu. There's a limited choice at lunch. In good weather the patio is open for less formal meals. *Bellevuebakken 9, tel. 55/31–02–40. Reservations required. Jacket and tie required. AE, DC, MC, V. Closed weekends.*

Lucullus. Although the decor seems a bit out of kilter—modern art matched with lace doilies and boardroom chairs—the food in this restaurant is always good. Sautéed monkfish with lobster sauce and rack of reindeer with blueberry sauce are two of many superb dishes. *Hotel Neptun, Walckendorfsgt. 8, tel. 55/90–10–00. Reservations required. Jacket and tie required. AE, DC, MC, V. No lunch. Closed Sun.*

Expensive

Fiskekrogen. It's right on Fisketorvet, and in good weather you can sit outside for lunch. The fish soup is a meal in itself, and the appetizer plate is a sampling of specialties, from smoked shrimp to marinated moose. The fish symphony features two or three kinds of fish with lobster sauce and a garnish of shellfish. Meat lovers should try the grilled moose or venison rib-eye steak with herb butter. *Zachariasbryggen, Fisketorvet, tel. 55/31–75–66. Reservations required. Dress: casual. AE, DC, MC, V. No lunch Sept. 16–Apr.*

To Kokker. The name means "two cooks," and that's what there are. It's on Bryggen, in a 300-year-old building complete with crooked floors. Try the roasted reindeer or the marinated salmon. Desserts feature local fruit. *Enhjørningsgården, tel. 55/32–28–16. Reservations required. Dress: casual but neat. AE, DC, MC, V. No lunch. Closed Sun.*

Moderate

Bryggestuen & Bryggeloftet. It's always full, upstairs and down. The menu's the same in both places, but only the first floor is authentically old. Poached halibut served with boiled potatoes and cucumber salad, a traditional favorite, is the specialty, but there's also sautéed ocean catfish with mushrooms and shrimp, and grilled lamb fillet. *Bryggen 11, tel. 55/31–06–30. Reservations advised. Dress: casual. AE, DC, MC, V.*

Munkestuen Cafe. With its five tables and red-and-white-check tablecloths this mom-and-pop place looks more Italian than Norwegian, but locals regard it as a hometown legend—make reservations as soon as you get into town. Try the monkfish with hollandaise sauce or the fillet of roe deer with morels. *Klostergaten 12, tel. 55/90–21–49. Reservations required. Dress: casual. AE, DC, MC, V. Closed Sat. and 3 weeks in July. No lunch.*

Inexpensive

Augusta and **Augustus.** You can't beat these two cafeterias under the same management for lunch or for cake and coffee in the afternoon. Vegetarians will be impressed by the number of salads and quiches, in addition to pâté and open-face sandwiches. *Augusta: C. Sundtsgt. 24, tel. 55/23–00–25. No reservations. Dress: casual. Augustus: Galleriet, tel. 55/32–35–25. No reservations. Dress: casual. No credit cards.*

Banco Rotto. The fanciest café in town used to be a bank, and appropriately for Norway—a country where a cocktail costs a fortune—the liquor is still kept in the safe. Depending upon the time of day, it changes its identity from café to restaurant to piano bar; it functions best at either end—as a lunch café in the afternoon and as an evening spot with music and dancing on Friday and Saturday nights. *Vågsalmenning 16, tel. 55/32–75–20. No reservations. Dress: casual. AE, DC, MC, V.*

Børskafe. What began as a beer hall in 1894 is now more of a pub, with hearty homemade food at reasonable prices. The corned beef with potato dumplings is served only on Thursday and Friday, while meat cakes with stewed peas and fried flounder plus the usual open-face sandwiches are always on the menu. *Strandgt. 15, tel. 55/32–47–19. No reservations. Dress: casual. No credit cards.*

Lodging

From June 20 through August 10, special summer double-room rates are available in 21 Bergen hotels; rooms can only be reserved 48 hours in advance. In the winter, weekend specials are often a fraction of the weekday rates, which are geared for business travelers. All rates include breakfast. The tourist information office will assist in finding accommodations in hotels, guest houses, or private houses.

Highly recommended hotels are indicated by a star ★.

Moderate–Very Expensive

Hotel Admiral. This dockside warehouse from 1906, right on the water across Vågen from Bryggen, was converted into a hotel in 1987. The building is geometric Art Nouveau, and although the small rooms are ordinary, the larger rooms overlooking the harbor have some of the best nighttime views in town. The harborside restaurant, Emily, has a small but good buffet table. *C. Sundts Gate 9–13, 5004, tel. 55/32–47–30, fax 55/23–30–92. 95 rooms with bath or shower, 12 suites. Facilities: restaurant, bar. AE, DC, MC, V.*

Hotel Norge. Other hotels come and go, but the Norge stays. It's a traditional luxury hotel in the center of town, right by the park. The architecture is standard modern, with large rooms.

Ole Bulls pl. 4, 5012, tel. 55/21–01–00, fax 55/21–02–99. 348 rooms with bath, 12 suites. Facilities: 4 restaurants, 2 bars, nightclub, pool, fitness center, conference center, shops. AE, DC, MC, V.

SAS Royal Hotel Bryggen. The hotel is behind the famous buildings at Bryggen, one story taller, with the same width and roof pitch, and very well designed. Finished in 1982, the smallish guest rooms, with their subdued woven spreads and dark wood beds, are beginning to look dated. More expensive rooms, on the top floor, have been refurbished. *Bryggen, 5003, tel. 55/54–30–00, fax 55/32–48–08. 267 rooms with bath, 7 suites. Facilities: 2 restaurants, 2 bars, nightclub, pool, fitness center, conference center. AE, DC, MC, V.*

Inexpensive–Moderate

Augustin Hotel. This small, family-run hotel, one block from the harbor, is just off the main pedestrian shopping street. The rooms are small but newly refurbished, and some overlook the harbor. The first-floor bistro offers simple meals, and the coffee shop, Augusta (*see* Dining, *above*), serves wonderful cakes. *C. Sundtsgate 24, 5004, tel. 55/23–00–25, fax 55/23–31–30. 38 rooms with shower. Facilities: 2 restaurants, conference room. AE, DC, MC, V.*

Hotell Dreggen. Restored in 1990, this hotel is between Bergenshus Fortress and Bryggen Museum. It's basically a bed-and-breakfast, but other meals can be arranged. Virtually every room is a different size or shape, but all are furnished in light wood and pale-colored textiles. *Sandbrugt. 3, 5003, tel. 55/31–61–55, fax 55/31–54–23. 21 rooms with bath. Facilities: restaurant, bar, conference room. AE, DC, MC, V.*

Hotel Park Pension. Near the university, this small family-run hotel is in a well-kept Victorian building. Both the public rooms and the guest rooms are furnished with antiques. It's a 10-minute walk from downtown. *Harald Hårfagres Gate 35, 5000, tel. 55/32–09–60, fax 55/31–03–34. 21 rooms with bath. Facilities: breakfast room, conference room. AE, V.*

Inexpensive

Fantoft Sommerhotell. This student dorm, 6 kilometers (3½ miles) from downtown, becomes a hotel from May 20 to August 20. Family rooms are available. Accommodation is simple but adequate. Take a bus from gate No. 18, 19, or 20 to Fantoft. *5036 Fantoft, tel. 55/27–60–10, fax 55/27–60–30. 72 rooms with shower. Facilities: restaurant. AE, DC, MC, V.*

The Arts and Nightlife

The Arts

Bergen is known for its **Festspillene** (International Music Festival), held each year during the last week of May and the beginning of June. It features famous names in classical music, jazz, ballet, the arts, and theater. Tickets are available from the Festival Office at **Grieghallen** (Lars Hillesgt. 3, 5015, tel. 55/31–09–54).

During the summer, twice a week, the **Bjorgvin folk dance group** performs a one-hour program of traditional dances and music from rural Norway at Bryggens Museum. Tickets are sold at the tourist information center and at the door. *Bryggen, tel. 55/24–89–29. Cost: NKr70. Performances June 8–mid-Aug., Tues. and Thurs. 8:30.*

A more extensive program, **Fana Folklore,** is offered in an evening of folklore, with traditional wedding food, dances, and folk music, plus a concert, at the 800-year-old Fana Church. *A/S Kunst (the Art Association) Torgalmenning 9, tel. 55/91–52–40. Admission: NKr160 (includes dinner). June 5–Aug. 31., Mon., Tues., Thurs., and Fri.*

Concerts are held at **Troldhaugen,** home of composer Edvard Grieg (*see* Tour 3, *above*), all summer. Tickets are sold at the tourist information center or at the door. Performances are given June 26–August 29, Wednesday and Sunday at 7:30; and September 1–October 15, Sunday at 1.

Nightlife

Most nightlife centers around the harbor area. **Zachariasbryggen** is a restaurant and entertainment complex right on the water. **Kjøbmandsstuen** is a piano bar with a crowd on weekends. **Engelen** (The Angel) at the SAS Royal Hotel attracts a mixed weekend crowd when it blasts hip-hop, funk, and rock. The **Hotel Norge** piano bar and disco are more low-key, with an older crowd. **Dickens** (8–10 Ole Bulls Plads, tel. 55/90–07–60), across from the Hotel Norge, is a relaxed meeting place for an afternoon or evening drink. **Maxime** (tel. 55/90–07–70) is a packed weekend disco, currently fashionable with the ripped-jean crowd. The complete opposite, **Wessel Stuen,** also on Ole Bull Plads (tel. 55/90–08–20) is a cozy place where you'll find students and the local intelligentsia. **Holbergstuen** (Torgalm. 6, tel. 55/31–80–15) is similar but often attracts a crowd of local sages who hold court.

Bergensers love jazz, and **Bergen Jazz Festival** (Georgernes Verft 3, N–5011 Bergen, tel. 55/32–09–76) is held here during the third week of August. During the winter, **Bergen Jazz Forum** (same address) is *the* place, but it's closed for much of the summer. For rock, **Hulen** (The Cave; Olav Ryesvei 47, tel. 55/32–32–87) has live music on weekends.

Bergen has an active gay community with clubs and planned events. **Homofil Bevegelse** (Gay Movement, Nygårdsgt. 2A, tel. 55/31–21–39) is open Sunday 2–8 PM. **Café Finken** (same address, tel. 55/31–21–39) is open daily until 1 AM.

6 Mountains and Valleys of the Interior

American Express offers Travelers Cheques built for two.

American Express® Cheques *for Two*. The first Travelers Cheques that allow either of you to use them because both of you have signed them. And only one of you needs to be present to purchase them.

Cheques *for Two* are accepted anywhere regular American Express Travelers Cheques are, which is just about everywhere. So stop by your bank, AAA* or any American Express Travel Service Office and ask for Cheques *for Two*.

The central portion of Norway lies in the shadow of the famed fjords but doesn't lack majestic scenery. A land of wide-open vistas and deep forests, it's veined with swift-flowing streams and scattered with peaceful lakes—a natural setting so powerful and silent that a few generations ago, trolls were the only reasonable explanation for what lurked in, or for that matter plodded through, the shadows. These legendary creatures, serious Norwegians explain, boast several heads, a couple of noses (used to stir their porridge of course), and can grow to the size of a village. Fortunately for humans, however, they turn to stone in sunlight.

The tourist board aptly calls the triangle between Oppland and Hedmark counties, south to Lillehammer (and including Peer Gynt country, in Jotunheimen), Troll Park. The otherworldly quality of oblique northern light against wildflower-covered hills has inspired centuries of folk tales, and artists from Wagner to Ibsen, who was awarded a government grant to scour the land for these very stories. Even today, locals claim he applied for the grant just to have the opportunity to hike the hills.

The southern part of the interior, around Hardangervidda, is prime vacation land for wilderness sports lovers, with fishing, canoeing, rafting, hiking, and horseback riding over the plateau in the summer, and skiing, particularly on the slopes of Geilo, in winter. Northward, the land turns to rolling hills and leafy forests, and the principal town, Lillehammer, attracts skiers from around the world to its slopes and trails; in 1994 it hosts the Winter Olympics. At the northern end of the region is the copper-mining town of Røros, which is on UNESCO's World Heritage List—a bucolic little town that's changed little over the past 100 years.

Essential Information

Important Addresses and Numbers

Tourist Information The main tourist offices of the region are in **Geilo** (tel. 62/98–63–00); **Hamar** (Vikingskipet, Olympia Hall, tel. 62/51–02–17 or 62/51–02–25); **Kongsberg** (Storgt. 35, tel. 32/73–50–00); **Lillehammer** (Lilletorget, tel. 61/25–92–99); **Lom** (tel. 61/21–12–86); **Notodden** (tel. 35/01–20–22); **Øyer** (tel. 61/27–79–50); **Rjukan** (Torget 2, tel. 35/09–12–90); **Røros** (Bergmannspl., tel. 72/49–17–22); and **Skien** (Reiselivets Hus, N. Hjellegt. 18, tel. 35/53–49–80).

Arriving and Departing by Car, Train, and Bus

By Car On Route E18 from Oslo, the drive southeast to Kongsberg (84 kilometers/52 miles) takes a little more than an hour. The wide, two-lane Route E6 north from Oslo passes through Hamar and Lillehammer. Route 3 follows Østerdalen (the eastern valley) from Oslo. Route 30 at Tynset leads to Røros and E6 on to Trondheim, 156 kilometers (97 miles) farther north.

By Train The train from Oslo S to Kongsberg takes 1 hour and 25 minutes. There are good train connections between Oslo and the major interior towns to the north.

By Bus The many bus lines that serve the region are coordinated through Nor-Way Bussekspress in Oslo (Bussterminalen, Galleri Oslo, tel. 22/17–52–90, fax 22/17–59–22).

Getting Around

By Car Roads in the southern part of the interior region are open and flat, while those to the north become increasingly hilly and twisty as the terrain roughens into the central mountains. E18 and Routes 11 and 7 are the chief routes of the south; the northern end of the region is threaded by E16, E6, and Routes 51 and 3. Don't exceed the speed limit: Particularly in the area of Vinstra and Otta, you'll see high-tech markers at the roadside that are actually cameras. Exceed the speed limit and you'll receive a ticket in the mail.

By Train The only train service in the southern part of the region is the Oslo–Stavanger line (via Kristiansand). The midregion is served by the Oslo–Bergen line, which is as much an attraction as a means of transportation. The northern part is served by the Oslo–Trondheim line and two other lines.

By Bus Buses in the region rarely run more than twice a day, so get a comprehensive schedule from the tourist office or Nor-Way Bussekspress and plan ahead. There are good bus connections between Kongsberg and Notodden, Heddal, and Rjukan.

Exploring Mountains and Valleys of the Interior

Numbers in the margin correspond to points of interest on the Mountains and Valleys of the Interior map.

Tour 1: Central Norway

The center of Norway is outdoor country for Norwegians and northern Europeans, who come to ski, hike, dogsled and, in recent years, river raft.

① **Geilo,** population 2,700, is dead-center between Bergen and Oslo. The country's most popular winter resort, it often draws more than a million visitors a year to its alpine slopes and cross-country trails; many people ski directly from their hotels and cabins. Recently Geilo has become a popular summer destination, with fishing, boating, hiking, and riding—although, admittedly, it still looks like a winter resort minus the snow. Plan ahead if you plan to visit at Easter, when Norwegians flock there for a final ski weekend.

② Geilo is the gateway to **Hardangervidda,** Europe's largest mountain plateau and Norway's biggest national park—10,000 square kilometers of unique scenery, with the largest herd of wild reindeer in Europe, and home to many birds and animals on the endangered list. It also has rich and varied flora, about 450 different species. Touring the plateau, either on horseback or on foot, you can find a trail for any level of proficiency, and along the trails, the Norwegian Touring Association (DNT) has built cabins.

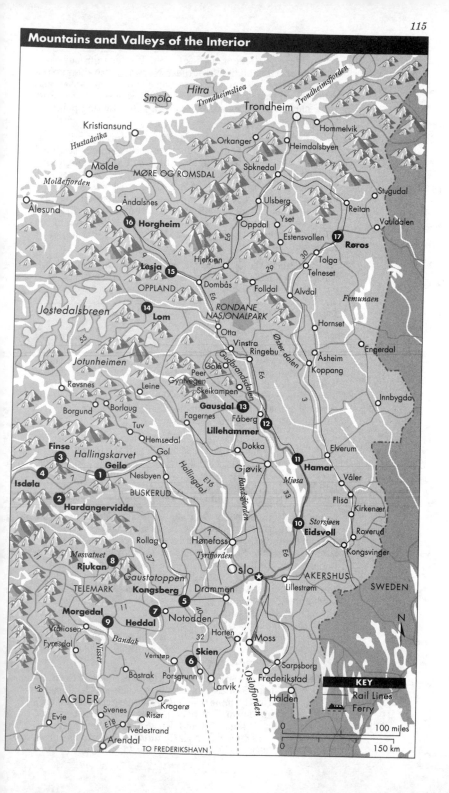

❸ The western settlement of **Finse** (on the Bergen railroad) is one of the most frigid places in southern Norway, with snow on the ground as late as August. Here polar explorers Nansen and Scott tested their equipment and the snow scenes in the *Star Wars* movies were filmed. It, too, is a good starting point for tours of Hardangervidda.

❹ At the western end of the vidda, 72 kilometers (44 miles) beyond Geilo, is **Isdøla**, at the junction of the 1-kilometer (0.62 miles, but it seems like 10) road to Fossli and Vøringfossen (Vøring Falls), which has a 141-meter (464-foot) vertical drop. The road down to the valley of Måbødalen was blasted into the mountain early in the century; it has been improved steadily, and now most of the difficult parts are tunneled. Cyclists and hikers can go down the side of the mountain to the base of the falls on the original trail, with 124 swings and 1,300 steps—it takes about 30 minutes—but it's not for amateurs.

At the base is the innermost arm of the **Hardangerfjord.** Although it's not as dramatic as some of the other fjords, it is pastoral, with royal-blue water and lush apple orchards.

Tour 2: Historic Kongsberg and Telemark

Kongsberg, Norway's first industrial town, rose to prominence because of the discovery there of silver in its purest form. The town of Rjukan was the site of the country's entrance into modern technology, with hydroelectric power. Telemark is the birthplace of skiing as we know it today, as well as the birthplace of many ancestors to Norwegian-Americans, for the poor farmers of the region were among the first to emigrate to the United States during the 19th century.

❺ **Kongsberg,** with 20,000 people, was Norway's silver town for more than 300 years. King Christian IV saw the town's natural potential when he discovered that a cow's horn had rubbed moss off a stone—to expose silver. Thereupon, the Danish builder king began construction of the town. The mines are now closed, but the Royal Mint is still going strong.

Norsk Bergverksmuseum (Norwegian Mining Museum) in the old smelting works, documents the development of silver mining and exhibits the pure silver along with gold, emeralds, and rubies from other Norwegian mines. The Royal Mint Museum, in the same building, is a treasure trove for coin collectors, with a nearly complete assemblage of Norwegian coins. Children can pan for silver all summer. *Hyttegt. 3, tel. 32/73–12–75. Admission: NKr25 adults, NKr15 children, NKr20 senior citizens. Open May 18–June 30, Aug. 16–31, daily 10–4; July 1– Aug. 15, weekdays 10–6, weekends 10–4; Sept. 1–30, daily noon–4; Oct. 1–May 17, Sun. noon–4. Guided tours of Underberget, with dinner: NKr220. Only for those 16 and older. Open July–mid-Aug. Tues.–Thurs. at 5.*

Gruvene (the Mines) are 8 kilometers (5 miles) outside town, toward Notodden. Guided mine tours include a 2.3-kilometer (1.4-mile) ride on the mine train into Kongensgruve (the King's mine) and a ride on the first personnel elevator. The temperature in the mine is about 7°C (43°F), so dress accordingly. *Tel. 35/02–02–50. Admission: NKr40 adults, NKr20 children, NKr30 senior citizens. Tours June–Aug. 15, daily 11, 12:30, 2* *and 3:30; May 18–31 and Aug. 16–31, daily 11, 12:30, 2; Sept., Sun. 2.*

Kongsberg Kirke (church), finished in 1761, was built during the heyday of the silver mines, with an impressive gilded Baroque altar, organ, and pulpit all on one wall. It seats 3,000. The royal box and the galleries separated the gentry and mineowners from the workers. *Admission: NKr10 adults, NKr5, children. Open May 18–Aug. 31, guided tours lasting 45 min. on the hour, weekdays 10–12, Sat. 10–1. Sun. services at 11 with tours afterward until 1:30. Organ concerts Tues. and Fri. at 11 during July.*

Time Out   **Peckels Resept** (Peckels gt. 12), in the center of town, is a café with personality. It serves sandwiches and hot dishes, along with delicious cakes for lunch.

6 South of Kongsberg on Routes 40 and 32 is **Skien,** the capital of the Telemark region. This town of 48,000 is best known as the birthplace of playwright Henrik Ibsen. **Fylkesmuseet** (the county museum), a manor house from 1780, has a collection of Ibsen memorabilia, including his study and bedroom and the "blue salon" from his Oslo flat (other interiors are at the Norsk Folkmuseum in Oslo). The museum also has a display of Telemark-style folk art, including rose painting and wood carving. *Øvregt. 41, tel. 35/52–35–94. Admission: NKr15 adults, NKr10 children. Garden open mid-May–Sept., daily 10–8. Museum open mid-May–Sept., daily 10–6.*

Venstøp, 5 kilometers (3 miles) northwest of the city, looks just as it did when the Ibsen family lived there from 1835 to 1843. The attic was a setting in *The Wild Duck.* The house is part of Skien's county museum. *Tel. 35/52–35–94. Admission: NKr15 adults, NKr10 children. Open mid-May–Sept., daily 10–6.*

7 **Heddal,** site of Norway's largest stave church, is 35 kilometers (20 miles) west of Kongsberg. The church dates from the middle of the 13th century and has exceptional animal-style ornament, along with grotesque human heads, on the portals. *Tel. 33/02–02–50. Admission: NKr15. Open June 21–Aug. 20, Mon.–Sat. 9–7, Sun. 1–7; May 15–June 20, Aug. 21–Sept. 20, 9–7, Sun. 1–5. Sun. services at 11. July 1–Aug. 10, organ concerts Tues. and Fri. at 11.*

Route 37 northwest from Kongsberg to Rjukan passes the 1,922-meter (6,200-foot) **Gaustatoppen Mountain,** a looming, snow-streaked table of rock popular with hikers. The town of **8** **Rjukan** may not ring a bell, but mention "heavy water," and anyone who lived through World War II or saw the film *The Heroes of Telemark* knows about the sabotage of the "heavy water" factory there, which thwarted German efforts to develop an atomic bomb. Heavy water was produced as a by-product in the manufacture of fertilizer at **Vemork,** 6 kilometers (4 miles) west of town, where a museum has been built. Exhibits document both the development of hydroelectric power and the World War II events. The first Saturday in July, the work of the saboteurs is commemorated, but their 8-kilometer (5-mile) path, starting at Rjukan Fjellstue (mountain lodge) and finishing at the museum, is marked and can be followed at any time. *Industriarbeidermuseet Vemork, tel. 35/06–51–53. Admission: NKr35 adults, NKr20 children. Open June 15–Aug. 15,* *daily 10–6; May 1–June 14, daily 10–4; Aug. 15–Sept. 30, weekdays 10–4, weekends 10–6; Oct. 1–31, weekends 11–4.*

Rjukan's history actually began in the decade between 1907 and 1916, when the population grew from a few hundred to 10,000 because of a different kind of water, hydroelectric power. Norsk Hydro, one of Norway's largest industries, which uses hydroelectric power to manufacture chemicals and fertilizer, was started here. It is also the site of northern Europe's first cable car, **Krossobanen,** built in 1928 by Hydro to transport people to the top of the mountain, where the sun shone year-round. *Admission: NKr20 adults, one-way, NKr10 children, NKr15 senior citizens. Open June 30–Aug. 25, daily 10–7; May 1–June 30 and Aug. 26–Sept. 30, daily 10–5; Oct. 1–Apr. 1, Fri.–Sun. 10–4.*

⑨ Farther into the heart of Telemark is **Morgedal,** the birthplace of modern skiing, thanks to a persistent Sondre Nordheim, who, in the 19th century, attached boards to his boots and practiced jumping from his roof. In 1868, after revamping his skis and bindings, he took off for a 185-kilometer (115-mile) trek to Oslo just to prove it could be done. A hundred years ago, skiers used one long pole, held diagonally, much like high wire artists. Eventually the use of two short poles became widespread, although purists feel that the one-pole version is the "authentic" way to ski. Traditional Telemark skiing is now the rage in Norway, though the trend was begun in the United States.

The **Bjaaland Museum** in Morgedal is named for Olav Bjaaland, who was chosen for Amundsen's expedition to Antarctica because he could ski in an absolutely straight line. The museum collections illustrate the development of Telemark skiing. Also on display are Bjaaland's streamlined polar sled and his photographs of the expedition. *Opposite Morgedal Turisthotell, tel. 036/54–156. Admission: NKr10 adults, NKr5 children. Open June–Aug., daily 10–5.*

Tour 3: Gudbrandsdal

The Gudbrandsdal (Gudbrand's valley) is one of Norway's longest, extending from Lake Mjøsa, north of Oslo, diagonally across the country to Åndalsnes. At the base of the lake is **Eidsvoll,** where Norway's constitution was signed on May 17, 1814. Most visitors come to the region for the beautiful scenery and the outdoor activities.

⑪ E6 follows the lake halfway to **Hamar.** During the Middle Ages, Hamar was the seat of a bishopric, and part of the cathedral wall, with four Romanesque arches, remains the symbol of the city. Oslo University has sponsored digs around the cathedral precinct just outside town that have turned up thousands of artifacts, which are displayed nearby at **Hedmarkmuseet og Domkirkeodden** (the Hedmark Museum and Cathedral ruins). *Hedmarkmuseet and Domkirkeodden, tel. 62/53–11–63. Admission: NKr30 adults, NKr10 children. Open June 15–Aug. 18, daily 10–6; May 20–June 14, Aug. 19–Sept. 8, daily 10–4. Utvandrermuseum, tel. 62/52–13–04. Open weekdays 8:30–3:30.*

⑫ The winter-sport center of **Lillehammer,** with 23,000 inhabitants, is next. As host for the 1994 Winter Olympics, the small town has built a massive arena blown out of the interior of a mountain and the world's largest indoor ice rink—designed to look like an upside-down Viking ship—in addition to other venues and accommodations. However, long-term efficiency and planning are keeping expansion surprisingly minimal—ensuring that the town will not be left in Olympic obsolescence. After the games, many of the buildings for the foreign media will be turned over to the local university, and one-third of the athletes' quarters will be transported to Tromsø to be used as housing. Extra beds for 7,000 visitors are located in private accommodations, and transportation to and from Oslo, where many visitors are staying is being increased (cars are not being allowed in Lillehammer). If you plan to attend, make your reservations as early as possible.

The **Lillehammer Olympic Information Center** outlines preparations for the big event through videos and exhibits that also describe Norway's place in international, especially winter, sports. There's a boutique with Olympic clothing and souvenirs, and a cafeteria. *Lillehammer Olympiske Informasjonssenter. Elevgt. 19, tel. 61/27-19-00, fax 61/27-19-50. Admission free. Open Mon.-Sat. 10-8, Sun. 12-8.*

Kulturhuset Banken (the Old Bank), a magnificent, century-old building, is the main venue for cultural events during the Olympics (and later on). It is decorated with both contemporary and turn-of-the-century art. Check out the murals on the ceiling of the ceremonial hall. *Kirkegt. 41, tel. 61/26-68-10. Tours by prior arrangement. Café open weekdays 10-9, Sun. 1-9.*

The new **Olympiaparken** (Olympic Park) includes the Lysgårdsbakkene ski jumping arena, where the Winter Olympics' opening and closing ceremonies are held. From the tower you can see the entire town. Also in the park are **Håkon Hallen,** used for ice hockey, and the **Birkebeineren Stadion** (ski stadium), which holds cross-country and biathlon events.

A highlight of Lillehammer's ski year is the Birkebeiner cross-country ski race, which commemorates the trek of two warriors, whose legs were wrapped in birchbark (hence *birkebeiner*—birch legs), across the mountains from Lillehammer to Østerdalen in 1205 carrying the 18-month-old prince Håkon Håkonsson away from his enemies. The race attracts 6,000 entrants annually. Cartoon figures of Viking children representing Håkon on skis and his aunt Kristin (on ice skates) have been created as official mascots for the games.

Lillehammer claims fame as a cultural center as well. Sigrid Undset, who won the Nobel Prize in literature, lived in the town for 30 years. It is also the site of **Maihaugen,** Norway's oldest (and, according to some, Scandinavia's largest) open-air museum, founded in 1887. The massive collection was begun by Anders Sandvik, an itinerant dentist who accepted folksy odds and ends—and eventually entire buildings—from the people of Gudbransdalen in exchange for repairing their teeth. Eventually Sandvik turned the collection over to the city of Lillehammer, which provided land for the museum. In addition to more than 130 structures and 50,000 objects from all over Norway, it has a main building with reconstructed artisans' workshops. *Maihaugvn 1, tel. 61/28-89-00. Admission: NKr50 adults, NKr20 children. Open June-Aug., daily 9-6; May, daily 10-4. Ticket includes guided tour.*

Lillehammer is also home to the **Norsk Vegmuseum** (Norwegian Museum of Transport History), a collection of vehicles ranging from the infancy of the horseless carriage to the present. *Hunder, 2638 Fåberg, tel. 61/27–71–10. Admission: NKr25 adults, NKr12 children. Open June 15–Aug. 31, daily 10–6.*

One of the most important art collections in Norway is housed at the **Lillehammer Bys Malerisamling** (Lillehammer Art Museum). In addition to Munch pieces, the gallery has one of the largest collections of works from the national romantic period. *Kirkegt. 71, Stortorget, tel. 61/26–94–44. Admission: NKr30 adults, NKr15 children. Open Tues.–Fri. 11–7, Sat. 11–3.*

🔞 At **Gausdal,** just north of Lillehammer, you can turn onto the scenic, well-marked **Peer Gynt Vegen** (the Peer Gynt Road), named after the real-life person behind Ibsen's character. A feisty fellow, given to tall tales, he is said to have spun yarns about his communing with trolls and riding reindeer backwards. Traveling along the rolling hills sprinkled with old farmhouses and rich with views of the mountains of Rondane, Dovrefjell, and Jotunheimen, the road is only slightly narrower and just 3 kilometers (2 miles) longer than the main route. It passes two major resorts, **Skeikampen/Gausdal** and **Golå/Wadahl,** before rejoining E6 at Vinstra. Between Vinstra and Harpefoss, at the Sødorp Church, you can visit Peer Gynt's stone grave and what is said to be his old farm. Although you can walk the grounds, the 15th-century farm is privately owned.

From Vinstra, the road continues along the great valley of the River Mjøsa, birthplace of Gudbrandsdalsost, a sweet, brown goat cheese. The route offers lovely, rolling views of red farmhouses and lush green fields stretching from the valley to the mountainsides are lovely.

At Otta, Route 15 turns off for the 62-kilometer (38-mile) ride
⑭ to **Lom,** in the middle of **Jotunheimen** national park. It is a picturesque, rustic town, with log cabin architecture, a stave church from 1170, and plenty of decorative rose painting.

Lom Stavkirke (Lom Stave Church), a mixture of old and new construction, is on the main road. The interior, including the pulpit, a large collection of paintings, pews, windows, and the gallery, is Baroque. *Open May 1–Sept. 30, Mon.–Sat. 10–5, Sun. noon–5.*

Upper Gudbrandsdal has breathtaking scenery. The area
⑮ around **Lesja** is trout-fishing country; Lesjaskogvatnet, the lake, has a mouth at either end, so the current changes in the middle. The landscape becomes more dramatic with every mile, as jagged rocks loom up from the river, leaving the tiny settlement of **Marstein** without sun for five months of the year.

⑯ **Horgheim** used to have a gingerbread hotel for elegant early tourists to view **Trollveggen,** the highest overhanging vertical rockface in Europe. Now the tourists have been replaced by expert rock climbers from around the world. Åndalsnes, the end station on the railroad, is the perfect departure point for tours of Central Fjord Country (*see* Chapter 7 *below*).

Tour 4: Røros

At the northern end of the Østerdal, the long valley to the east of Gudbrandsdalen, lies **Røros,** for more than 300 years a company town: Practically everyone who lived there was connected with the copper mines. The last mine in the region closed in 1986 but the town has survived thanks to other industries, including tourism, especially after it was placed on UNESCO's World Heritage List.

The main attraction is the **old town,** with its 250-year-old workers' cottages, slag dumps, and managers' houses, one of which is now City Hall. Descendants of the man who discovered the first copper ore in Røros still live in the oldest of the nearly 100 protected buildings. The tourist office has 75-minute guided tours of this part of town, starting at the information office and ending at the church. *Admission: NKr25 adults, NKr20 senior citizens and students, NKr15 children. Tours: June 1–21 and Aug. 19–Sept. 29, Mon.–Sat. at 11; June 22–Aug. 18, Mon.–Sat. at noon and 3, Sun. at 3. Oct.–May, Sat. at 11.*

The **Røroskirke** (Røros Church), which towers over all the other buildings in the town, is an eight-sided stone structure from 1784, with the mines' symbol on the tower. It can seat 1,600, impressive in a town with a population of only 5,000 today. The pulpit looms above the center of the altar, and seats encircle the top perimeter. Two hundred years ago wealthy locals paid for the privilege of sitting there. *Admission: NKr15 adults, NKr12 senior citizens and students, NKr6 children. Open June 1–21 and Aug. 19–Sept. 29, weekdays 2–4, Sat. 11–1; June 22–Aug. 18, Mon.–Sat. 10–5. Oct.–May, Sat. 11–1.*

Olavsgruva (Olaf's mine), outside town, is now a museum. The guided tour of Olavsgruva takes visitors into the depths of the mine, complete with sound and light effects. Remember to bring warm clothing and good shoes, as the temperature below ground is about 5°C (41°F) year-round. *Rte. 31, tel. 72/41–05–00. Admission: NKr35 adults, NKr25 senior citizens and students, NKr20 children. Guided tours June 1–21 and Aug. 19–Sept. 29, Mon.–Sat. at 1 and 3, Sun. at noon; June 22–Aug. 18, daily at 10:30, noon, 1:30, 3, 4:30, 6. Oct.–May, Sat. at 3.*

Back in town, in the old smelting plant, is **Rørosmuseet** (the Røros Museum), which documents the history of the mines, with working models in one-tenth scale demonstrating the methods used in mining. *Tel. 72/41–05–00. Admission: NKr30 adults, NKr25 senior citizens and students, NKr15 children. Open weekdays 11–3:30, weekends 11–2.*

What to See and Do with Children

Hamar   **Jernbanemuseet** (the Railway Museum) documents the development of rail transportation in Norway, with locomotives and rolling stock on both normal and small-gauge track. *Tertittoget,* NSB's last steam locomotive, gives rides from mid-May to mid-August. *Strandvn. 132, tel. 62/51–31–60. Admission: NKr25 adults, NKr10 children. Open June and Aug., daily 10–4; July, daily 10–6.*

Lillehammer   **Hunderfossen Park,** 13 kilometers (8 miles) north of Lillehammer, has rides and a petting zoo for small children, plus an energy center, with Epcot-influenced exhibits about oil and gas and a five-screen theater for everyone. There's also the world's biggest troll. *2638 Fåberg, tel. 61/27–72–22. Admission: NKr60 adults, NKr50 children and senior citizens. Open early June, daily 10–4; mid-June–mid-Aug., daily 10–5.*

Just beyond Hunderfossen is **Lilleputthammer,** a miniature version of Lillehammer as it looked at the turn of the century, complete with animated figures in period dress. There are also rides, a swimming pool, and a water discothèque. *Øyer Gjestegård, 2636 Øyer, tel. 61/27–73–35. Admission to Lilleputthammer and swimming complex: NKr40. Open June 22–Aug. 18, daily 10–7; swimming complex, daily 11–6.*

Off the Beaten Track

Geilo   About 35 kilometers (21 miles) northeast of Geilo on Route 7 is **Torpo,** site of a stave church dating from the late 12th century. Its colorful painted ceiling is decorated with scenes from the life of St. Margaret. *Open June–Aug., daily 9:30–5:30.*

Hamar   Take a ride on the world's oldest paddleboat, 130-year-old *Skibladner,* also called the "white swan of the Mjøsa," which connects the towns along the lake. The schedule is complicated, with only three stops a week in Eidsvoll and Lillehammer but three stops daily three times a week in Gjøvik. Ask for a schedule from the tourist information or the *Skibladner* office. *Strandgt. 23, 2300 Hamar, tel. 62/52–70–85. June 15–Aug. 10.*

Hell   West of Gudbrandsdalen you will find the lush Espedalen valley and some of Europe's biggest stone caldrons. The sight alone is worth a look, and barbecues are held on Sunday throughout the summer, so you can shamelessly "fry in Hell."

Lillehammer   The composer of Norway's national anthem and the 1903 Nobel Prize winner in literature, Bjørnstjerne Bjørnson lived at **Aulestad,** in Gausdal, 18 kilometers (11 miles) northwest of Lillehammer, from 1875 until he died in 1910. After his wife, Karoline, died in 1934, their house was opened as a museum. *2620 Follebu, tel. 61/22–03–26. Admission: NKr25 adults; NKr15 children and senior citizens. Open July, daily 10–5:30; June, Aug., daily 10–3:30; Sept., daily 11–2:30.*

Skien   From Skien you can take boat tours on the **Telemark waterways,** a combination of canals and natural lakes between Skien and either **Dalen** or **Notodden.** (For trips to Dalen, contact Telemarkreiser, tel. 35/53–03–00; Notodden is served by Telemarksbåtene, 3812 Akkerhaugen, tel. 35/95–82–11, fax 35/95–82–96.) The trip to Dalen takes you through **Ulefoss,** where you can leave the boat and visit neoclassical **Ulefoss Manor,** which dates from 1807. *Ulefoss, tel. 35/94–56–10. Admission: NKr20 adults, NKr10 children. Open June–mid-Aug., Sun–Fri. noon–3.*

Shopping

Geilo   **Brusletto & Co.,** in central Geilo (tel. 32/09–02–00), is a purveyor of high-quality hunting knives with silver-inlaid handles made from burnished metal, walnut, and rosewood. Norwegian men wear these knives, used for hunting and hiking, on their belts—something akin to jewelry.

Lillehammer In Lillehammer, most of the stores along Storgate sell souvenirs. Try **Fakkelmannen** (Elvegt. 17, tel. 61/07–13–55) and **Pins'etten** (Storgt. 79, tel. 61/25–96–50) for pins; **Ingeborg Svarstad's Vevstugu** (Reichweinsgt. 20, tel. 61/25–12–42), **Marihøna** (Storgt. 79, tel. 61/25–99–80), **Husfliden** (Storgt. 47, tel. 61/25–30–03), and **Reidun's Rosemaling og Brukskunst** (Storgt. 84A, tel. 61/25–84–50) for traditional Norwegian sweaters and handicrafts; and **Toves Brukthandel** (Storgt. 81, tel. 61/25–45–11) and **Loftet Bruktklaer** (Storgt. 81) for good bargains in the secondhand market.

Sports and Outdoor Activities

Although skiing, especially cross-country, is the most popular sport in the area, striking scenery, and fresh air make outdoor possibilities endless—summer or winter. The following is only a sampling of what is available. For additional information on outdoor activities, contact the regional tourist boards or **Telemarkreiser** (tel. 35/53–03–00). Some of the organized activities operate only in summer. If you can't reach them, call the local tourist board.

Bicycling You can rent a bike and get local maps through any local tourist board. **Askeladdens Eventrreiser** in Oslo (tel. 22/55–55–66, fax 22/44–20–48) organizes a six-day trip that begins in Finse and heads west to the fjords; most of it is on relatively flat or downhill terrain. Students can make the same trip with the more youth-oriented **Terra Nova** in Bergen (tel. 55/32–23–77, fax 55/32–30–15). For details about a five-day mountain-biking trip across Hardangervidda, contact **Ashland's Adventures** (Huk Aveny 17, 1287 Oslo, tel. 22/55–55–66).

Dog-sledding In **Jotunheimen,** Magnar Aasheim and Kari Steinaug (tel. 61/23–87–50, fax 61/23–87–51) have one of the biggest kennels in Norway, with more than 80 dogs. You can travel as a sled-bound observer or control your own team of four to six dogs, most of which are ridiculously friendly Siberian and Alaskan huskies.

Fishing Fishing throughout the region is excellent, and lakes and rivers are well stocked with trout, grayling, and char. Among the highlights is the Hardanger area, with the Eidefjord, Granvin, and Jondal good choices for salmon and trout. In Kvam, salmon run in the Strandadalselva, Moelven, and Øysteselva (rivers), and trout are plentiful in the mountain lakes. Within the Troll Park, the Gudbrandsdalåen is touted as one of the best-stocked rivers in the country, and the size of Mjøsa trout (locals claim 25 pounds) is legendary. For seasons, permits (you'll need both a national and a local license), and tips, call local tourist boards.

Hiking You can pick up maps and the information-packed **"Peer Gynt"** pamphlet at the tourism office in Vinstra; then hike anywhere along the 50-kilometer (31-mile) circular route, passing Peer's farm, cottages, and monument. The national parks are also a good hiking choice (*see also* National Parks, *below*).

Elsewhere in the area, hiking possibilities are limitless—particularly around Hardanger and Troll Park. Check with the local tourist board for maps and tips. Overnighting in cabins or hotels is particularly popular on the Peer Gynt trail, where you can walk to each of the **Peer Gynt Hotels** (Box 115, N-2647 Hundorp, tel. 61/29-66-88).

In summer you can hike single-file (for safety purposes, in case of calving or cracks) on the ice and explore ice caves on the **Galdhøpiggen** glacier. Call Lom Fjellføring (tel. 61/21-13-88) or the tourist board (tel. 61/21-12-86).

Horseback Riding For day- or week-long trips to the Hardangervidda, on horses or husky Norwegian ponies, contact **Eivindplass Fjellgard** (tel. 32/09-48-45) or **Geilo Hestesenter** (tel. 32/09-01-81). There are several stables in the Peer Gynt area, including **Sulseter Riding School** (tel. 61/29-01-58) and the **Peer Gynt Summer Arena** (tel. 61/29-55-18), both of which offer mountain trips.

Hunting Just south of Lillehammer you can hunt for beaver, and the Østerdalen offers good elk and reindeer hunting. As elsewhere in Norway, you'll need local and national licenses, and in some regions you are permitted to hunt only with a Norwegian. For information, call **Troll Park** (Lillehammer, tel. 61/26-92-00).

Mountaineering and Touring Near **Hardangerjøkulen** (the Hardanger Glacier), about an hour's drive north of Geilo, you can take a guided hike to the archaeological digs of 8,000-year-old Stone Age settlements. Contact **Hallingdal Mountaineering** (tel. 32/08-86-11).

From 1932 to 1953, **musk ox** were transported from Greenland to the Dovrefjell, where about 60 still roam—but it's a good idea to bring binoculars to see them. For information on safaris, call the **Dombaas Tourist Office** (tel. 61/24-14-44). **Elk safaris,** in the Bjødnhovd (not far from Fagernes), and **bear safaris,** in southern Valdres, are also organized. Call the **Valdres Tourist Office** (tel. 61/36-04-00).

National Parks The interior offers several varied national parks. The **Hardangervidda,** Europe's largest plateau and Norway's biggest park, is flat in the east and at its center and more mountainous in the west. Europe's largest herd of reindeer roam the plateau, and trout and char abound in the lakes and streams. About 150 kilometers (94 miles) north is **Ormtjernkampen,** a virgin spruce forest, and **Jotunheimen,** a rougher area spiked with glaciers, as well as Norway's highest peak, the Galdhøpiggen. Farther north is the scrubby, flat, and wide **Rondane** and the **Dovrefjell,** peaked to the west with some of the country's steepest mountains and home to wild musk ox, reindeer, and birds.

Rafting and Canoeing In Geilo they've combined rafting and canoeing with skiing, outfitting rubber rafts with a wood rudder and taking off down the slopes for a bracing, if peculiar, swoosh. Contact the tourist board for details. For rafting in **Dagali** or **Voss, Dagali-Voss Rafting** (Geilo, 32/09-38-20) organizes trips.

The **Sjoa River,** closer to Lillehammer, offers some of the most challenging rapids in the country. Contact **Sjoa Rafting** (tel. 61/23-87-50). **Flaate Opplevelser** (tel. 63/97-29-04) and **Norwegian Wildlife and Rafting** (tel. 61/23-87-27) also have trips in the **Sjoa** and **Dagali** areas.

Skiing **Telemark** is famous as the cradle of skiing, and the region is a center for ski touring. Just to the north, between Bergen and Oslo, is **Geilo** (tel. 32/09-16-95) (24 kilometers/15 miles of Alpine slopes, 130 kilometers/81 miles of cross-country trails; 18 lifts; also a ski-board tunnel). Among the area's other four ski centers, **Vestlia** (tel. 32/09–01–88), west of the Ustedalsfjord, is a good choice for families, as children can play under the guidance of the Troll Klub while parents ski; **Halstensgaard** (no tel.) and **Slaatta** (tel. 32/09–17–10) have a range of alpine and cross-country trails; and **Havsdalsenteret** (tel. 32/09–17–77) attracts a young crowd to its long alpine slopes. One ski pass (NKr140 for adults, NKr90 for children, tel. 32/09–18–09) gives access to all lifts in all five centers. Vestlia is connected to the eastern ski centers by ski taxis (NKr13, tel. 32/09–01–80).

North of Geilo is **Hemsedal** (34 kilometers/21 miles of alpine slopes, 175 kilometers/108 miles of cross-country trails; 17 ski lifts), which together with several nearby areas offers hundreds of miles of alpine and cross-country trails along with comfortable, modern facilities.

North of Oslo, **Lillehammer,** the 1994 Winter Olympics town, is another major skiing center (20 kilometers/12 miles of alpine, 400 kilometers/248 miles of cross-country trails; 7 ski lifts). Within the Lillehammer area, there are five ski centers: **Hafjell** (tel. 61/27–70–78), 10 kilometers (6.3 miles) north, is an Olympic venue with moderately steep alpine slopes; **Kvitfjell** (tel. 61/28–07–95), 50 kilometers (31 miles) north, another Olympic site, has some of the most difficult slopes in the world; **Skei** (tel. 61/22–85–55), near Gausdal, 30 kilometers (19 miles) north, has both cross-country and alpine trails; **Galdhøpiggen** (tel. 61/21–21–42), 135 kilometers (84 miles) northwest of Lillehammer, sits on a glacier, which makes it great for summer skiing; **Peer Gynt** (tel. 61/29–85–28), 80 kilometers (50 miles) northwest, has respectable downhill but is stronger as a cross-country venue. One ski lift ticket, called a **Troll Pass** (NKr175 for adults, NKr135 for children), is good for admission to all the lifts at all five sites.

To the east of the Gudbrandsdalen is the **Troll-løype** (Troll Trail), 250 kilometers (156 miles) of country trails that vein across a vast plateau that's bumped with mountains, including the Dovrefjells to the north. Ski as much or as little of the tracks as you want, and you can also choose accommodation en route. For information, contact the **Otta Tourist Office** (N-2640 Otta, tel. 61/23–02–44, fax 61/23–09–60).

Beitostølen (9 kilometers/5 miles of downhill slopes, 150 kilometers/93 miles of cross-country trails; 7 ski lifts), on the southern slopes of the Jotunheim range, has everything from torchlit night skiing to paragliding. At the northern end of the region is **Oppdal** (45 kilometers/27 miles of alpine pistes, 186 kilometers/115 miles of cross-country trails; 10 ski lifts), another World Cup venue. Like most other areas, it has lighted trails and snow-making equipment.

Dining and Lodging

Highly recommended establishments are indicated by a star★.

Elveseter
Dining and Lodging

Elveseter Hotell. Located 136 kilometers (85 miles) north of Lillehammer in Bøverdalen, this family-owned hotel is like a museum. Imagine a swimming pool in a barn dating from 1579. Every room has a history, and doors and some walls have been painted by local artists. In the public rooms are museum-quality paintings and antiques. There's no place like it. *2687 Bøverdalen, tel. 61/21–20–00, fax 61/21–21–01. 90 rooms with* *bath or shower. Facilities: 2 restaurants, bar, swimming pool, conference rooms, parking. No credit cards. Closed Sept. 25– May 31. Inexpensive.*

Geilo
Dining and Lodging

Dr. Holms Hotell. Renovated in 1989 to include two new wings and a new kitchen, Dr. Holms is among Norway's top resort hotels. Chef Jim Weiss has made the gourmet restaurant (not to be confused with the dining room) worth a special trip. His game sausages are full of flavor, and his butterscotch pudding with crunchy topping is sensational. An après-ski stop at Dr. Holms is a must. *3580 Geilo, tel. 32/09–06–22, fax 32/09–16–20. 110 rooms with bath or shower, 14 suites. Facilities: 2 restaurants, 3 bars, fitness room, swimming pool, conference center, garage. AE, DC, MC, V. Expensive.*

Golå
Dining and Lodging
★

Golå Høyfjellshotell og Hytter. Tucked away in Peer Gynt territory, this peaceful hotel is furnished in Norwegian country, with all the extras. The restaurant has a down-to-earth menu of fresh local fish and game, prepared simply and elegantly. *2646 Golå, tel. 61/29–81–08, fax 61/29–85–40. 42 rooms with shower. Facilities: restaurant, ski slopes, outdoor swimming pool, conference rooms, children's Troll Klub, half- and full-board, parking. AE, DC, MC, V. Expensive.*

Kongsberg
Dining and Lodging

Grand. A statue of Kongsberg's favorite son, Olympic ski-jumper Birger Ruud, stands in the park in front of this modern, centrally located hotel. All rooms were refurbished in 1990. *Kristian Augustsgt. 2, 3600, tel. 32/73–20–29, fax 32/73–41–29. 92 rooms with bath or shower, 2 suites. Facilities: 2 restaurants, 2 bars, nightclub, fitness room, swimming pool, conference rooms, parking. AE, DC, MC, V. Inexpensive–Moderate.*

Lillehammer
Dining

Birkebeinerstuene. Centrally located between Storgata and the LOOC Information Center are a ground-floor café and a second-floor restaurant. The café is in traditional Norwegian style, serving cakes, sandwiches, and hot dishes. The restaurant serves lunch specials and à la carte evening meals. The interior is light and airy, the cuisine traditional, and the staff service-minded. *Elvegt. 18, tel. 61/26–44–44. AE, DC, MC, V. Closed Sun. Cafe: Moderate, restaurant: Expensive.*

Lundegården Brasserie & Bar. A piece of the Continent in the middle of Storgata, this restaurant, with its exquisite interior, is a haven where guests can enjoy a light snack in the rattan-furnished bar area or a full meal in the inviting dining room with starched white tablecloths. No detail is overlooked. The varied menu offers such dishes as baked salmon with pepper-cream sauce and seasonal vegetables. *Storgt. 108A, tel. 61/26–90–22. Reservations required. Dress: casual but neat. AE, DC, MC, V. No lunch. Moderate–Expensive.*

Shanghai Chopstick. This is a nice, clean café serving typical Chinese food. *Storgt 83, tel. 61/25–98–68. Inexpensive.*

Zeki Grill og Gatekjøkken. When your purse is empty, everything else is closed, or homesickness overcomes you, a Chicago hot dog costs NKr25. *Storgt 83, tel. 61/25–85–81. Inexpensive.*

Dining and Lodging

Hammer Hotel. The Home Hotel on Storgatan opened in August 1991. It's named for the old Hammer farm, which first opened its doors to guests in 1665. The rooms are decorated in shades of green with oak furniture, both modern and rustic. Light beer, waffles, and an evening meal are included in the price. *Storgt. 108, 2600, tel. 61/26–35–00, fax 61/26–37–30. 72* rooms with shower. *Facilities: fitness room, conference center, garage. AE, DC, MC, V. Moderate–Expensive.*

Lillehammer Hotel. A five-minute walk from Maihaugen, the hotel has the prime location for the Olympics—next door to Olympic Park, the hub of the games. The rooms are big but anonymous. *Turisthotellvn. 27B, 2600, tel. 61/25–48–00, fax 61/25–73–33. 196 rooms with bath or shower. Facilities: 2 restaurants, bar, nightclub, fitness room, 2 swimming pools, parking. AE, DC, MC, V. Expensive.*

Mølla Hotell. This converted mill houses one of Lillehammer's new hotels. The intimate reception area on the ground floor gives the feeling of a private home. The bar, Toppen, on the top floor, has a good view of Mjøsa, the town, and the ski jump arena. The restaurant, Kvernhuset, winds down into the basement with old mill equipment kept for atmosphere among seating nooks. Try the Norwegian fillet of lamb with creamed potatoes. *Elvegt. 12, tel. 61/26–92–94, fax 61/26–92–95. 58 rooms with bath. Facilities: wheelchair access, sauna, solarium, exercise equipment. AE, DC, MC, V. Moderate–Expensive.*

Gjestehuset Ersgaard. Dating from the 1500s, originally called "Eiriksgård" (Eirik's Farm), Ersgaard today has all modern facilities. With a homey atmosphere in beautiful surroundings, this white manor house offers views of Lillehammer and Lake Mjøsa. *Nordseterveien 201 (at the Olympic Park), tel. 61/25–06–84, fax 61/25–06–84. 30 rooms, 20 with bath. Facilities: terrace, children's play yard. DC, MC, V. Moderate.*

Birkebeineren Motell & Apartments. Central accommodation at reasonable prices. Breakfast included except in apartments. *Olympiaparken, tel. 61/26–47–00, fax 61/26–47–50. Facilities: 310 beds and 40 chalets, sauna, dining room. AE, DC, MC, V. Inexpensive–Moderate.*

Dølaheimen Breiseth Hotell. This friendly hotel is located by the railroad station and within walking distance of shops and businesses. The Dølaheimen Kafe serves hearty Norwegian meals. *Jernbanegt. 1–3, tel. 61/25–88–66, fax 61/26–95–00. 89 rooms. Facilities: allergy rooms, sauna, solarium, wheelchair access. AE, DC, MC, V. Inexpensive–Moderate.*

Lom
Dining and Lodging

Fossheim Turisthotell. Arne Brimi's cooking has made this hotel famous. He's a self-taught champion of the local cuisine; his dishes are based on nature's kitchen, with liberal use of game, wild mushrooms, and berries. Anything with reindeer is a treat in his hands, and his thin, crisp wafers with cloudberry parfait make a lovely dessert. *2686, tel. 61/21–20–05, fax 61/21–15–10. 54 rooms with bath or shower. Facilities: restaurant, bar, parking. AE, DC, MC, V. Inexpensive–Moderate.*

Oppdal
Dining and Lodging

Oppdal Hotell. A rather severe, modern, concrete-and-glass, slope-front addition obscures this fine brick building, but inside the mood is lighter. The public rooms are overdecorated, but the bedrooms are understated, small but tastefully furnished, with light wood and pale woven textiles. It's basically a resort, with sports year-round. *O. Skasliens v., 7340, tel. 72/42–11–11, fax 72/42–08–24. 75 rooms with bath or shower. Facilities: 2 restaurants, bar, nightclub, fitness center, conference center, parking. AE, DC, MC, V. Inexpensive–Moderate.*

Øyer
Dining and Lodging

Hafjell Hotell. The largest hotel between Oslo and Trondheim, near the Olympic alpine facilities, opened in the spring of 1992. It is built in a modern, yet rustic Norwegian style. Stig Søvik, one of Norway's finest chefs, prepares updated versions of Norwegian classics at the restaurant. *2636, tel. 61/27–77–77, fax 61/27–77–80. 138 rooms with bath. Facilities: restaurant, bar, parking. AE, DC, MC, V. Moderate–Expensive.*

Rjukan
Dining and Lodging

Gaustablikk Høyfjellshotell. Built at the foot of Gaustadtoppen Mountain near Rjukan, this modern timber hotel is a popular ski resort, with nine downhill slopes and 80 kilometers (50 miles) of cross-country trails. In summer, these marked trails are perfect for walks and hikes. *N–3660, tel. 35/09–14–22, fax 35/09–19–75. 91 rooms with bath or shower, 14 suites. Facilities: restaurant, bar, nightclub, fitness room, swimming pool, parking. AE, DC, MC, V. Moderate.*

Park Hotell. This newly refurbished hotel is in the center of town. The rooms are tastefully decorated in light colors. *Sam Eydes gt. 67, 3660, tel. 35/09–02–88, fax 35/09–05–05. 39 rooms with bath or shower. Facilities: restaurant, bar, nightclub. AE, DC, MC, V. Moderate.*

Røros
Dining and Lodging

Bergstadens Hotel. The lobby is big, but when there's a fire in the stone fireplace, it is quite cozy. Most of the rooms are decorated in shades of light blue, rose, and gray. The main draw here is the dining room: Chef Kjell Sund sticks to local traditions and products—fish from mountain streams and berries from the nearby forest. *Oslovn. 2, 7460, tel. 72/41–11–11, fax 72/41–01–55. 71 rooms with bath or shower, 2 suites. Facilities: 2 restaurants, bar, nightclub, pool, conference center. AE, DC, MC, V. Moderate.*

Skien
Dining

Boden Spiseri. In the 1970s, Norwegians began their love affair with pepper steak. Boden serves an excellent version, but it also has Norwegian-style food, such as medallions of reindeer. For dessert, the cream-puff swan with ice cream and chocolate sauce is a delight. *Landbrygga 5, tel. 35/52–61–70. Dress: casual. AE, DC, MC, V. No lunch. Moderate.*

Lodging

Høyers Hotell. The old-fashioned exterior, all cornices and pedimented windows, is reflected in the Høyers's lobby, which is an incongruous mixture of old and new. The rooms are modern and light, thanks to the big windows. *Kongensgt. 6, 3700, tel. 35/52–05–40, fax 35/52–26–08. 69 rooms with bath, 1 suite. Facilities: restaurant, bar, nightclub, conference center. AE, DC, MC, V. Inexpensive–Moderate.*

The Arts

Bø i Telemark

During the second week in August, Bø holds its annual **Telemarksfestival** for international folk music and dancing, featuring musicians and dancers from distant lands as well as Norwegian and Sami artists. Nearly every weekend during the summer there's entertainment at **Telemark Sommarland** in Bø—everything from gospel singers to jazz.

Kongsberg

Every June jazz fans descend on Kongsberg for its annual **jazz festival.**

Skien

Henrik Ibsen's home town celebrates its favorite son every August with the **Ibsen-Kultur-festival** (Skien Tourist Office, Box 192, 3701 Skien, tel. 35/53–49–60), which includes concerts as well as drama.

Vinstra   Henrik Ibsen's *Peer Gynt* is performed (in Norwegian) on the first two weekends in August at a small outdoor theater on the shores of Lake Golaa. Contact the Vinstra Tourist Board (Nedregt. 5A, 2640 Vinstra, tel. 61/29–01–66) for additional information.

7 Central Fjord Country

Drawing from all directions, this fjord-riddled coast, from south of Bergen to Kristiansund, is stippled with islands and grooved with deep barren valleys, with most of the fertile land edging the water. The farther north one travels, the more rugged and wild the landscape. The motionless Sognefjord is the longest inlet, snaking 190 kilometers (110 miles) inland. It is 4,000 feet deep—a depth that often makes it appear black. Some of its sections are so narrow, with rock walls looming on either side, that they look as if they've been sliced from the mountains.

At the top of Sogn og Fjordane county are a succession of fjords referred to as Nordfjord, with Jostedalsbreen, mainland Europe's largest glacier, to the south. Sunnfjord is the coastal area between Nordfjord and Sognefjord, with Florø, the county seat, on an island close to Norway's westernmost point.

The mountains of Møre og Romsdal county are treeless moonscapes of gray rock, stone cliffs that hang out over the water far below. Geirangerfjord is the most spectacular fjord, with a road zigzagging all the way down from the mountaintops to the water beside a famous waterfall.

There is more to the central region than fidgety coasts and peaks. In fact, tourists have been visiting central fjord country ever since the English "discovered" the area some 150 years ago in their search for the ultimate salmon. One of these tourists was Kaiser Wilhelm, who spent every summer except one, from 1890 to 1913, in Molde and helped rebuild Ålesund into one of the most fantastic fits of architectural invention in Scandinavia.

Essential Information

Important Addresses and Numbers

Tourist Information Ålesund (Rådhuset, tel. 70/12–12–02); **Åndalsnes** (corner Nesgata/Romsdalsvn., tel. 71/22–16–22); **Balestrand** (dockside, tel. 57/69–12–55); **Flåm** (railroad station, tel. 57/63–21–06); **Geiranger** (dockside, tel. 70/26–30–99); **Hellesylt** (dockside, tel. 70/26–50–52); **Loen** (tel. 57/87–76–77); **Lærdal** (tel. 57/66–65–09); **Molde** (Storgt 1, tel. 71/25–43–30); **Olden** (tel. 57/87–31–26); **Stryn** (tel. 57/87–15–26); **Ulvik** (dockside, tel. 56/52–63–60); **Voss** (Hestevangen 10, tel. 56/51–17–16).

Emergencies *Ålesund* **Police:** tel. 112 or 70/12–13–21. **Fire:** tel. 111. **Ambulance:** tel. 113. **Hospital Emergency Rooms/Doctors/Dentists:** tel. 70–12–33–48. **Car Rescue:** tel. 70/14–18–33.

Late-night Pharmacies *Ålesund* **Nordstjernen** (Kaiser Wilhelmsgt. 22, Ålesund, tel. 70/12–59–45) is open Wednesday until 6 and Saturday and Sunday from 6 to 8.

Arriving and Departing by Plane

Ålesund's **Vigra** airport is 15 kilometers (9 miles) from the center of town. Braathens SAFE (tel. 70/12–58–00 Ålesund, 70/18–32–45 Vigra) has nonstop flights from Oslo, Bergen, Trondheim, and Bodø. It's a 25-minute ride from Vigra to town with Flybussen. Tickets cost NKr50. Buses are scheduled according to flights—they leave the airport about 10 minutes after all arrivals and leave town about 60 or 70 minutes before each flight.

Arriving and Departing by Car, Train, and Boat

By Car From Oslo, it is 570 kilometers (353 miles) on Route E6 to Dombås and then Route 9 through Åndalsnes to Ålesund. The well-maintained two-lane road is inland to Åndalsnes and then follows the coastline out to Ålesund.

The 380-kilometer (235-mile) drive from Bergen to Ålesund covers some of the most breathtaking scenery in the world. Roads are narrow two-lane affairs much of the time; passing is difficult, and in summer traffic can be heavy.

By Train The **Raumabanen** between Oslo S and **Åndalsnes** runs three times daily in each direction for the 6½-hour ride. At Åndalsnes, buses wait outside the station to pick up passengers for points not served by the train. The 124-kilometer (76-mile) trip to Ålesund takes close to two hours.

By Boat *Hurtigruten* (the coastal steamer) stops at Skansekaia in **Ålesund,** northbound at noon, departing at 3, and stops southbound at midnight, departing at 1. A catamaran runs between Ålesund and Molde at least twice daily.

Getting Around

By Car Ferries are a way of life in western Norway, but they are seldom big enough or run often enough during the summer, causing built-in delays. Considerable hassle can be eliminated by reserving ahead, as cars with reservations board first.

By Bus Bus routes are extensive. The tourist office has information about do-it-yourself tours by bus to the outlying districts. Three local bus companies serve **Ålesund;** all buses depart from the terminal on Kaiser Wilhelms Gate.

By Boat In addition to regular ferries to nearby islands, boats connect Ålesund with other points along the coast. Excursions by boat are available through the tourist office.

Guided Tours

Orientation A 1½-hour guided stroll through **Ålesund,** concentrating mostly on the Art Nouveau buildings, departs from the tourist information center (Rådhuset) Saturday and Tuesday at 1 PM from June 15 to August 21.

Special-interest The **M/S *Geirangerfjord*** (tel. 70/26–30–07) offers 105-minute
Cruises guided minicruises (at 10, 1, 3, 5, and 8) on the Geirangerfjord. Tickets are sold at the dock in **Geiranger.**

Flying Firdafly A/S (tel. 57/86–53–88), based in **Sandane,** offers air tours over Jostedalsbreen. Hotel Alexandra in Loen (*see* Lodging, *below*) arranges group flights. Mørefly A/S (tel. 70/18–35–00) offers 20-minute fjord and mountain-sightseeing trips by helicopter from **Ålesund.**

Hiking **Aak Fjellsport** (mountain sport) **Center** (tel. 71/22–64–44) in **Åndalsnes** specializes in walking tours of the area, from rambling in the hills for beginners and hikers to full-fledged rockclimbing, along with rafting on the Rauma River. These are the guys who hang out of helicopters to rescue injured climbers, so they know what they're doing.

From Easter through September, **Jostedalen Breførlag** (5828 **Gjerde,** tel. 56/68–32–73) offers glacier tours, from an easy 1½-hour family trip on the Nigard branch (equipment is provided) to advanced glacier courses with rock and ice climbing.

Diving   Ålesund **Dykkersenter** (Storgt. 38, tel. 70/12–34–24) has equipment for hire. All certificates are accepted.

Exploring Central Fjord Country

The best way to see fjord country is to make an almost circular tour—from Oslo to Åndalsnes, out to the coastal towns of Åle-sund, Molde, and Kristiansund, then over Trollstigveien to Geiranger, a ferry to Hellesylt, down to Stryn, around Loen and Olden and through the subglacial tunnel to Fjærland, a ferry to Balestrand, connecting with another ferry down to Flåm, where the railroad connects with Myrdal on the Bergen line (*see* Excursions from Bergen, *above*). Then the trip can either continue on to Bergen or back to Oslo.

Numbers in the margin correspond to points of interest on the Central Fjord Country map.

Tour 1: Åndalsnes and the Coast

❶ **Åndalsnes,** an industrial town of 3,000 people, has at least three things going for it: As the last stop on the railroad, it is a gateway to fjord country; **Trollstigveien** (the Trolls' Path), one of Europe's most fantastic zigzag roads, starts here; and **Trollveggen** (the Trolls' Wall), the highest sheer rock wall in Europe (1,000 meters/3,300 feet), which attracts climbers from around the world, is just outside of town.

❷ West 240 kilometers (150 miles), on three islands and between two bright blue fjords, is Ålesund, home to 35,000 inhabitants and one of Norway's largest harbors for exporting dried and fresh fish. Nearly 800 buildings in the center of town were destroyed by fire in 1904, which is said to have been started by a tipped oil lamp. In the rush to shelter the 10,000 homeless victims, Kaiser William II led a mercurial rebuilding that married the German Art Nouveau with Viking roots—much of it carried out by an army of young, foreign architects who threw in their own rabid flourishes. Delightfully, nothing has changed. Winding streets are crammed with warehouses topped with turrets, spires, gables, dragonheads, and curlicues, all in a delirious spirit that's best seen while wandering behind the local dock to Kongensgate, the walking street.

You can drive or take a bus (tel. 70/12–65–82) up nearby Aksla Mountain to a vantage point, **Kniven** (the knife), for a splendid view of the city—which absolutely glitters at night.

Time Out   **Fjellstua,** a modern lodge at the very top of the mountain, has a terrace with a cafeteria, where the view is especially good.

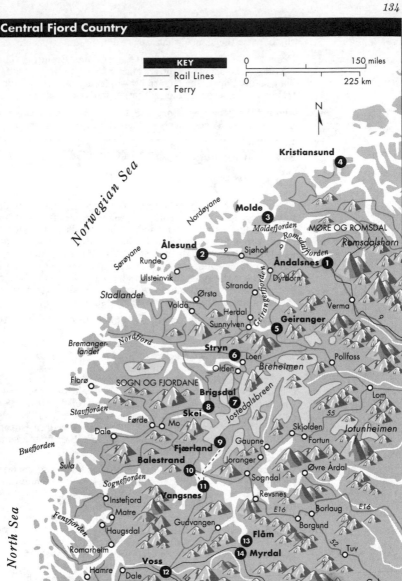

Central Fjord Country

KEY
— Rail Lines
---- Ferry

0 — 150 miles
0 — 225 km

N

Norwegian Sea

Kristiansund ④

Molde ③

Moldefjorden MØRE OG ROMSDAL

Romsdalfjorden

Romdal fjorden

Romsdalshorn

Nordøyane

Ålesund ② Sjøholt 9

Åndalsnes ①

Dyrdron

Verma

Sørøyane

Runde

Ulsteinvik

Stadlandet

Stranda

Geirangerfjorden

Ørsta

Volda

Herdal

Sunnylven

Geiranger ⑤

Bremanger-landet

Nordfjord

Stryn ⑥

Loen

Olden

Breheimen

Pollfoss

Florø

SOGN OG FJORDANE

Brigsdal ⑦

Jostedalsbreen

Lom

Stavfjorden

Førde Mo

Skei ⑧

Skjolden

Fortun

55

Jotunheimen

Dale

Buefjorden

Sula

Fjærland ⑨

Gaupne

Joranger

Øvre Årdal

Balestrand

Sognefjorden

⑩

⑪

Sogndal

Instefjord

Matre

Vangsnes

Revsnes

E16

Borlaug

E16

Haugsdal

Gudvangen

Borgund

Fensfjorden

Romarheim

Flåm ⑬

52

Tuv

Myrdal ⑭

Hamre

Voss ⑫

Dale

Ia

Gol

Bergen

HORDALAND

Ålvik

Eidfjord

Geilo

Nesbyen

Os

Hardangerfjorden

Kinsarvik

Maurset

Fagerheim

Tunnhovdfj

Tyssedal

Dagali

North Sea

Odda

Hardangervidda

Uvdal

Nore

Tynesøya

Stord

Bømlo Leirvik

Seljestad

Sprogen

Rjukan Miland

Møsvatnet

Near Ålesund is **Runde,** Norway's southernmost major bird rock, one of the largest in Europe, and a breeding ground for some 130 species, including puffins, gannets, and shags. The island is otherwise known for the "Runde Hoard," 1,300 kg of silver and gold coins, which were retrieved from a Dutch ship that sank in 1725. The catamaran leaves from Skateflua quay for the 25-minute trip to Hareid, where it connects with a bus for the 50-kilometer (31-mile) trip to Runde. A path leads from the bus stop to the nature reserve. It is also possible to sail around the rock on the yacht *Charming Ruth,* which leaves from Ulsteinvik at 11 on Wednesday and Sunday.

❸ North of Ålesund is **Molde.** During World War II the German air force suspected that King Haakon VII was staying in a red house here and bombed every red house in town. These days the city is known for its yearly jazz festival at the end of July, when big names from around the world gather for a huge jam session. Tickets can be purchased at all post offices in Norway.

Although Molde is a modern town, rebuilt almost entirely after **❹** the war, **Kristiansund** was spared the destruction of its historic harbor, Vågen. Many buildings in the town—which celebrated its 250th birthday in 1992—are well preserved, including **Woldbrygga,** a cooper's (barrelmaker's) workshop from 1875 to 1965, with its original equipment still operational. *Admission: NKr10 adults, NKr5 children. Open weekdays 2–4, Sun. 1–4.*

Tour 2: Geirangerfjord to Sognefjord

Geiranger is the ultimate fjord, Norway at its most dramatic, with the finest sightseeing in the wildest nature compressed into a relatively small area. The mountains lining the Geiranger Fjord tower 2,000 meters (6,600 feet) above sea level. The most scenic route to Geiranger is the two-hour drive along Route 63 over **Trollstigveien** (the Trolls' Path) from Åndalsnes. This road took 100 men 20 summers (from 1916 to 1936) to build, in a constant fight against rock and water. Trollstigveien and Ørneveien (at the Geiranger end) zigzag over the mountains separating two fjords. They're open only during the summer, but there's enough snow for skiing well into July. Trollstigveien has 11 giant hairpin turns, each one blasted from solid rock. Halfway up, the spray from **Stigfoss** (Stig Falls) blows across the bridge.

Time Out | **Trollstigen Fjellstue,** near the top of Trollstigveien, is cozy and rustic inside. The *medisterkaker* with *surkål* (mild sausage cakes with caraway-flavored sauerkraut) is a good, hearty meal—be sure to pick up a little tub of *tyttebær* (lingonberry).

❺ Ørneveien (the Eagles' Road), down to **Geiranger,** completed in 1952, with 11 hairpin turns, leads directly to the fjord. The 16-kilometer-long (10-mile-long), 960-foot- (-298-meter-) deep Geirangerfjord's best-known attractions are its waterfalls— the Seven Sisters, the Bridal Veil, and the Suitor—and the abandoned farms at **Skageflå** and **Knivsflå,** which are visible (and accessible) only by boat (*see* Guided Tours, *above*). Perhaps the inhabitants left because provisions had to be carried from the boats straight up to Skageflå—a backbreaking 800 feet (248 meters).

If you continue on to Stryn, take the ferry across The Geiranger Fjord to Hellesylt, a 75-minute ride. It's about 50 kilometers (30 miles) from Hellesylt to Stryn on Route 60. Stryn, Loen, and Olden, at the eastern end of Nordfjord, were among the first tourist destinations in the region more than 100 years ago. **Stryn** is famous for its salmon river and summer ski center, while Loen and Olden are starting points for expeditions to branches of Europe's largest glacier, **Jostedalsbreen.**

6

7 **Brigsdal** is the most accessible arm of the Jostedal glacier. Take a bus (from Stryn, Loen, or Olden) or drive to Brigsdalsbre Fjellstove. The glacier is a 45-minute walk from the end of the road, or you can ride there with pony and trap, as tourists did 100 years ago. Local guides lead tours (*see* Guided Tours, *above*) over the safe parts of the glacier. These perennial ice masses are more treacherous than they look, for there's always the danger of calving (breaking off), and deep crevasses are not always visible.

Time Out **Briksdalsbre Fjellstove** celebrated its 100th anniversary in 1992. Stop at the gift shop or at the cafeteria for delicious homemade cakes, or spend the night at the modern lodge.

It is also possible to visit the **Kjenndal** arm of the glacier on the *M/B Kjendal* (tel. 57/87-76-60), which departs from Sande, near Loen. It sails down the 14-kilometer (9-mile) arm of the lake under mountains covered by protruding glacier arms and past Ramnefjell (Ramne Mountain), scarred by rock slides, to **Kjenndalsbreen Fjellstove.** A bus runs from the lodge (which serves excellent trout) to the glacier.

For many years **Olden** was the home of American landscape artist William H. Singer (d. 1943), scion of a Pittsburgh steel family. A philanthropist, he paid for the road and the regional hospital. His **studio** (open July and August, weekends noon–2) can be visited.

8 From Olden it's 62 kilometers (37 miles) of easy though not particularly inspiring terrain to **Skei,** at the base of Lake Jølster, where the road goes under the glacier for more than 6 kilometers (4 miles) of the journey to **Fjærland,** which, until 1986, was without road connections altogether. In 1991 the **Norsk Bremuseum** (Norwegian Glacier Museum) opened just north of Fjærland. It has a huge screen with a film about glacier trekking and a fiberglass glacial maze, complete with special effects courtesy of the *Star Wars* movies' set designer. *Tel. 57/69-32-88. Admission: NKr60 adults; NKr30 children and senior citizens. Open May–Sept., daily 10–6; Apr., Oct., daily 10–4.*

9

10 By 1996 Fjærland should have road connections with Sogndal, but until then, the only way to travel is by ferry, which stops at both **Balestrand,** one of the famous destinations of old, and **11** **Vangsnes** across from it on the southern bank of **Sognefjord,** one of the longest and deepest fjords in the world, snaking 200 kilometers (136 miles) into the heart of the country. Along its wide banks are some of Norway's best fruit farms, with fertile soil and lush vegetation (the fruit blossoms in May are spectacular). Ferries are the lifeline of the region.

12 From Vangsnes it is 80 kilometers (50 miles) south to **Voss,** birthplace of football hero Knut Rockne, and a good place to stay the night, either in the town itself or 36 kilometers (23 miles) away at Stalheim. The road to Stalheim, an old resort, has 13 hairpin turns in one 1½-kilometer (1-mile) stretch of road—and it's 550 meters (1,800 feet) straight down. Voss is connected with Oslo and Bergen by train and by 114 kilometers (71 miles) of roads (some sections are narrow and steep).

⑬ It is also possible to ride a ferry from Balestrand to **Flåm,** from which you can make Norway's most exciting railway journey, **⑭** to **Myrdal.** Only 20 kilometers (12 miles) long, it takes 40 minutes to travel 884 meters (2,850 feet) up a steep mountain gorge, and 53 minutes to go down. Don't worry about the brakes. The train has five separate systems, any one of which is able to stop it. A masterpiece of engineering, the line includes 20 tunnels. From Flåm it is also an easy drive back to Oslo on E16 along the Lærdal River, one of Norway's most famous salmon streams and King Harald's favorite.

Off the Beaten Track

Halfway across the southern shore of Lake Jølster (about a 10-minute detour from the road to Fjærland) is **Astruptunet,** the farm of artist Nicolai Astrup (1880–1928). The best of his primitive, mystical paintings sell in the $500,000 range, making him second only to Edvard Munch among Norwegian artists. His home and studio are in a cluster of small turf-roofed buildings on a steep hill overlooking the lake. *Tel. 57/82–77–82. Admission: NKr30 adults, NKr15 children and senior citizens. Open May 19–June 9, Aug. 12–Sept. 1, weekdays, Sun. noon–5, Sat. noon–3; June 10–Aug. 11, weekdays, Sun. 10–6, Sat. 10–4.*

Shopping

Skei in Jølster **Audhild Vikens Vevstove** (Skei, tel. 57/72–81–25, Førde, tel. 57/82–00–84) specializes in the handicrafts, particularly woven textiles, of the Jølster region as well as handicrafts from neighboring areas, including brass, porcelain, and leather goods.

Stryn **Strynefjell Draktverkstad** (6890 Oppstryn, tel. 57/87–72–20) is a women's workshop, started in 1988, that specializes in stylish knickers, trousers, and skirts made of heavy wool fabric. It's a 10-minute drive east of Stryn on Route 15.

Sports and Outdoor Activities

Fishing There are numerous lakes, rivers, and streams around Voss, with trout everywhere; char, salmon, and sea trout reside in these waters. There's also good salmon fishing in the Vosso River (June–mid-August), and the Vangsvatnet and Lønavatnet lakes are good for ice fishing. You can also go sea fishing among the islands south of Bergen near Sunde (call the culture board, at tel. 56/33–75–00), or fish for more trout and salmon in the Etne River in Sunnhordland. As always, a license is required.

Hiking Walks and hikes are especially rewarding in this region, with spectacular mountain and water views everywhere. Be prepared for abrupt weather changes in spring and fall. Voss is a starting point for mountain hikes in Slølsheimen, Vikafjell, and the mountains surrounding Voss. Contact the Voss Tourist

Board (Uttraagata 9, tel. 56/51–17–16) for tips. There's also good walking in Sunnhorldland, Osterfjorden, Sotra-Øygarden (among the islands), and the more rugged Nordhorland. The local tourist boards can help you plan hikes.

Skiing Voss (40 kilometers/25 miles of alpine slopes; 1 cable car, 8 ski lifts; 8 illuminated and 2 marked cross-country trails) is an important alpine skiing center in Norway, although it doesn't have the attractions or traditions of some of its resort neighbors to the east. The area includes several schools and interconnecting lifts that will get you from run to run. Call the tourist-information office (tel. 56/51–17–16) for details.

Dining and Lodging

Outside of some roadside snack bars and simple cafeterias, restaurants are few in fjord country. Most visitors dine at the hotels, where food is often abundant and simple. Most feature a cold table at either lunch or dinner.

Highly recommended establishments are indicated by a star★.

Ålesund **Gullix.** The decor is a bit much, with stone walls, plants hang-
Dining ing from the ceiling, musical instruments, and even the odd old-fashioned record player, but you can't fault the food, which ranges from sautéed monkfish garnished with shrimp, mussels, and crayfish to grilled marinated filet mignon of lamb. *Rådstugt. 5B, tel. 70/12–05–48. Reservations advised. Dress: casual but neat. AE, DC, MC, V. Moderate.*

Sjøbua. Within walking distance of the new hotels, this fish restaurant is typical Ålesund. Pick your own fish from the large tank. The mixed fish and shellfish platter is the most popular dish on the menu. The lobster soup is excellent, too, but leave room for the raspberry ice cream with nougat sauce. *Brunholmgt. 1, tel. 70/12–71–00. Reservations advised. Dress: casual but neat. AE, DC, MC, V. Closed Sun. Moderate.*

Brosundet Cafe. Hotel Atlantica's coffee shop is one of the most popular restaurants in town. It has its own bakery, so there's always homemade bread and rolls. The *sirupsnipper* (spice cookies) are very popular. You can order anything from *bløtkake* (cream cake) and coffee, with free refill, to peppersteak. *R. Rønnebergsgt. 4, tel. 70/12–91–00. No reservations. Dress: casual. AE, DC, MC, V. Inexpensive.*

Vesle Kari. This tiny maritime-theme café serves typical Norwegian fare—open-face sandwiches and such hot dishes as *kjøttkaker* (meat patties), predictable but tasty. *Apotekergaten 2, tel. 70/12–84–04. No reservations. Dress: casual. No credit cards. Inexpensive.*

Lodging **Bryggen.** Right on Brosundet, Bryggen, formerly a turn-of-the-century fish warehouse, was restored by the Home hotel chain in early 1990. The decor in both lobby and guest rooms illustrates the importance of the fishing industry to Ålesund. A hot meal is included in the room price, and waffles and coffee are always available. *Apotekergt. 1–3, N–6021, tel. 70/12–64–00, fax 70/12–11–80. 76 rooms, 6 suites. Facilities: Fitness room, conference rooms, fishing, parking. AE, DC, MC, V. Moderate.*

Hotel Scandinavie. The impressive building with towers and arches dates from 1905, but the rooms are newly refurbished, with dark modern Scandinavian furniture, while some textiles pay a token tribute to Art Nouveau. *Løvenvoldgt. 8, N-6002, tel. 70/12-31-31, fax 70/12-94-88. 75 rooms with bath, 2 suites. Facilities: 2 restaurants, bar, fitness room, conference room, garage. AE, DC, MC, V. Moderate.*

Rica Parken. This modern business hotel near Aksla offers panoramic views from most of the small but well-appointed rooms, which were redecorated in 1990 with rattan furniture and pastel colors. *Storgt. 16, N-6002, tel. 70/12-50-50, fax 70/12-21-64. 132 rooms with bath, 6 suites. Facilities: restaurant, bar, nightclub, fitness center, conference rooms, parking. AE, DC, MC, V. Moderate.*

Scandic. This large postmodernist building complex stands next to the Exhibition Hall. Its interior design has a maritime theme. The rooms are both spacious and tastefully decorated. *Molovn. 6, N-6004, tel. 70/12-81-00, fax 70/12-92-10. 120 rooms with bath. Facilities: restaurant, bar, nightclub, swimming pool, fitness center. AE, DC, MC, V. Moderate.*

Åndalsnes
Lodging

Grand Hotel Bellevue. It looks like a white stucco apartment building from the 1950s. The rooms are spare but adequate, all with a view of either the mountains or the fjord. *Åndalsgt. 5, N-6300, tel. 71/22-10-11, fax 71/22-60-38. 46 rooms with bath or shower. Facilities: 2 restaurants, bar, conference room, parking. AE, DC, MC, V. Moderate.*

Balestrand
Lodging

Kvikne's Hotel. This huge wood gingerbread house at the edge of the Sognefjord has been a landmark since 1913. It is fjord country's most elaborate old hotel, with rows of open porches and balustrades. The rooms are comfortable—those in the old section have more personality, but the view's the best part. *N-5850, Balholm, tel. 57/69-11-01, fax 57/69-15-02. 190 rooms with bath or shower. Facilities: restaurant, nightclub, fitness room, fishing, water sports. AE, DC, MC, V. Moderate.*

Fjærland
Lodging

Hotel Mundal. This small, old-fashioned yellow-and-white gingerbread hotel celebrated its 100th anniversary in 1991. All rooms are individually and simply decorated. The dining room is rather dreary, but the food is good. *N-5855, tel. 57/69-31-01, fax 57/69-31-79. 36 rooms with bath. Facilities: 2 restaurants, bar, conference rooms, fishing, parking. No credit cards. Moderate-Expensive.*

Flåm
Lodging

Fretheim Hotell. With the fjord in front and mountains in back, the setting is perfect. The hotel is anonymous, white, and functional. The inside has comfortable lounges, but the rooms won't win any decorating prizes. *N-5743, tel. 57/63-22-00, fax 57/63-23-03. 56 rooms with bath or shower, 28 without. Facilities: 2 restaurants, bar, fishing. AE, MC, V. Moderate.*

Geiranger
Lodging

Union Turisthotel. This family-owned hotel celebrated its 100th anniversary in 1991. The old building was torn down, but the present hotel is a tribute to the old style. It is modern and comfortable, with lots of windows facing the view and light furniture in the relatively large rooms. *N-6216, tel. 70/26-30-00, fax 70/26-31-61. 145 rooms with bath or shower, 10 suites. Facilities: restaurant, bar, nightclub, fitness room, indoor and outdoor swimming pools, parking. AE, DC, MC, V. Expensive.*

Grande Fjord Hotell. Idyllically situated at the edge of the fjord, this small hotel complex has more charm than the big hotels in the area. The rooms are simple but comfortable. *N-6216, tel. 70/26-30-67 (Apr.-Oct.), 70/26-31-77 (Nov.-Mar.).*

10 rooms with bath, 5 without, 18 cabins with bath. Facilities: restaurant, parking. No credit cards. Inexpensive.

Kristiansund N
Lodging

Inter Nor Grand. Practically every Norwegian town has a Grand Hotel. This one's primarily a conference hotel, but the rooms are nicer than most (certainly much nicer than the lobby), with brass beds and light wood furniture. *Bernstorff-stredet 1, N–6500, tel. 71/67–30–11, fax 71/67–23–70. 130 rooms with bath/shower. Facilities: 2 restaurants, bar, nightclub, fitness room, conference center, parking. AE, DC, MC, V. Moderate–Expensive.*

Loen
Dining and Lodging
★

Alexandra. It looks like a huge white hospital: More than 100 years ago, English and German tourists stayed here. Even though the original dragon-style building exists only in pictures in the lobby, it is still the most luxurious hotel around. The facilities are first-rate and the dining room was renovated in January 1993, but the food, prepared by Chef Wenche Loen, is the best part. *N–6878, tel. 57/87–76–60, fax 57/87–77–70. 198 rooms with bath. Facilities: 2 restaurants, bar, nightclub, swimming pool, fitness room, gift shop, tennis, boating, conference center. AE, DC, MC, V. Expensive.*

Molde
Dining and Lodging

Inter Nor Alexandra Molde. Spisestuen, the restaurant of Molde's premier hotel, is worth a special trip. Kåre Monsås offers such dishes as pepper-marinated veal fillet. The ice-cream soufflé is an excellent dessert. The rooms, many of which overlook the water, are nondescript but comfortable, with dark-brown wood furniture and textiles in shades of blue. *Storgt. 1–7, N–6400, tel. 71/25–11–33, fax 71/21–66–35. 139 rooms with bath/shower, 11 suites. Facilities: 3 restaurants, 2 bars, swimming pool, fitness room, conference rooms, garage. AE, DC, MC, V. Moderate–Expensive.*

Runde
Lodging

Christineborg Turisthotel. This modern hotel faces the sea and the bird rocks. It's surprisingly comfortable and civilized, a welcome setting for unwinding. *N–6096, tel. 70/08–59–50, fax 70/08–59–72. 31 rooms with shower. Facilities: restaurant, fishing boat. MC, V. Inexpensive.*

Stalheim
Lodging

Stalheim Hotel. A large, rectangular building, much like other Norwegian resort hotels, the Stalheim has been painted dark red and blends into the scenery better than most hotels. It has an extensive collection of Norwegian antiques and even its own open-air museum with 30 houses. *N–5715, tel. 56/52–01–22, fax 56/52–00–56. 127 rooms with bath or shower, 3 suites. Facilities: restaurant, bar, fishing, shop. AE, DC, MC, V. Expensive–Very Expensive.*

Stryn
Lodging

King Oscar's Hall. Mike and Møyfrid Walston have brought back to life a derelict but magnificent hotel from the heyday of the dragon style, 1896, complete with a tower with dragonheads on the eaves. The Great Hall gives new meaning to the word *great* and the number of royal guests, present and past, is impressive. *N–6880, tel. and fax, 57/87–19–53. 5 suites. Facilities: restaurant, parking. V. Closed Sept.–Apr. Expensive.*

Voss
Lodging

Fleischers Hotel. The modern addition along the front detracts from the turreted and gabled charm of this old hotel. Inside, the old style has been especially well maintained, particularly in the restaurant. The rooms in the old section are comfortable and pleasantly old-fashioned; in the rebuilt section (1993) they are modern and inviting. The motel section offers apartments.

Evangervegen 13, N–5700, tel. 56/51–11–55, fax 56/51–22–89. 86 rooms with bath or shower; 30 apartments. Facilities: restaurant, bar, nightclub, indoor pool, fitness room, tennis, children's playroom, parking. AE, DC, MC, V. Moderate.

8 Trondheim and the North

The coast of northern Norway fidgets up from Trondheim, scattering thousands of islands and skerries along the way, until it reaches the northernmost point of Europe. Then it continues even farther, straggling above Sweden and Finland to point a finger of land into Russia.

Long and thin, this area covers an astonishing variety of land- and cityscapes, from bustling Trondheim to elegant Tromsø to colorful Karasjok, capital of the Sami. Some areas, especially when seen from the deck of the mail boats, seem like endless miles of wilderness marked by an occasional dot—a lonely cabin or a herd of reindeer. Views are often exquisite: glaciers, fjords, rocky coasts, and celestial displays of the midnight sun in summer and northern lights (aurora borealis) in winter.

Nordkapp (the North Cape) has a character that changes with the seasons. In summer it teems with visitors and tour buses, and in winter, under several feet of snow, it is bleak, subtle, and astonishingly beautiful. It is accessible then only by squealing snow cat: a bracing and thoroughly Norwegian adventure.

Essential Information

Important Addresses and Numbers

Tourist Information
Trondheim (Munkegt. 19, tel. 73/92–93–94). Other tourist offices in the region: **Bodø** (Sjøgt. 21, 8000, tel. 75/52–60–00); **Harstad** (Rikard Kaarbøsgt. 20, 9400, tel. 77/06–32–35); **Lofoten** (8300 Svolvær, tel. 76/07–30–00); **Mo i Rana** (8600 Mo, tel. 75/15–04–21); **Narvik** (Kongensgt. 66, 8500, tel. 76/94–33–09); **Tromsø** (Storgt. 61, 9000, tel. 77/61–00–00); **Vesterålen Reiselivslag** (8400 Sortland, tel. 77/02–15–55); and **Nordkapp,** (Nordkapphuset, Honningsvåg, tel. 78/47–28–94).

Emergencies
Trondheim
Police: tel. 112. **Fire:** tel. 111. **Ambulance:** tel. 113. **Car rescue:** tel. 73/96–82–00. **Doctors:** tel. 73/99–88–00. **Dentists:** tel. 73/52–25–00.

Other Towns
Bodø: tel. 112; **Harstad:** tel. 112; **Narvik:** tel. 112; **Tromsø:** tel. 112.

Late-night Pharmacies
Trondheim
St. Olav Vaktapotek (Kjøpmannsgt. 65, tel. 73/52–66–66) is open Monday through Saturday 8:30 AM–midnight and Sunday 10 AM–midnight.

Tromsø
Svaneapoteket (Fr. Langes Gate 9, tel. 77/68–64–24) is open daily 8:30–4 and 6–9.

Arriving and Departing by Plane

Airports and Airlines
Trondheim's **Værnes Airport** is 35 kilometers (22 miles) northeast of the city. **SAS** (tel. 74/82–49–22), **Braathens SAFE** (tel. 74/82–32–00), and **Widerøe** (tel. 74/82–49–22) are the main domestic carriers. SAS also has one flight between Trondheim and Copenhagen daily, except Sunday, and daily flights to Stockholm.

With the exception of Harstad, all cities in northern Norway are served by airports less than 5 kilometers (3 miles) from the center of town. Tromsø is a crossroads for air traffic between northern and southern Norway and is served by Braathens

SAFE, SAS, and Widerøe. SAS flies to eight destinations in northern Norway, including Bodø, Tromsø, Alta, and Kirkenes. Braathens SAFE flies to five destinations, including Bodø and Tromsø. Widerøe specializes in northern Norway and flies to 19 destinations in the region, including Honningsvåg, the airport closest to the North Cape.

Arriving and Departing by Car, Train, Bus, and Boat

By Car Trondheim is about 500 kilometers (310 miles) from Oslo: seven to eight hours of driving. Speed limits are 80 kmh (50 mph) much of the way. There are two alternatives, E6 through Gudbrandsdalen or Route 3 through Østerdalen. Roads are decent, for the most part, but can become thick with campers during midsummer, sometimes making the going slow. It's 727 kilometers (450 miles) from Trondheim to Bodø on Route E6, which goes all the way to Kirkenes.

By Train The **Dovrebanen** has five departures daily, four on Saturday, in both directions on the Oslo–Trondheim route. Trains leave from Oslo S Station for the seven- to eight-hour journey. Trondheim is the gateway to the North, and two trains run daily in both directions on the 11-hour Trondheim–Bodø route. For information about trains out of Trondheim, call 73/53–00–10. The **Nordlandsbanen** has two departures daily in each direction on the Bodø–Trondheim route, an 11-hour journey. The **Ofotbanen** has one departure daily in each direction on the Stockholm–Narvik route, a 21-hour journey.

By Bus Buses run only from Oslo to Otta, where they connect with the train to Trondheim. Buses connect Bergen, Molde, Ålesund, and Røros with Trondheim. **Nor-Way Bussekspress** (tel. 22/17–52–90) can help you to put together a bus journey to the North. The Express 2000 travels three times a week between Oslo, Kautokeino, Alta, and Hammerfest. The journey, via Sweden, takes 24, 26, and 29 hours, respectively.

By Boat **Hurtigruten** (the coastal express boat, which calls at 35 ports from Bergen to Kirkenes) stops at Trondheim, southbound at St. Olav's Pier, Quay 16, northbound at Pier 1, Quay 7.

Getting Around

By Plane Northern Norway has excellent air connections through SAS, Braathens SAFE, and Widerøe. (*See* Arriving and Departing by Plane, *above*.)

By Bus
Trondheim Most local buses in **Trondheim** stop at the Munkegata/ Dronningens Gate intersection. Some routes end at the bus terminal (Skakkes Gate 40, tel. 73/52–44–74). Tickets cost NKr12 and allow free transfer between buses (tel. 73/54–71–00) and streetcars (**Gråkallbanen**, tel. 72/55–21–63).

The North North of **Bodø** and **Narvik** (a five-hour bus ride from Bodø), beyond the reach of the railroad, buses go virtually everywhere, but they don't go often. Get a comprehensive bus schedule from a tourist office or travel agent before making plans. Local bus companies include **Saltens Bilruter** (Bodø, tel. 75/52–50–25), **Ofotens Bilruter** (Narvik, tel. 76/94–64–80), **Tromsbuss** (Tromsø, tel. 77/67–02–33), **Tromsøexpressen** (Tromsø, tel. 77/

Spend your
vacation
touring
castles.
Not train
stations.

Vacation Cars. Vacation Prices. Wherever your destination in Europe, there is sure to be one of more than 1,000 Budget locations nearby. Budget offers considerable values on a wide variety of quality cars, and if you book before you leave the U.S., you'll save even more with a special rate package from the Budget World Travel Plan.℠ For information and reservations, contact your travel consultant or call Budget in the U.S. at **800-472-3325.** Or, while traveling abroad, call a Budget reservation center.

THE SMART MONEY IS ON BUDGET.

We feature Ford and other fine cars. *A system of corporate and licensee owned locations.*

MCI brings Europe and America closer together.

Call the U.S. for less with MCI CALL USA.®

It's easy and affordable to call home when you use MCI CALL USA!

- Less expensive than calling through hotel operators
- Available from over 80 countries and locations worldwide
- You're connected to English-speaking MCI® Operators
- Even call 800 numbers in the U.S.†

†Regular MCI CALL USA rates apply to 800 number calls.

Call the U.S. for less from these European locations.

Dial the toll-free access number for the country you're calling from. Give the U.S. MCI Operator the number you're calling and the method of payment: MCI Card, U.S. local phone company card or collect. Your call will be completed!

Austria	022-903-012	Hungary	00*-800-01411	Poland	0*-01-04-800-222
Belgium	078-11-00-12	Ireland	1-800-551-001	Portugal	05-017-1234
Czech/Slovak	00-42-000112	Italy	172-1022	San Marino	172-1022
Denmark	8001-0022	Liechtenstein	155-0222	Spain	900-99-0014
Finland	9800-102-80	Luxembourg	0800-0112	Sweden	020-795-922
France	19*-00-19	Monaco	19*-00-19	Switzerland	155-0222
Germany	0130-0012	Netherlands	06*-022-91-22	United Kingdom	0800-89-0222
Greece	00-800-1211	Norway	050-12912	Vatican City	172-1022

* Wait for 2nd dial tone.
Collect calls not accepted on MCI CALL USA calls to 800 numbers.
Some public phones may require deposit of coin or phone card for dial tone.

Call 1-800-444-3333 in the U.S. to apply for your MCI Card® now!

67–27–87), and **Finnmark Fylkesrederi og Ruteselskap** (Alta, tel. 78/43–52–11, Hammerfest, tel. 78/41–16–55).

By Boat Boat is the ideal transportation in Nordland. The **Hurtigruten** stops twice daily (north and southbound) at 20 ports in northern Norway. It is possible to buy tickets between any harbors right on the boats. **Saltens Dampskibsselskab** (Bodø, tel. 75/52–10–20) has express boats between Bodø and Hamarøy and Svolvær, while **OVDS** (Narvik, tel. 76/94–40–90) ferries and express boats serve many towns in the region. **TFDS, Troms Fylkes Dampskibsselskap** (Tromsø, tel. 77/68–60–88) operates various boat services in the region around Tromsø.

By Car The roads aren't a problem in northern Norway—most are quite good, although there are always narrow and winding stretches, especially along fjords. Distances are formidable. Route 17—*Kystriksvegen* (the Coastal Highway) from Namsos to Bodø—is an excellent alternative to E6. Getting to Tromsø and the North Cape involves additional driving on narrower roads off E6. In the northern winter, near-blizzard conditions and icy roads sometimes make it necessary to drive in a convoy. You'll know it when you see it: Towns are cut off from traffic at access roads, and vehicles wait until their numbers are large enough to make the crossing safely.

You can also fly the extensive distances and then rent a car for sightseeing within the area, but book a rental car as far in advance as possible. There's no better way to see the Lofoten and Vesterålen islands than by car. Nordkapp (take the plane to Honningsvåg) is another excursion best made by car.

By Taxi Taxi ranks are located in strategic places in downtown **Trondheim.** All taxis are connected to the central dispatching office (tel. 73/52–76–00). Taxi numbers in other towns are: **Harstad,** tel. 77/06–20–56; **Narvik,** tel. 76/94–65–00; **Røst,** tel. 77/89–62–90; and **Tromsø,** tel. 77/68–80–20.

Guided Tours

Tromsø The tourist information office sells tickets for **City Sightseeing** (Dampskipskaia) and **M/S *Polstjerna,*** an original Arctic vessel that offers a fishing tour in the waters around Tromsø Island.

Trondheim The Trondheim Tourist Association offers a number of tours. Tickets are sold at the tourist information office or at the start of the tour.

Samiland **Contact Sami Travel A/S** (Kautokeino, tel. 78/48–62–03) for adventure trips to Sami settlements.

Svalbard **Svalbard Polar Travel** (9170 Longyearbyen, tel. 79/02–19–71) arranges combination air-sea visits, from three-day mini-cruises to 12-day trekking expeditions on the rim of the North Pole. **Spitsbergen Travel** (9170 Longyearbyen, tel. 79/02–24–00) offers specialized "exploring" tours, which focus on the plant and animal life of the region.

Exploring Trondheim and the North

Numbers in the margin correspond to points of interest on the Trondheim and the North map.

Tour 1: Trondheim

❶ **Trondheim's** original name, Nidaros (still the name of the cathedral), is a composite word referring to the city's location at the mouth of the Nid River. After a savage fire in 1681, the wood town was rebuilt according to the plan of General Cicignon, a military man from Luxembourg, who also designed its fort. The wide streets of the city center are still lined with brightly painted wood houses and picturesque warehouses.

Start at Torget, the town square, with the statue of St. Olav in the middle. South on Munkegate is one of the finest collections in Scandinavia, the **Nordenfjeldske Kunstindustrimuseum** (Decorative Arts Museum). It has superb period rooms from the Renaissance to 1950s Scandinavian modern. The Tiffany windows are also magnificent. *Munkegt. 5, tel. 73/52–13–11. Admission: NKr20 adults, NKr10 children. Open June 20–Aug. 20, Mon.–Sat. 10–6, Sun. noon–5; Aug. 21–June 19, Mon.–Sat. 10–3, Thurs. 10–7, Sun. noon–4.*

Continue on Munkegate to **Nidaros domen** (Nidaros Cathedral), built on the grave of St. Olav, who formulated a Christian religions code for Norway in 1024 while he was king. He was killed in battle against the Danes at Stikle Stad. After he was buried water sprang from his grave, and people began to believe that his nails and hair continued to grow beneath the ground. After a series of other miracles, the town became a pilgrimage site for the Christians of northern Europe, and Olav was canonized in 1164.

Although construction was begun in 1070, the oldest existing parts of the cathedral date from around 1150. During the Catholic period, it attracted crowds of pilgrims, but after the Reformation, its importance declined and fires destroyed much of it. The 1814 Constitution decreed that Norway's kings should be crowned at the cathedral. Restoration began around 1870 and the interior was completed in 1930. The facade is still being restored, and the western front, with twin towers and a rose window, has been reinstalled during the past 60 years. The first king of modern Norway, Haakon VII, and Queen Maud, daughter of Edward VII of England, were crowned in the cathedral in 1906. Two years later, the Constitution was altered to eliminate the coronation ceremony, but in 1957, King Olav, and in 1991, King Harald and Queen Sonja, were formally blessed here. *Kongsgårdsgt. 2, tel. 73/50–12–12. Castle admission: NKr10 adults; NKr5 children, senior citizens, students. Ticket also permits entry to Erkebispegården (see below). Open June 1–Aug. 15, weekdays 9:30–12:30, Sun. 1–4; Apr. 1–May 31 and Aug. 16–Oct. 31, Fri. noon–4. Tower Admission: NKr5. Open June 19–Aug. 15, daily every half hour during regular opening hours.*

Next door is Scandinavia's oldest secular building (actually two buildings connected by a gatehouse), from around 1160,

Trondheim and the North

20 Svalbard

Nordkyn-
halvøya   Berlevåg   Vardø

Nordkapp 14

13   Båtsfjord

Honningsvåg   Grense
                                       Jakobselv
Hammerfest   Kåfjord   Tana bru   98
          12   Kistrand   Storskog
                                    17   18
          Rypefjord   E6 Kirkenes
Sørøya Seiland   Lakselv
Øksfjordjøkulen   19
Norwegian   Alta   Øvre Pasvik
Sea   10   Karasjok   RUSSIA
          Alteidet 11   16
     Hjemmeluft   FINNMARK
            Kvænangsfjellet

          Olderdalen
Tromsø 9   Kautokeino
       Seljelvnes   FINLAND
         TROMS   15
Andenes   Senja Andselv Øverbygd
          Andøya Setermoen
Harstad 8
Vesterålen Islands 7
                HINNØYA 5
Austvågøya Lofoten Lødigen Narvik
Vestvågøya 6 Svolvær
Flakstadøya E10 Skutvika
   Sund Nusfjord Stamsund
Moskenesøya Reine
    Verøy Sørland
  Røst   3 4 Fauske
        Bodø Saltstraumen   Arctic Circle
Polarsirkelsenteret
          17 812
             2
                Mo i Rana
Trænfjorden   SWEDEN
Sandnessjøen Korgen
    Mosjøen
Norwegian   Hommelstø
Sea   Vegafjorden BØRGEFJELL
         Vik NASJONALPARK
Hortafjorden Terråk
        Salsbruket Gædde
Folla   Namsos
    NORD- Snåsa
TRØNDELAG
715 Steinkjer
  Trondheims-
  fjorden 1
Hitra   Trondheim
  Kristiansund

KEY
- - - Ferry

0   150 miles
0   225 km

Erkebispegården (the Archbishop's Palace), the residence of the archbishop until the Reformation. After that, it was a Danish governor's palace, and later a military headquarters. *Tel. 73/50-12-12. Admission: NKr10 adults; NKr5 children, senior citizens, students. Ticket also permits entry to cathedral. Open June 1-Aug. 15, weekdays 9-3, Sat. 9-2, Sun. noon-3.*

Within the Erkebispegården is **Forsvarsmuseet** (the Army Museum), with displays of uniforms, swords, and daggers. **Hjemmefrontmuseet** (the Resistance Museum), also there, documents the occupation of Norway during World War II through objects and photographs. *Tel. 73/51-51-11, ext. 182. Admission: NKr5 adults, NKr2 children. Open June 1-Aug. 31, weekdays 9-3; year-round, weekends 11-3.*

On Bispegate turn right and follow the river. You'll pass Gamle Bybro (the Old Bridge) and reach Kjøpmannsgata, where you can turn left on Kongensgate. Behind **Biblioteket** (the Library, Kongensgate 2) are the remains of St. Olavskirke (St. Olav's Church). The crypt of another medieval church can be seen inside **Trondhjems og Strindens Sparebank** (a savings bank at Søndregate 2) during normal banking hours.

Time Out Two short blocks farther is Nordregate, a pedestrian mall. Pop into **Erichsens** restaurant/coffee shop (Nordregt. 10) for a quick lunch, cake and coffee, or a three-course meal.

Continue on Nordregate and turn left on Dronningens Gate. On the left is **Stiftsgården,** Scandinavia's largest wood building, built in 1778 as a private home, the result of a competition between two sisters who were trying to outdo each other with the size of their houses. Today it is the king's official residence in Trondheim. The interior is sparsely furnished in threadbare Rococo, Empire, and Biedermeier. *Tel. 73/52-24-73. Admission: NKr20 adults, NKr10 children. Open June 1-Aug. 20, Mon.-Sat. 10-3, Sun. 10-4.*

The street on the far side of Stiftsgården is Munkegate. To the right is **Ravnkloa Fiskehall** (fish market), by the water, where you can see an immense variety of seafood. Past the railroad station and the quay across the water, you'll come to a former prison that now houses **Sjøfartsmuseet** (the Maritime Museum). Inside are galleon figureheads, ship models, a harpoon cannon from a whaling boat, and a large collection of seafaring pictures. *Fjordgt. 6A, tel. 73/52-89-75. Admission: NKr10 adults, NKr5 children and senior citizens. Open Mon.-Sat. 9-3, Sun. noon-3; closed Sat. in winter.*

Time Out Down Kjøpmannsgata from the museum is a modern shopping mall, Olavskvartalet; in its center is **Torgcafeen,** run by the Grand Hotel Olav, which serves sandwiches, salads, and cakes.

Across the street is the Royal Garden Hotel, built in the same Hansa style as the buildings that line the wharf. Farther down are the oldest buildings on the river, dating from the 1700s.

For an unusual museum visit, you can take a half-hour ride to Fagerheim and the **Ringve Music Museum** at Ringve Gård, the childhood home of the naval hero Admiral Tordenskiold. Guides (music students) demonstrate the instruments on display and tell about their role in the history of music. Concerts are held regularly. *Lade allé 60, tel. 73/92-24-11. Admission:*

NKr40 adults, NKr20 senior citizens and students, NKr10 children. Guided tours in English May 20–June 30, daily at noon, 2; July 1–Aug. 10, daily at 11, 12:30, 2:30; Aug. 11–Aug. 31, daily at 11, 12:30, 2:30; Sept. 1–31, daily at noon; Oct. 1– May 19, Sun. at 1:30. Tour lasts approximately 75 minutes.

At the other end of town, **Trøndelag Folkemuseum** has a collection of rustic buildings from the turn of the century, including a dental office and a lace-and-ribbon-maker's workshop. *Sverresborg, tel. 73/53–14–90. Admission: NKr30 adults, NKr10 children, senior citizens. Open May 20–Sept. 1, daily 11–6.*

Tour 2: Trondheim to Narvik

Nord Trøndelag, as the land above Trondheim is called, is largely agricultural. Taken on its own, it's beautiful, with farms, mountains, rock formations, and clear blue water, but compared with the rest of Norway, it is subtle, with only an undulating landscape—so many tourists just sleep through it on the night train, or fly over it on their way to the North.

The first town of any size is **Steinkjer,** a military base, boot camp for 3,000 Norwegian army recruits every year. North 350 kilometers (218 miles) is **Mo i Rana** (the poetic name means Mo on the Ranafjord), a center for iron and steel production using ore from nearby mines. Glacier fans can hike on the **Svartisen** (literally Black Ice), an ice cap 30 kilometers (19 miles) north of town.

On a bleak stretch of treeless countryside 80 kilometers (50 miles) north of **Mo i Rana** is the Arctic Circle. **Polarsirkelsenteret** (The Arctic Circle Center), on E6, presents a multiscreen show about Norway. The post office has a special postmark, and you can get your Arctic Circle Certificate stamped. There's also a cafeteria and gift shop. *8242 Polarsirkelen, tel. 75/16– 60–60. Admission: NKr30. Open May 1–Sept. 30 (Apr., Oct., cafeteria only).*

Bodø, a modern city of about 37,000 just above the Arctic Circle, is best known as the end station of the Nordlandsbanen railroad and the gateway to the Lofoten islands and the North. At Bodø, the Midnight Sun is visible from June 2 to July 10. Like many other coastal towns, it began as a small fishing community, but today it is a commercial and administrative center.

Saltstraumen, 33 kilometers (20 miles) southeast of Bodø on Route 80/17, is a 3-kilometer- (2-mile-) long and 500-foot-wide section of water between the outer fjord, which joins with the sea, and the inner fjord basin. During high tide, the volume of water rushing through the strait and into the basin is so great that whirlpools form. This is the legendary mælstrøm—and the strongest one in the world. Sometimes as many as four separate whirlpools can be seen, and the noise made by these "cauldrons" can be both loud and eerie. All that rush of water brings enormous quantities of fish, making the mælstrøm a popular fishing spot.

Time Out **Saltstraumen Hotel** (tel. 75/58–76–85) is practically on top of the mælstrøm. The restaurant to the left of the entrance serves delicious steamed halibut in butter sauce.

⑤ **Narvik,** 336 kilometers (210 miles) north, is more easily reached by rail from Stockholm than from most places in Norway, as it is the end station on the Ofotbanen, the Norwegian railroad that connects with the Swedish railroad's northernmost line. It was originally established as the ice-free port for exporting Swedish iron ore mined around Kiruna.

On May 9, 1940, the German army invaded Norway through Narvik, and German occupying forces stayed for more than five years. After the war, Narvik, which had been leveled by the bombing, was rebuilt. **Krigsminnemuseet** (the War Memorial Museum) documents wartime events with artifacts, models, and pictures. *Torget, tel. 76/94–44–26. Admission: NKr20 adults, NKr10 children and senior citizens. Open June 15– Sept. 15, daily 10–10; Sept. 16–June 14, daily 10–2.*

Tour 3:The Lofoten Islands

⑥ Extending out into the ocean north of Bodø are the **Lofoten Islands,** a 190-kilometer (118-mile) chain of jagged peaks, mountaintops rising from the bottom of the sea like open jaws. The midnight sun is visible here from May 26 to July 17. In the summer, the idyll of farms, fjords, and fishing villages makes it a major tourist attraction, while in the winter, the coast facing the Arctic Ocean is one of Europe's stormiest.

Until about 40 years ago, fishing was the only source of income. Cod and haddock were either dried or salted and sold on the Continent. Up to 6,000 boats with 30,000 fishermen would mobilize between January and March for the Lofotfiske, the annual cod-fishing event. During the season they fished in open boats and took shelter during stormy nights in *rorbuer,* simple cabins built right on the water. Today many rorbuer have been converted into lodgings, and much of the fishing has been taken over by year-round factory ships, but many fishing villages, still with the criss-crossing wood racks set out in the open air for drying fish, remain, and individual fishermen still go out.

Svolvær, the main town, connected with the other islands by express boat and ferry and by coastal steamer and air to Bodø, has a thriving summer art colony. A drive on E10, from Svolvær to the outer tip of the Lofotens (130 kilometers/80 miles)—the town with the enigmatic name of Å—is an opportunity to see how the islanders really live. Scenic stops include **Nusfjord,** a 19th-century fishing village on the UNESCO list of historic monuments; **Sund,** with its smithy; and **Reine.**

Time Out   **Gammelbua,** in Reine, serves excellent steamed halibut, homemade fish soufflé, and inspired desserts and cakes.

Off the tip of Moskenesøy, the last island with a bridge, is **Moskenesstraumen,** another mælstrøm, not quite as dramatic as Saltstraumen, but inspiration to both Jules Verne, who wrote about it in *Journey Beneath the Sea,* and Edgar Allan Poe, who described it in his short story "A Descent into the Maelstrom."

⑦ North of the Lofotens are the **Vesterålen Islands,** with more fishing villages and rorbuer, and diverse vegetation.

Tour 4: Harstad to the North Cape

East of Vesterålen on Hinnøya, Norway's largest island, is **Harstad,** where the year-round population of 22,000 swells to 42,000 during the annual June cultural festival (the line-up includes concerts, theater, and dance) and its July deep-sea fishing festival.

Tromsø, the most important city north of the Arctic Circle, and home to 50,000 people, is 318 kilometers (197 miles) northeast. At 2,558 square kilometers (987 square miles), it's Norway's largest city in terms of area, just about the same size as the country of Luxembourg. The midnight sun shines from May 21 to July 23, and the 13,000 students at the world's northernmost university are one reason the nightlife here is more lively than in many other northern cities.

Certainly **Ishavskatedralen** (the Arctic Cathedral) is the city's best-known structure. A looming peak of 11 descending triangles of concrete and glass, it is meant to evoke the shape of a Sami tent and the iciness of a glacier. Inside, an immense jewel-colored stained-glass window by Norwegian artist Viktor Sparre depicts the Second Coming. At the back of the church is a silver-and-copper organ, a modern adaptation of the omnipresent ships that hang in Scandinavian churches.

The **Tromsø Museum,** part of Tromsø University, offers an extensive survey of local history, lifestyles, and nature, with dioramas on Sami culture, arctic hunting practices, and wildlife. *Universitetet, tel. 77/64–50–00. Admission: NKr10 adults, NKr5 children. Open June–mid-Aug., daily 9–6; mid-Aug.–May, Mon.–Fri. 8:30–3:30, Sat. noon–3, Sun. 11–4. At other times, call for hours.*

Polarmuseet (the Polar Museum), in an 1830s customs warehouse, documents the history of the polar region, with skis and equipment from Roald Amundsen's expedition to the South Pole and a reconstructed Svalbard hunting station from 1910. *Søndre Tollbugt. 11b, tel. 77/68–43–73. Admission: NKr20 adults, NKr5 children. Open May 15–Aug. 31, daily 11–6; Sept. 1–May 14, daily 11–3.*

There are more museums in Tromsø, but to get a real sense of its northerly immensity and peace, take the **Fjellheisen** (cable car) from behind the cathedral up to the mountains, just a few minutes out of the city center. In the late afternoon and on weekends, summer and winter, this is where locals go to ski, picnic, walk their lucky dogs, and admire the view. *Tel. 77/63–51–21. Admission: NKr40 adults, NKr20 children. Open May–Sept., daily 10–5; June–Aug., daily 10–midnight if it's sunny. At other times, call for hours.*

It's 409 kilometers (253 miles) to Alta on coastal road most of the way. Kautokeino Sami spend the summer in turf huts at **Kvænangsfjellet,** so you might see a few of their reindeer. **Øksfjordjøkelen,** the only glacier in Norway that calves into the sea, is 13 kilometers (8 miles) west of Alteidet.

Alta is the last marker on the way to the North Cape and a major transportation center into Finnmark, the far north of Norway. Most people come just to spend the night before making the final ascent, but it's worth a trek to **Hjemmeluft,** southwest of the city, to see four groupings of 2,500- to 6,000-year-old **pre-**

historic rock carvings, the largest in northern Europe. The pictographs, featuring ships, reindeer, and even a man with a bow and arrow, were discovered in 1973. *Tel. 78/43-53-77 (Alta Museum). Admission: NKr10 adults, NKr5 children. Open June 1-June 14 and Aug. 16-Aug. 31, daily 8-8; June 15-Aug. 15, daily 8 AM-11 PM; Sept. 1-May 31, weekdays 9-3, weekends 11-4.*

A detour on the way to the North Cape is to the world's northernmost town, **Hammerfest,** an important fishing center 145 kilometers (90 miles) from Alta. At these latitudes the "most northerlies" become numerous, but certainly the lifestyles here are a testament to determination, especially in winter, when night lasts for months. In 1891 Hammerfest decided to brighten the situation and purchased a generator from Thomas Edison. It was the first city in Europe to have electric street lamps.

The journey from Alta to the Cape is 217 kilometers (134 miles) and includes a 45-minute ferry ride from Kåfjord to **Honningsvåg,** the last village before the Cape. Honningsvåg was completely destroyed at the end of World War II, when the Germans retreated and burned everything they left behind. Only a single wood church, which still survives, was not left in embers. **Nordkappmuseet** (the North Cape Museum), on the third floor of Nordkapphuset (the North Cape House), documents the history of the fishing industry in the region as well as the history of tourism at the North Cape. *9750 Honningsvåg, tel. 78/47-28-33. Admission: NKr15 adults, NKr5 children. Open June 15-Aug. 15, Mon.-Sat. 11-8, Sun. 6-8; Aug. 16-June 14, weekdays 11-3.*

From Honningsvåg, it's 34 kilometers (21 miles) to **Nordkapp,** on treeless tundra, with crumbling mountains and sparse dwarf plants. The contrast between this near-barren territory and the new **North Cape Hall** is striking. Blasted into the interior of the plateau, it includes a panorama restaurant. A tunnel leads past a small chapel to a grotto with a panoramic view of the Arctic Ocean and to the cliff wall itself. You'll pass exhibits that trace the history of the Cape, from Richard Chancellor, an Englishman who drifted around it and named it in 1533, to Oscar II, king of Norway and Sweden, who climbed to the top of the plateau in 1873, and King Chulalongkorn of Siam (now Thailand), who visited the Cape in 1907. Out on the plateau itself, a hollow sculptured globe is illuminated by the Midnight Sun, which shines from May 11 to August 31. *9764 Nordkapp. Admission: NKr95 adults, NKr35 children.*

Although this area is notoriously crowded in the summer, with endless lines of tour buses, it's completely different from fall through spring, when the snow is yards deep and the sea is frosty gray. Because the roads are closed in winter, the only access is from the tiny fishing village of Skarsvåg via snow cat, a thump-and-bump ride that's as unforgettable as the beautifully bleak view. For winter information, contact the **Skarsvåg Tourist Information Office** (tel. 78/47-52-80). Knivsjellodden, slightly west and less dramatic than the North Cape, is actually a hair farther north.

Tour 5: Samiland

Everyone has heard of Lapland, but few know its real name, Samiland. The Sami recognize no national boundaries, as their territory stretches from the Kola Peninsula in the Soviet Union through Finland, Sweden, and Norway. These indigenous reindeer herders are a distinct ethnic group, with a language related to Finnish. Although still considered nomadic, they no longer live in tents or huts, except for short periods during the summer, when their animals graze along the coast. They have had to conform to today's lifestyles, but their traditions survive through their language, music (called Joikk), art, and handcrafts. Norwegian Samiland is synonymous with the communities of Kautokeino and Karasjok in Finnmark.

⑮ Kautokeino, 129 kilometers (80 miles) southeast of Alta, is the site of the Sami theater and the Nordic Sami Institute, dedicated to the study of Sami culture. It is a center for Sami handicrafts and education, with even a school of reindeer herding.

Guovdageainnu (Kautokeino in the Sami language) **Gilisillju,** the local museum, documents the way of life of both the nomadic and the resident Sami of that area prior to World War II, with photographs and artifacts, including costumes, dwellings, and art. *9520 Kautokeino, tel. 78/45–62–03. Admission: NKr10 adults, children free. Open weekdays 9–3.*

⑯ Karasjok, on the other side of the Finnmark plateau, is the seat of the 39-member Sami Parliament and capital of Samiland. It has a typical inland climate, with the accompanying temperature extremes. The best time to come is at Easter, when the communities are celebrating the weddings and baptisms of the year and taking part in reindeer races and other colorful festivities. In summer, when many of the Sami go to the coast with their reindeer, the area is not nearly as interesting.

Samid Vuorku-Davvirat (the Sami Collections), is a comprehensive museum of Sami culture, with emphasis on the arts, reindeer herding, and the status of women in the Sami community. *Museumsgt. 17, tel. 78/46–63–05. Admission: NKr15 adults, NKr5 children. Open Mon.–Sat. 9–3, Sun. noon–3.*

From late fall to early spring you can go **reindeer sledding.** A Sami guide will take you out on a wood sled tied to a couple of unwieldy reindeer, and you'll clop through the barren, snow-covered scenery of Finnmark. Wide and relatively flat, the colorless winter landscape is veined by inky alder branches and little else. You'll reach a *lavvu*, a traditional Sami tent, and be invited in to share a meal of boiled reindeer, bread, jam, and strong coffee next to an open alder fire. It's an extraordinary experience. *Karasjok Opplevelser, tel. 78/46–73–60.*

Tour 6: The Finnish-Russian Connection

At its very top, Norway hooks over Finland and touches Russia for 122 kilometers (75 miles). The towns in east Finnmark have a more heterogeneous population than those in the rest of the country. A century ago, during hard times in Finland, many industrious Finns settled in this region, where their descendants keep the language alive.

⑰ A good way to visit this part of Norway is to fly to **Kirkenes** and then explore the region by car. Only Malta was bombed more than Kirkenes during World War II, so virtually everything has been built within the past 40 years.

From Kirkenes, it's about 60 kilometers (37 miles) to **Grense Jakobselv,** the Russian border. As a protest against constant Russian encroachment in the area, King Oscar II built a chapel

⑱ right at the border in 1869. Just east of Kirkenes is **Storskog,** for many years the only official land crossing of the border between Norway and Russia.

The southernmost part of Finnmark, a narrow tongue of land

⑲ tucked between Finland and Russia, is **Øvre Pasvik** national park. This subarctic evergreen forest is the western end of Siberia's *taiga* and supports many varieties of flora found only here. The area is surprisingly lush, and in good years all the cloudberries make the swamps shine orange.

Tour 7: Svalbard

⑳ North of the North Cape are the islands of **Svalbard,** the largest of which is Spitsbergen. Officially part of Norway only since 1925, they might have remained wilderness, with only the occasional visitor, if coal had not been discovered late in the 19th century. Today both a Norwegian and a Russian coal company have operations there, and there are two Russian coal miners' communities. The islands offer ample opportunities for ski, dogsled, and skidoo exploring.

The best way to experience Svalbard is by ship, as accommodations on the islands themselves are sparse. The capital, **Longyearbyen,** is 90 minutes by air from Tromsø. It was named for an American, John Monroe Longyear, who established a mining operation there in 1906. Only three species of land mammals—polar bear, reindeer, and Arctic fox—and one species of bird—ptarmigan—have adapted to Svalbard winters, but during the summer months, more than 30 species of birds nest on the steep cliffs of the islands, and white whales, seals, and walruses also come for the season.

Because Svalbard is so far north, it has four months of continual daylight, from April 21 to August 21. Summers can be lush, with hundreds of varieties of wildflowers. The season is so compressed that buds, full-blown flowers, and seed appear simultaneously on the same plant.

What to See and Do with Children

Tromsø   Take bus No. 28 to the mainland to ride Fjellheisen (*see* Tour 4, *above*) cable car to **Storsteinen** (the Big Rock), 420 meters (1,386 feet) above sea level, for a great view of the city.

Nordlysplanetariet (the Northern Lights Planetarium), at Breivika, is just outside town. Here, 112 projectors guarantee a 360-degree view of programs, which include a tour through the Northern Lights, the Midnight Sun, and geological history, as well as a film and multimedia show about the city. *Breivika, tel. 77/67–60–00. Admission: NKr50 adults, NKr25 children, NKr40 senior citizens. Open June 1–June 15, weekdays 12:30–7; June 16–Aug. 15, 10–7; Sept.–Apr., weekends 11:30–6.*

At **Tromsø Museum** (*see* Tour 4, *above*) children can listen to animal sounds over earphones, match animal puzzles to their tales, and play with a nearly lifesize dinosaur. An open-air museum is on the same grounds. *Folkeparken, tel. 77/64–50–00. Admission: NKr10 adults, NKr5 children. Open June 1–Aug. 31, daily 9–7; Sept. 1–May 31, weekdays, 8:30–3:30, Wed. also 7–10; Sat. noon–3, Sun. 11–4. Aquarium only: Open June 1– Aug. 31, daily 10–5; Sept. 1–May 31, Sun. only 11–2.*

Off the Beaten Track

In winter this entire region, blanketed by snow and cold, is off the beaten track. As the Norwegians say, there is no bad weather, only bad clothes—so bundle up and explore.

Kirkenes From mid-June to mid-August, the *FFR* (Hammerfest, tel. 78/ 59–25–44) operates visa-free day cruises to Murmansk on a high-speed catamaran. Booking is required two weeks in advance.

St. Georgs kapell, 45 kilometers (28 miles) west of Kirkenes, is the only Russian-Orthodox chapel in Norway, where the Orthodox Skolt-Sami had their summer encampment. It's a tiny building, and services are held outside, weather permitting.

Mo i Rana Sætergrotta and Grønligrotta are two of around 200 caves 26 kilometers (16 miles) northwest of Mo i Rana. Sætergrotta, with 2,400 meters (7,920 feet) of charted underground paths, many narrow passages, natural "chimneys," and an underground river, is for serious cave explorers. *Tel. 75/15–04–21. Admission: NKr140 at tourist office. Two-hour guided tours daily at 11 and 2.*

Grønligrotta, Scandinavia's best-known show-cave, even has electric lights. The 20-minute tour goes deep into the limestone cave to the underground river. *Admission: NKr30 adults, NKr15 children. Tours daily on the hour 10–7. Open June 15– Aug. 15.*

Svartisen Saltens Dampskibsselskap (tel. 75/72–10–20) offers seven-hour boat tours from Bodø to Svartisen, the second-largest glacier in Norway, near Mo i Rana, on Saturday in summer. The easiest way to get to the glacier is from Mo, 32 kilometers (20 miles) by car to Svartisvatn lake. A boat crosses the lake every hour to within 2½ kilometers (1.5 miles) of the Østerdal arm of the glacier. If you plan to get to the glacier on your own, you should inquire at the tourist office about connecting with a guide. Glacier walking is extremely hazardous and should never be done without a professional guide, because even though a glacier may appear fixed and static, it is always changing; there's always the danger of crevasses.

Shopping

Harstad Trastadsenteret (Rik. Kaarbøsgt. 19) sells pottery, weavings, and textile prints by local artists.

Kåfjord Grenbu (tel. 77/71–62–73) at Løkvoll in Manndalen on E6 about 15 kilometers (9 miles) west of Alta is a center for Coastal Sami weaving, on vertical looms. Local weavers sell their rugs and wall hangings along with other regional crafts.

Karasjok The specialties of the region are Sami crafts, particularly handmade knives. In Samelandssenter (tel. 78/48–73–60) is a large collection of shops featuring northern specialties, including **Knivsmed Strømeng** (tel. 78/48–71–05).

Kautokeino The Frank and Regina **Juhls** silver gallery (tel. 78/48–61–89) sells Sami crafts as well as their own modern jewelry.

Lofoten Lofoten is a mecca for artists and craftspeople; a list of galleries and crafts centers, with all locations marked on a map, is available from tourist offices.

Probably the best-known craftsperson in the region is Hans Gjertsen, better known as **Smeden i Sund** (the blacksmith at Sund; tel. 76/09–36–29). Watch him make wrought iron cormorants in many sizes, as well as candlesticks and other gift items.

Tromsø The city has two major shopping centers: **Veita** (Storgaten 102, tel. 77/65–87–55) and **Pyramiden** (Tromsdalen, tel. 77/63–82–00).

Trondheim Trondheim has an extraordinary number of high-quality art and handicraft stores. In addition to **Husfliden** (Olav Tryggvasonsgt. 18, tel. 73/52–18–74). **Yvonne Verkstedutsalg og Galleri** (Ørjaveita 6, tel. 73/52–73–27) also sells works of local artists. **Olavskvartalet,** across from the Royal Garden Hotel, is a shopping center with many specialty stores.

Sports and Outdoor Activities

Bird-watching From Moskenes, just north of Å (or from Bodø), you can take a ferry to the bird sanctuaries of **Værøy** and **Røst**. Hundreds of thousands of seabirds inhabit the cliffs of the islands, in particular the eider ducks, favorites of the local population, which build small shelters for their nests. Eventually the down collected from these nests ends up in *dyner* (feather comforters).

There are even more birds in Gjesvær on the east coast of the Honningsvåg. Contact Ola Thomassen (tel. 78/47–57–73) for organized outings.

Dog-sledding **Canyon Huskies** (tel. 78/43–33–06), in Alta, arranges all kinds of personalized tours, whether you want to stay in a tent or hotel, and whether you want to drive your team or stay in the sled. Like most Norwegian sled dogs, these are very friendly.

Fishing In **Trondheim** the Nidelven (Nid River) is one of Norway's best salmon and trout rivers. You can fish right in the city, but, as usual, you'll need a license. Ask at any sports store. In the waters of **Tromsø**, there are cod, coalfish, haddock, and the occasional catfish. Elsewhere in Finnmark, ice fishing is a passion, often with the entire family involved. (The Sami sometimes ice fish from tiny houses they pull onto the ice with snow cats.) Check with the tourist board to find out if and where any competitions are scheduled. Bring at least your own ice drill.

Hiking In **Tromsø** there's good hiking in the mountains above the city, reachable by funicular. Other regional possibilities begin anywhere outside the cities (usually only a few minutes away). In between the Alta and Karasjok areas, the **Finnmarksvidda** has marked trails with overnight possibilities in lodges. Contact the Norwegian Mountain Touring Association (Stortinsgata

28, N-0161 Oslo) and the Finnmark Travel Association (tel. 78/
43–54–44).

Hunting Two licenses are needed to hunt, and for large game, especially moose, lots must be drawn among applicants. Contact the Finnmark Travel Association (tel. 78/43–54–44).

Rafting Deep-sea rafting is a relatively new sport in the area, but one that is as exhilarating as it is beautiful. Several tours are offered, including a three-hour trip to the North Cape. Call **Nordkapp Safari** (tel. 78/47–27–94).

Reindeer Sledding Reindeer sledding is a wonderful Finnmark experience (*see* Tour 5, *above*).

Skiing **Bymarka** and **Estenstadmarka,** the wooded areas on the periphery of Trondheim, are popular among cross-country skiers. At **Skistua** (ski lodge) in Bymarka, and at **Vassfjellet** south of the city, there are downhill runs. In Tromsø, the mountains, only eight minutes away by funicular, are not only a great place to ski, but also to hike (*see* Tour 4, *above*). Elsewhere, you'll have to ask specifics from the tourist board. Listen to the weather reports and pay heed to warnings. Blizzards come in quickly over the water; the wind alone can knock an ample person clear off his or her feet.

Beaches

In Trondheim, the island of Munkholmen, easily reached by ferry from Ravnkloa, has a popular sandy beach. Elsewhere, most beaches are rocky, and the water is, as the Norwegians say, fresh. However, some of the beaches of Nordland are long and sandy, with temperatures reaching as high as 20°C (68°F).

Dining and Lodging

Dining **Trondheim** is known for several dishes, including *surlaks* (pickled salmon), marinated in a sweet-and-sour brine with onions and spices, and served with sour cream. A sweet specialty is *tekake* (tea cake), which looks like a thick-crust pizza topped with a lattice pattern of cinnamon and sugar.

If you visit northern Norway between May and August, try the specialty of *måsegg* and *Mack-øl*, more for curiosity value than for taste. *Måsegg* (seagulls' eggs), are always served hard-boiled and halved in their shells. They're larger than chicken eggs, and they look exotic, with greenish-gray speckled shells and bright orange yolks, but they taste like standard supermarket eggs. *Mack-øl* (similar to pils), is brewed in Tromsø at the world's northernmost brewery. Otherwise, as in the rest of provincial Norway, most better restaurants are in hotels.

Lodging Most Trondheim hotels have summer rates, but for some, a hotel pass or special booking method is required. Unless otherwise noted, breakfast is included.

At times it seems as though the SAS and Rica hotel chains are the only ones in northern Norway, and often that is true. These are always top-rate, usually the most expensive hotel in town, with the best restaurant and the most extensive facilities. Rustic cabins and campsites are also available everywhere, as well as independent hotels.

In the Lofoten and Vesterålen islands, rorbuer, which have been converted into lodgings or modern versions of these simple dwellings, are the most popular form of accommodation. These rustic quayside cabins, with minikitchens, bunk beds, living rooms, and showers are reasonably priced, and they give an authentic experience of the region. *Sjøhus* (sea houses) are larger, usually two- or three-storied buildings similar to rorbuer.

Highly recommended establishments are indicated by a star★.

Alta
Dining and Lodging

SAS Alta Hotell. This new glass-and-white hotel does everything it can to make you forget that you are in a place where it is dark much of the time. Everything is light, from the reflectors on the ceiling of public rooms to the white furniture in the rooms. *Box 1093, N-9501, tel. 78/43-50-00, fax 78/43-58-25. 155 rooms with bath or shower, 2 suites. Facilities: 3 restaurants, 2 bars, nightclub, conference center, parking. AE, DC, MC, V. Expensive.*

Bodø
Dining

Løvolds' Kafeteria. Freshly caught fish (the Løvolds also sell fishing gear) and traditional Norwegian dishes are featured at this upstairs cafeteria with a harbor view. It's a good place for coffee and cake, too, for all pastries are made in-house. *Tollbugt. 9, tel. 75/52-02-61. No reservations. Dress: casual. No credit cards. Moderate.*

Dining and Lodging

Bodø Hotell. This pale blue-gray modern building has an identity of its own yet fits well into the Bodø street scene. The facade is more interesting than the rooms. *Professor Schyttesgt. 5, N-8000, tel. 75/52-69-00, fax 75/52-57-78. 63 rooms with bath or shower, 3 suites. Facilities: restaurant. AE, DC, MC, V. Moderate.*

Diplomat. This hotel near the harbor is a short walk from the shopping district. The modern rooms are soberly decorated. The restaurant has live entertainment, but the food could be more imaginative. *Sjøgt. 23, N-8000, Bodø, tel. 75/52-70-00, fax 75/52-24-60. 104 rooms with shower (no bathtubs). Facilities: 3 restaurants, bar, nightclub, fitness room, conference center, garage. AE, DC, MC, V. Moderate.*

Hammerfest
Dining and Lodging

Rica Hotel Hammerfest. The entire hotel was redecorated in 1989. The rooms are functional and small, but the furniture is light and comfortable. *Sørøygt. 15, tel. 78/41-13-33, fax 78/41-13-11. 88 rooms with bath or shower. Facilities: restaurant, bar, nightclub, fitness center, conference center, parking. AE, DC, MC, V. Moderate-Expensive.*

Harstad
Dining

Røkenes Gård. This large, white wood building with an intricately carved portal was built in 1750 as a commercial trading house and inn. Recently it was restored by the ninth generation of descendants, and it is now a cozy restaurant serving regional specialties, such as reindeer and cloudberry parfait. *9400 Harstad, tel. 77/01-74-65. Reservations required at least 24 hours in advance. Dress: casual but neat. AE, DC, MC, V. Closed Sun. Expensive.*

Dining and Lodging

Grand Nordic. It's a neat, brickred building in the Bauhaus style, with Norwegian 1970s-look leather furniture in the public rooms. Bedrooms, no bigger than necessary, are furnished with dark woods. The restaurant and conference rooms are lighter and more modern. *Strandgt. 9, N-9400, Harstad, tel. 77/06-21-70, fax 77/06-77-30. 85 rooms with bath or shower, 3* *suites. Facilities: 2 restaurants, bar, nightclub, parking, conference center. AE, DC, MC, V. Moderate-Expensive.*

Honningsvåg **Hotel Havly.** This simple hotel is cozy and centrally located,
Dining and Lodging with small, spic-and-span rooms, and an ample breakfast buffet. Because this is a seamen's hostel, no alcohol is served. *N-9751 Honningsvåg, tel. 78/47-29-66, fax 78/47-30-10. 35 rooms with shower. Facilities: restaurant, conference rooms. AE, MC, V. Closed Easter, Dec. 24-Jan 2. Inexpensive.*

Karasjok **Karasjok SAS Hotell.** This feels more like a ski chalet than a ho-
Dining and Lodging tel, with bright rooms, done in warm blues and reds, that are
★ cozy rather than industrial. The lobby is more staid, with a seating arrangement up front. The hotel's wonderful Sami restaurant, Goathi, serves traditional fare, including reindeer cooked over open fires. *Box 38, N-9731 Karasjok, tel. 78/46-74-00, fax 78/46-68-02. 56 rooms with shower. Facilities: restaurant, conference rooms, bar, saunas. AE, DC, MC, V. Closed Dec. 24-Jan. 2. Expensive-Very Expensive.*

Kirkenes **Rica Arctic Hotel.** Do not confuse this new hotel with the Rica
Dining and Lodging Hotel Kirkenes, an older establishment, which ends up costing the same during the summer. Rooms here are spacious and pretty, with white painted furniture and light print textiles. *Kongensgt. 1-3, N-9900, Kirkenes, tel. 78/99-29-29, fax 78/99-11-59. 80 rooms with bath. Facilities: restaurant, bar, nightclub, fitness room, swimming pool, conference center, shopping center, parking. AE, DC, MC, V. Moderate-Very Expensive.*

Lofoten Islands **Fiskekrogen.** This quayside restaurant in the fishing village of
Dining Henningsvær will prepare your own catch. Chef/owner Otto Asheim's specialties include smoked *gravlaks* (smoking the dill-marinated salmon gives it extra depth of flavor) and sautéed ocean catfish garnished with mussels and shrimp. *8330 Henningsvær, tel. 76/07-46-52. Reservations required. Dress: casual. DC, MC, V. Moderate.*

Dining and Lodging **Nyvåga Rorbu og Aktivitetssenter.** Built in 1990, this hotel and recreation complex is a 15-minute drive from the airport. It looks old, but it's brand new. Activities are well organized, with fishing-boat tours, eagle safaris, and deep-sea rafting, plus planned evening entertainment. *8310 Kabelvåg, Storvågan, tel. 76/07-89-00, fax 76/07-89-50. 60 rooms with shower. Facilities: 2 restaurants, conference rooms. AE, DC, MC, V. Moderate-Expensive.*

Henningsvær Rorbuer. This small group of renovated turn-of-the-century rorbuer, all facing the sea, is just outside the center of Lofoten's most important fishing village. Breakfasts can be ordered from the cafeteria/reception, where there's a fireplace and a TV. Reservations are essential for July. *8330 Henningsvær, tel. 76/07-46-00. 14 1- or 2-bedroom rorbuer with shower. Facilities: cafeteria, sauna, laundry, grill. MC, V. Inexpensive.*

Narvik **Inter Nor Grand Royal.** It looks like an office building from the
Dining and Lodging outside, but inside it is a comfortable top-class hotel, with big, rather formal rooms. The main restaurant is also quite formal. *Kongensgt. 64, N-8500 Narvik, tel. 76/94-15-00, fax 76/94-55-31. 112 rooms with bath or shower. Facilities: 2 restaurants, 2 bars, fitness room, conference center. AE, DC, MC, V. Moderate-Expensive.*

Tromsø   **Brankos.** Branko and Anne Brit Bartolj serve authentic Yugo-
Dining   slavian food, including *cevapcici* (small, spicy meatballs) and
raznici, accompanied by their own imported Yugoslavian
wines, in their art-filled dining room. *Storgt. 57, tel. 77/68–26–
73. Reservations required. Dress: casual but neat. AE, DC,
MC, V. No lunch. Moderate–Expensive.*
Compagniet. An old wood trading house from 1837 is now a styl-
ish restaurant serving modern Norwegian food. Chef Morten
Lønstad, formerly of Oslo's Feinschmecker, prepares sautéed
shrimp with garlic and mussels baked in an herb sauce for
starters, while main dishes include grilled monkfish with
Dijon-mustard hollandaise sauce. *Sjøgt. 12, tel. 77/65–57–21.
Reservations required. Dress: casual but neat. AE, DC, MC,
V. No lunch in winter. Moderate–Expensive.*

Dining and Lodging   **SAS Royal Hotel.** It's a new, modern hotel with splendid views
over the Tromsø shoreline, but standard rooms are tiny, and
even the costlier "Royal Club" rooms aren't big enough for real
desks and tables, so modular ones have been attached to the
walls. *Sjøgt. 7, N–9000, tel. 77/65–60–00, fax 77/68–54–74. 193
rooms with bath, 6 suites. Facilities: restaurant, bar, nightclub, business center, parking. AE, DC, MC, V. Moderate–
Expensive.*
Hotel With. This recently constructed building on the waterfront in the dock area has spacious rooms decorated in shades of
gray with the occasional colorful accent. The sauna/relaxation
room on the top floor has the best view in town. As a Home hotel, it offers alcohol-free beer, a hot meal included in the room
price, and waffles and coffee at all times. *Sjøgt. 35–37, N–9000,
tel. 77/68–70–00, fax 77/68–96–16. 76 rooms with shower. Facilities: fitness room, conference rooms, parking. AE, DC,
MC, V. Moderate–Expensive.*
Polar Hotell. This no-frills hotel gives good value for money in
the winter, when none of the bigger hotels have special rates.
Rooms are small, and the orange/brown color scheme is a bit
dated, but it's a pleasant, unassuming place to stay.
*Grønnegaten 45, N–9000, tel. 77/68–64–80, fax 77/68–91–36.
64 rooms with shower (no bathtubs). Facilities: restaurant,
bar, conference room. AE, DC, MC, V. Inexpensive–Moderate.*

Trondheim   **Bryggen.** The furnishings are in bleached wood, with dark-blue
Dining   and red accessories, and the atmosphere is intimate. The menu
★   features a reindeer fillet salad with cranberry vinaigrette and
an herb cream soup with both freshwater and ocean crayfish for
starters. Meat dishes include breast of chicken with a red-wine
sauce and lamb medley. *Øvre Bakkelandet 66, tel. 73/52–02–30.
Reservations required. Dress: casual but neat. AE, DC, MC,
V. Closed Sun. No lunch. Expensive.*
Havfruen. "The Mermaid" has a maritime dining room with an
open kitchen at street level, while in the cellar, 200-year-old
stone walls from the original building frame the setting. Fish
soup is the most popular starter, while summer main dishes include poached halibut. Desserts are simple—the citrus parfait
is especially good. *Kjøpmannsgt. 7, tel. 73/53–26–26. Reservations advised. Dress: casual but neat. AE, DC, MC, V. Closed
Sun. No lunch. Moderate–Expensive.*
Hos Magnus. The price/value ratio is excellent at this old-fashioned, cozy restaurant in the new part of Bryggen. The menu
ranges from such modern dishes as cognac-marinated moose
fillet with mustard dressing to the old local specialty surlaks

for appetizers. Grilled, marinated spiral pork chop and fillet of beef with mushrooms and onions are featured on the meat menu. There are ample fish and vegetarian choices, too. *Kjøpmannsgt. 63, tel. 73/52–41–10. Reservations advised. Dress: casual but neat. AE, DC, MC, V. Moderate.*

Lian. In the heights above the city, Lian offers beautiful scenery and Norwegian standards. The oldest part of the restaurant dates from 1700, but the round section, from the 1930s, commands the best view. The food is solid, honest, and hearty, with roast beef, reindeer, smoked pork loin, and the old standby, *kjøttkaker* (Norwegian meat cakes). *Lian, tel. 72/55–90–77. Dress: casual. No credit cards. Closed Mon. Moderate.*

★ **Tavern på Sverresborg.** This big, yellow, wood former ferryman's house at the Trondelag Folkemuseum has been an inn since 1739. The food is authentic Norwegian, including meat and fish prepared with old methods—pickled, salted, and dried. Choices include a plate with four different kinds of herring, roast lamb ribs, trout, meat cakes, and rømmegrøt. Homemade oatmeal bread and rolls accompany all dishes. *Sverresborg allé, tel. 73/52–09–32. Dress: casual but neat. MC, V. No lunch Sept. 2–May 19. Moderate.*

De 3 Stuer. This small bistro chain serves everything homemade, and the daily special features such dishes as fish soufflé, fried fish with sour-cream sauce, split-pea soup with sausage, boiled beef, and lamb stew, all served with dessert and coffee. For lunch, there's smørbrød, crescent rolls, salads, and cakes. *Trondheim Torg, tel. 73/52–92–20; Gågaten Leuthenhaven, tel. 73/52–43–42; Dronningens Gate 11, tel. 73/52–63–20. No reservations. Dress: casual. No credit cards. Dronningens closed Sun. Inexpensive.*

Lodging **Prinsen.** Rooms in this recently remodeled hotel in the center of the city are light, monochromatic to the point of being dull, and decorated with classic furniture. Teatergrillen, named after a nearby theater, serves a good early dinner. *Kongensgt. 30, N-7002, tel. 73/53–06–50, fax 73/53–06–44. 85 rooms with bath or shower, 1 suite. Facilities: 3 restaurants, 3 bars, nightclub. AE, DC, MC, V. Moderate–Very Expensive.*

Royal Garden. The city's showcase hostelry, right on the river, was built in the same style as the old warehouse buildings that line the waterfront, only in glass and concrete. It's a luxury hotel, with big rooms, light wood furniture, and predominantly blue textiles. *Kjøpmannsgata 73, N-7010, tel. 73/52–11–00, fax 73/53–17–66. 297 rooms with bath, 8 suites. Facilities: 3 restaurants, bar, pool, fitness room, shops. AE, DC, MC, V. Moderate–Very Expensive.*

Grand Hotel Olav. Situated in the center of town, this hotel boasts 27 different room models, all impeccably decorated. It is part of a complex that contains shops, conference rooms, and the Olavshallen Concert Hall (home of the Trondheim Philharmonic). *Kjøpmannsgto 48, tel. 73/53–53–10, fax 73/53–57–20. 106 rooms, 5 no-smoking rooms. Facilities: 3 restaurants, bar, pub, nightclub, parking. AE, DC, MC, V. Expensive.*

★ **Bakeriet.** Built as a bakery in 1863, Trondheim's newest hotel opened in March 1991. There's no restaurant, but a hot evening meal is included in the room rate. You can borrow a track suit, and there's free light beer in the lounge by the sauna. Every room has a VCR and a window thermometer. Few rooms look alike, but all are large, with natural wood furniture, beige-and-red-stripe textiles, and stylish in their simplicity. *Brattørgt. 2,*

N–7011, Trondheim, tel. 73/52–52–00, fax 73/50–23–30. 91 rooms with bath or shower, 1 suite. Facilities: sauna. AE, DC, MC, V. Inexpensive–Moderate.

Trondheim. If you've always wanted to try mead, the fermented honey drink of the Vikings, you can do it here—it's produced on the premises. The building is old on the outside, with a curved corner and wrought-iron balconies, but inside it's completely remodeled. The rooms are big and light, with what is now considered to be classic Scandinavian bentwood furniture. Kongensgt. 15, N–7013, tel. 73/50–50–50, fax 73/51–60–58. 140 rooms with shower or bath. Facilities: restaurant, bar, conference room. AE, DC, MC, V. Inexpensive–Moderate.

Singsaker Sommerhotell. A student dorm that becomes a hotel from June 15 to August 20, it is not much cheaper than many downtown hotels. It's good for the single traveler, though, as the lounge fills up in the evening with other loners. Rogertsgt. 1, N–7016, tel. 73/52–00–92, fax 73/52–06–35. 104 rooms, 16 with bath. Facilities: bar, fitness room. AE, DC, MC, V. Inexpensive.

The Arts and Nightlife

The Arts

Trondheim **Olavshallen** (Kjøpmannsgt. 44, tel. 73/53–40–50), a concert and cultural center built in 1989, is the home of Trondheim's symphony and the nearly 3,000 music students in the city. The auditorium seats 1,300. The concert and entertainment season is from September through May.

During the last week in July, the *St. Olav Play* is performed at the outdoor amphitheater in **Stiklestad,** 98 kilometers (60 miles) from Trondheim. The play, with a cast of 300, commemorates the life of King Olav Haraldsson, who united and brought Christianity to Norway. Tickets are available from any post office or from Stiklestad Nasjonale Kulturhus (tel. 74/07–12–00).

Tromsø Every year in January the city celebrates **Nordlysfestivalen** (the Northern Lights Festival) with a series of concerts by distinguished visiting artists at Kulturhuset (the Culture House) (Grønnegata 87, tel. 77/68–20–64). For concert information and reservations, contact the festival (tel. 77/68–08–63, fax 77/68–01–09).

The North Nature takes precedence over the arts in northern Norway, but Harstad hosts the yearly **Northern Norway Festival** in June.

From June 15 to August 15, **Beaivas Sami Theater** (9250 Kautokeino, tel. 78/48–68–11) offers summer programs of traditional Sami folk songs and modern works.

Nightlife

Trondheim **Olavskvartalet** (*see* Shopping, *above*) is the center of much of the city's nightlife, with a disco, a jazz and blues club, and a bar and beer hall in the cellar. **Hotell Prinsen** (*see* Lodging, *above*) has a summer restaurant, **Sommer'n,** open from mid-May to the end of August, with live music and dancing. **Restauranthuset Norrein** (Dronningens Gate 12, tel. 73/52–24–23) is an entertainment complex with the **Sunset Club,** a piano bar, and **Beverly,** a postmodern café straight out of California.

Tromsø Tromsø brags that it has 10 nightclubs, not bad for a city of 50,000 at the top of the world. **Compagniet** (*see* Dining, *above*) has the classiest nightclub; **Charly's** at the SAS Royal Hotel, and **Papagena** at the Grand Nordic hotel (*see* Lodging, *above*) are also popular.

Norwegian Vocabulary

	English	Norwegian	Pronunciation
Basics	Yes/no	Ja/nei	yah/nigh
	Please	Vær så snill	**vehr** soh snihl
	Thank you very much.	Tusen takk	**tews**-sehn tahk
	You're welcome.	Vær så god	**vehr** soh goo
	Excuse me.	Unnskyld	**ewn**-shewl
	Hello	God dag	goo **dahg**
	Goodbye	Adjø	ah-**dyur**
	Today	i dag	ee **dahg**
	Tomorrow	i morgen	ee **moh**-ern
	Yesterday	i går	ee **gohr**
	Morning	morgen	**moh**-ern
	Afternoon	ettermiddag	**eh-terr**-mid-dahg
	Night	natt	naht
Numbers	One	en	ehn
	Two	to	too
	Three	tre	tray
	Four	fire	**feer**-eh
	Five	fem	fehm
	Six	seks	sehks
	Seven	syv, sju	shew
	Eight	åtte	**oh**-teh
	Nine	ni	nee
	Ten	ti	tee
Days of the Week	Monday	mandag	**mahn**-dahg
	Tuesday	tirsdag	**teesh**-dahg
	Wednesday	onsdag	**oonss**-dahg
	Thursday	torsdag	**tohsh**-dahg
	Friday	fredag	**fray**-dahg
	Saturday	lørdag	**loor**-dahg
	Sunday	Søndag	**suhn**-dahg
Useful Phrases	Do you speak English?	Snakker De engelsk?	**snahk**-kerr dee **ehng**-ehlsk
	I don't speak Norwegian.	Jeg snakker ikke norsk.	yay **snahk**-kerr ik-keh nohrshk

I don't understand.	Jeg forstår ikke.	yay fosh-**tawr** **ik**-keh
I don't know.	Jeg vet ikke.	yay veht **ik**-keh
I am American/ British.	Jeg er amerikansk/ engelsk.	yay ehr ah-mehr- ee-kahnsk/ehng- ehlsk
I am sick.	Jeg er dårlig.	yay ehr **dohr**-lee
Please call a doctor.	Vær så snill og ring etter en lege.	vehr soh snihl oh ring **eht**-ehr ehn **lay**-geh
Do you have a vacant room?	Jeg vil gjerne ha et rom.	yay vil **yehr**- neh hah eht room
How much does it cost?	Hva koster det?	vah **koss**-terr deh
It's too expensive.	Det er for dyrt.	deh ehr for **deert**
Beautiful	vakker	**vah**-kehr
Help!	Hjelp!	yehlp
Stop!	Stopp!	stop
How do I get to . . .	Hvor er	voor **ehr**
. . . the train station?	jernbanestasjonen	yehrn-bahn-eh sta-**shoon**-ern
. . . the post office?	posthuset	**pohsst**-hewss
. . . the tourist office?	turistkontoret	tew-**reest**-koon- toor-er
. . . the hospital?	sykehuset	**see**-keh-hoo-seh
Does this bus go to . . . ?	Går denne bussen til . . . ?	gohr **den**-nah boos teel
Where is the W.C.?	Hvor er toalettene?	voor ehr too- ah-**leht**-ter-ner
On the left	Til venstre	teel **vehn**-streh
On the right	Til høyre	teel **hooy**-reh
Straight ahead	Rett fram	reht **frahm**

Dining Out	menu	meny	meh-**new**
	fork	gaffel	**gahff**-erl
	knife	kniv	kneev
	spoon	skje	shay
	napkin	serviett	ssehr-**vyeht**
	bread	brød	brur
	butter	smør	smurr
	milk	melk	mehlk
	pepper	pepper	**pehp**-per

salt	salt	sahlt
sugar	sukker	**sook**-kerr
water/bottled water	vann	vahn
The check, please.	Jeg vil gjerne betale.	yay vil **yehr**-neh beh-**tah**-leh

Index

Personal Itinerary

Departure *Date*

Time

Transportation

Arrival *Date*   *Time*

Departure *Date*   *Time*

Transportation

Accommodations

Arrival *Date*   *Time*

Departure *Date*   *Time*

Transportation

Accommodations

Arrival *Date*   *Time*

Departure *Date*   *Time*

Transportation

Accommodations

Fodor's Travel Guides

Available at bookstores everywhere, or call 1–800–533–6478, 24 hours a day.

U.S. Guides

Alaska

Arizona

Boston

California

Cape Cod, Martha's Vineyard, Nantucket

The Carolinas & the Georgia Coast

Chicago

Colorado

Florida

Hawaii

Las Vegas, Reno, Tahoe

Los Angeles

Maine, Vermont, New Hampshire

Maui

Miami & the Keys

New England

New Orleans

New York City

Pacific North Coast

Philadelphia & the Pennsylvania Dutch Country

The Rockies

San Diego

San Francisco

Santa Fe, Taos, Albuquerque

Seattle & Vancouver

The South

The U.S. & British Virgin Islands

The Upper Great Lakes Region

USA

Vacations in New York State

Vacations on the Jersey Shore

Virginia & Maryland

Waikiki

Walt Disney World and the Orlando Area

Washington, D.C.

Foreign Guides

Acapulco, Ixtapa, Zihuatanejo

Australia & New Zealand

Austria

The Bahamas

Baja & Mexico's Pacific Coast Resorts

Barbados

Berlin

Bermuda

Brazil

Brittany & Normandy

Budapest

Canada

Cancun, Cozumel, Yucatan Peninsula

Caribbean

China

Costa Rica, Belize, Guatemala

The Czech Republic & Slovakia

Eastern Europe

Egypt

Euro Disney

Europe

Europe's Great Cities

Florence & Tuscany

France

Germany

Great Britain

Greece

The Himalayan Countries

Hong Kong

India

Ireland

Israel

Italy

Japan

Kenya & Tanzania

Korea

London

Madrid & Barcelona

Mexico

Montreal & Quebec City

Morocco

Moscow & St. Petersburg

The Netherlands, Belgium & Luxembourg

New Zealand

Norway

Nova Scotia, Prince Edward Island & New Brunswick

Paris

Portugal

Provence & the Riviera

Rome

Russia & the Baltic Countries

Scandinavia

Scotland

Singapore

South America

Southeast Asia

Spain

Sweden

Switzerland

Thailand

Tokyo

Toronto

Turkey

Vienna & the Danube Valley

Yugoslavia

Special Series

Fodor's Affordables

Caribbean

Europe

Florida

France

Germany

Great Britain

London

Italy

Paris

**Fodor's Bed &
Breakfast and
Country Inns Guides**

Canada's Great
Country Inns

California

Cottages, B&Bs and
Country Inns of
England and Wales

Mid-Atlantic Region

New England

The Pacific
Northwest

The South

The Southwest

The Upper Great
Lakes Region

The West Coast

The Berkeley Guides

California

Central America

Eastern Europe

France

Germany

Great Britain &
Ireland

Mexico

Pacific Northwest &
Alaska

San Francisco

**Fodor's Exploring
Guides**

Australia

Britain

California

The Caribbean

Florida

France

Germany

Ireland

Italy

London

New York City

Paris

Rome

Singapore & Malaysia

Spain

Thailand

Fodor's Flashmaps

New York

Washington, D.C.

Fodor's Pocket Guides

Bahamas

Barbados

Jamaica

London

New York City

Paris

Puerto Rico

San Francisco

Washington, D.C.

Fodor's Sports

Cycling

Hiking

Running

Sailing

The Insider's Guide
to the Best Canadian
Skiing

Skiing in the USA
& Canada

**Fodor's Three-In-Ones
(guidebook, language
cassette, and phrase
book)**

France

Germany

Italy

Mexico

Spain

**Fodor's
Special-Interest
Guides**

Accessible USA

Cruises and Ports
of Call

Euro Disney

Halliday's New
England Food
Explorer

Healthy Escapes

London Companion

Shadow Traffic's New
York Shortcuts and
Traffic Tips

Sunday in New York

Walt Disney World
and the Orlando Area

Walt Disney World
for Adults

**Fodor's Touring
Guides**

Touring Europe

Touring USA:
Eastern Edition

**Fodor's Vacation
Planners**

Great American
Vacations

National Parks
of the East

National Parks
of the West

**The Wall Street
Journal Guides to
Business Travel**

Europe

International Cities

Pacific Rim

USA & Canada

WHEREVER YOU TRAVEL, ℋELP IS NEVER FAR AWAY.

From planning your trip to providing travel assistance along the way, American Express® Travel Service Offices* are always there to help.

Norway

BERGEN
Winge Reisebureau
Chr. Michelsensgt. 1-3
5-901-290

STAVANGER
Winge Reisebureau
Ostervaag 20
4-530-065

KRISTIANSAND
Winge Reisebureau
Radhusgaten 3
42-21540

TROMSØ
Winge Reisebureau
Gronnegaten 86-88
83-88000

OSLO
American Express
Travel Service Office
Karl Johansgatan 33-35
2-286-1300

TRONDHEIM
Winge Reisesenter A/S
Sondre Gate 16
7-553-000

AMERICAN EXPRESS® Travel Service